Describing Data Patterns
A general deconstruction of metadata standards

DISSERTATION
in support of the degree of

Doctor philosophiae
(Dr. phil.)

by Jakob Voß

submitted at January 7th 2013
defended at May 31st 2013

at the Faculty of Philosophy I
Humboldt-University Berlin
Berlin School of Library and Information Science

Reviewer:
Prof. Dr. Stefan Gradman
Prof. Dr. Felix Sasaki
Prof. William Honig, PhD

The full source code of this document, its variants and corrections are available at `https://github.com/jakobib/phdthesis2013`. Selected parts and additional content are made available at `http://aboutdata.org`

A digital copy of this thesis (with same pagination but larger margins to fit A4 paper format) is archived at `http://edoc.hu-berlin.de/`.

A printed version is published through CreateSpace and available by Amazon and selected distributors.

ISBN-13: 978-1-4909-3186-9
ISBN-10: 1-4909-3186-4

Cover: the Arecibo message, sent into empty space in 1974 (image CC-BY-SA Arne Nordmann, `http://commons.wikimedia.org/wiki/File:Arecibo_message.svg`)

SIMPLY EXPLAINED:
METADATA

Abstract

Many methods, technologies, standards, and languages exist to structure and describe data. The aim of this thesis is to find common features in these methods to determine how data is actually structured and described. Existing studies are limited to notions of data as recorded observations and facts, or they require given structures to build on, such as the concept of a record or the concept of a schema. These presumed concepts have been deconstructed in this thesis from a semiotic point of view. This was done by analysing data as signs, communicated in form of digital documents. The study was conducted by a phenomenological research method. Conceptual properties of data structuring and description were first collected and experienced critically. Examples of such properties include encodings, identifiers, formats, schemas, and models. The analysis resulted in six prototypes to categorize data methods by their primary purpose. The study further revealed five basic paradigms that deeply shape how data is structured and described in practice. The third result consists of a pattern language of data structuring. The patterns show problems and solutions which occur over and over again in data, independent from particular technologies. Twenty general patterns were identified and described, each with its benefits, consequences, pitfalls, and relations to other patterns. The results can help to better understand data and its actual forms, both for consumption and creation of data. Particular domains of application include data archaeology and data literacy.

Zusammenfassung

Diese Arbeit behandelt die Frage, wie Daten grundsätzlich strukturiert und beschrieben sind. Im Gegensatz zu vorhandenen Auseinandersetzungen mit Daten im Sinne von gespeicherten Beobachtungen oder Sachverhalten, werden Daten hierbei semiotisch als Zeichen aufgefasst. Diese Zeichen werden in Form von digitalen Dokumenten kommuniziert und sind mittels zahlreicher Standards, Formate, Sprachen, Kodierungen, Schemata, Techniken etc. strukturiert und beschrieben. Diese Vielfalt von Mitteln wird erstmals in ihrer Gesamtheit mit Hilfe der phenomenologischen Forschungsmethode analysiert. Ziel ist es dabei, durch eine genaue Erfahrung und Beschreibung von Mitteln zur Strukturierung und Beschreibung von Daten zum allgemeinen Wesen der Datenstrukturierung und -beschreibung vorzudringen. Die Ergebnisse dieser Arbeit bestehen aus drei Teilen. Erstens ergeben sich sechs Prototypen, die die beschriebenen Mittel nach ihrem Hauptanwendungszweck kategorisieren. Zweitens gibt es fünf Paradigmen, die das Verständnis und die Anwendung von Mitteln zur Strukturierung und Beschreibung von Daten grundlegend beeinflussen. Drittens legt diese Arbeit eine Mustersprache der Datenstrukturierung vor. In zwanzig Mustern werden typische Probleme und Lösungen dokumentiert, die bei der Strukturierung und Beschreibung von Daten unabhängig von konkreten Techniken immer wieder auftreten. Die Ergebnisse dieser Arbeit können dazu beitragen, das Verständnis von Daten — das heisst digitalen Dokumente und ihre Metadaten in allen ihren Formen — zu verbessern. Spezielle Anwendungsgebiete liegen unter Anderem in den Bereichen Datenarchäologie und Daten-Literacy.

Contents

Contents

List of Examples

List of Figures

List of Tables

Chapter 1

Introduction

> Beginning thinkers in this area often suppose that what will be offered to the screen reader will be merely individual stored documents, available on line quickly, but based somehow on conventional documents ensiling in conventional computer files.
>
> Our point of view is different.
>   — Ted Nelson (1981): *Literary Machines*, page 1/9

1.1. Motivation

Bibliographic data conceals a sneaky complexity. At first glance it is all quite familiar and simple: there is an author, a title, and a date of publication. Not by chance computer science publications frequently exemplify data by bibliographic data and metadata by library catalogs. On closer inspection everything falls apart: how about multiple authors, editors, publishers, and translators? What if authors are unknown or known under different names? What about subtitles and abbreviations? Which date does one specify in which detail and when does it change? Library science has elaborated detailed cataloging rules to answer these questions. But bibliographic data is not created, stored, modified, and used solely by skilled librarians — even they do not commit to a single schema. Moreover the subject of cataloging is changing. Although Ted Nelson's vision of a purely digital ecosystem of interconnected documents has not become reality yet, more and more publications appear in digital form. Traditional concepts such as 'document', 'page', 'edition', and 'copy' blur or change meaning — the continuing popularity of print-oriented techniques like the portable document format (PDF) is only a sign of reaction to this process.

In library and information science the description of physical documents is still relevant but it has largely been solved as research topic. The topic of this thesis is the description of *digital* documents which are given as data. While there is an increasing research interest in (digital) documents — see Buckland (1998b), Pédauque (2006), and Skare, Vårheim, and Lund (2007) for approaches — the nature of these documents as data has received less attention. Digital documents and all digital content share two crucial and basic properties, that have long been neglected in library science: bits can freely be copied and rearranged. Despite their nature as artifacts of communication, physical documents are still considered as stable, distinguishable, and atomic entities. But given a digital document one can create any number of identical copies, indistinguishable from the original. With same ease one can create modifications, that may or may not constitute documents in their own right. These properties of digital documents complicate their bibliographic description by metadata. Despite the success of full text search for simple retrieval, the importance of metadata for digital content is even higher than for physical objects: if metadata is used to differentiate digital copies from each other, it does not only describe but also constitute the document. Digital documents are also much more likely processed, transformed, and aggregated than physical documents. In doing so, metadata is needed to state when two different strings of bits represent the same document. Lacking a physical structure of pages, we also require metadata to structure documents into parts.

As documents become digital, so does metadata. To understand the nature of bibliographic data, we must first understand the nature of data. If it is 'something given' (as indicated by the Latin origin *datum*) where does the act of giving originate? If data describes other data, what properties does it refer to? We will approach this questions by analysis of existing methods of structuring and describing data. The results apply to both data and metadata. Later it will be shown what constitutes the relationship between data and metadata and how the results apply to metadata about digital documents in particular. A clear distinction between data and metadata is difficult for several reasons. Sometimes it is not even clear whether metadata is added as description about a piece of data or whether it is part of it. Can citations be considered as metadata only if extracted from a document? Are they metadata about the citing document, the cited document, or both? We may answer this question by metadata about metadata, but does this lead to an infinite chain of descriptions? Furthermore not only metadata but also most data is about something. Its referent may be no document and not digital, but it is not directly accessible: in digital environments the association between data and its referent is always constructed by a document because non-documents, such as people, places, and ideas, are not directly accessible in the digital realm. The affinity between metadata and data has an effect on every new system and method to structure data. For instance it has been mentioned from the beginning of the Semantic Web (Tim Berners-Lee 1997; R. Guha and Bray 1997; Ora Lassila and Swick 1999) although it took some time to shift the focus from information about documents ('information resources') to information about any objects ('non-information resources'). Meanwhile concrete forms of data are undervalued in favor of a common data language such as the Resource Description Framework (RDF). However, a look at existing data shows that there is not one common data language but a multiplicity of formats, languages, systems, and structures. Data and metadata is structured in many forms, e.g. file systems, databases, markup, formats, encodings, schemas, and queries. It is unlikely that this plurality will be replaced by one type of data only.

This thesis will look into this variety without proposing one method of data structuring as superior to the other. Instead I want to find common patterns as frequent strategies that occur over and over again in data and metadata. Just like linguistic analysis of natural language reveals insights to (social) reality, a deeper understanding of structures in data and metadata can give insight to structures of the world, that is reflected in data. Grammar, dialects, rhetoric figures, and other patterns that shape natural language are deeply studied in linguistics. A similar approach to data, which could be called 'data linguistics', is still to be founded. A deeper understanding of data patterns is crucial especially for libraries and archival institutions. Future librarians and archivists will likely be confronted with more and more digital documents that have been structured and described by outdated methods. Knowledge of common patterns in data can help when digital preservation has failed, by application of what could be called 'data archaeology'. It could be argued that there is no need for data patterns, because concrete data structures and models already implement and define data much more precisely. Yet existing approaches are not enough, because they each focus to one specific formalization method. This practical limitation blocks the view to more general data patterns, independent from a particular encoding, and it conceals blind spots and weaknesses of a chosen formalism. Even a perfect theoretical system of data, metadata and digital documents may not suffice. In practice data is often far less organized than it was meant to be. Standards are misinterpreted or ignored. Documentation is sketchy. Markup and formats are unknown or broken. Eventually documents turn out to be inherently as fuzzy as the reality that they deal about. At least digital libraries cannot just reject data if it lacks appropriate descriptions, so they must recognize their complexity and uncertainty. To understand and reveal concealed structures in data, we must not only know the techniques that have been applied to it, but also the patterns that underlie and motivated the application of specific technologies. This thesis will hopefully provide at least some basic guidance for this challenge.

1.2. Background

> We do not, it seems, have a very clear and commonly
> agreed upon set of notions about data.
> — George Mealy (1967): *Another look at data*

The main topic of this thesis is the structure and description of data in digital documents. The concept of data is relevant to many disciplines with various meanings: a summary of different philosophies of data is given by Ballsun-Stanton (2010, 2012) with data as the product of objective, reproducible measurements ("data as hard numbers"), data as product of any recorded observations ("data as observations"), and data as processable encodings of information and knowledge ("data as bits"). This research commits to the third understanding of data, which is found both in computer science and library and information science. Without committing to a specific definition of information and knowledge, we assume that data is given as processable encoding of something, at least as a sequence of bits. This definition is compatible with notions of data in some disciplines that provide tools and related works for data research. Chapter 2 gives an overview of basic concepts and foundations from mathematics (section 2.1), computer science (section 2.2), library and information science (section 2.3), philosophy (section 2.4), semiotics (section 2.5), and pattern theory (2.6). This thesis can best be located between library and information science on the one hand and computer science on the other. Both disciplines do not deal with data as primary topic but they prefer the term *information* which data is related to as secondary form. The scope of library and information science includes the description of documents with data as one aspect of digital documents. Computer science neither deals with data as such but with computation and the implementation of automatic processes. This involves data, but data was never the central object of research as suggested by Naur (1966). Over the past years there has been an increasing interest in data motivated by the growing amount of *Open Data* and tools for data analysis. This has brought up ideas of "data science" and "data journalism" (Bradshaw and Rohumaa 2011). However, both commit to the philosophies of data as hard numbers or data as observations as they deal with aggregating, filtering, and visualizing large sets of data, based on statistical methods of data analysis. Such analyses require a basic understanding of data as prerequisite but they do not make it to their primary object of investigation. The main concern of data science is "big data", that is "when the size of the data itself becomes part of the problem" (Loukides 2010). In contrast, the problem of this research is the inherent complexity of data, which exists independent from its size. It is my aim to show how data is actually structured and described, independent from particular application for which, and independent of particular technologies in which data is processed.

For the most part, the research question is focused on digital documents as instances of data. The *document* is a core concept of library and information science (see section 2.3). Nevertheless, there exists no commonly agreed upon definition, even within the discipline. As described by Buckland (1997, 1998a) the nature of (digital) documents can better be defined in terms of function rather than format: whatever functions as a document can be a document. The document must only be usable as recorded "evidence in support of a fact" (Briet 1951).[1] A digital document, in short, can be any data object that eventually exists as sequence of bits. Such data objects are often referred to as 'information'. However Ted Nelson (2010, p. 300) is right as he writes in response to a misleading summary of his hypertext system Xanadu by Tim Berners-Lee: "not 'all the world's information', but all the world's *documents*. The concept of 'information' is arguable, documents much less so."[2] An important distinction between digital documents, that are subject to bibliographic description, and general data objects or information, that are subject to general data management in business, is the stability of documents. While business databases are designed to cover the *current* state, bibliographic data is designed to cover what *has been* published or recorded. Description and interpretation of a digital document may change, be extended, reduced, or turn out to be wrong. Still there is the assumption of facts, which a document is evidence for, even if both the facts and the documents can be expressed in several ways. Business data in contrast describes facts that change in time: products are created and sold, people are hired and fired, etc. Most information systems cover both types of data: static data, that is not changed, and dynamic data, that may change. For instance a library system holds description of publications: these publications are documents which are not changed after they have been published. At the same time the system holds descriptions of dynamic holdings, which are bought, lend, and sort out. Dynamic data can be transformed into static data by just 'freezing' it – this process of archiving or preservation is one major task of library institutions. This 'frozen data' is what constitutes a digital document. This finding, however, does not answer which data constitutes a document and how one determines its relevant parts. The definition of a document is either passed on to the eye of the beholder or to the level of metadata about documents. The former cannot be automatized, and the latter forms a digital document on its own. As there is no obvious distinction between data and metadata, metadata only shifts the problem of document identity to another level. Nevertheless metadata provides useful methods to tackle the nature of digital documents in particular and data in general. To further identify digital documents, we need to reveal structures in data and metadata, which will be described by data patterns.

---

[1] Translation from French by Buckland (1997). In practice a fact that is supported by a document can be any statement, whether valid and true or not.

[2] The quote from Tim Berners-Lee and Fischetti (1999) that Nelson refers to is: "Ted described a futuristic project, Xanadu, in which all the world's information could be published in hypertext."

1.3. Method and scope

My research method is based on a phenomenological description of existing methods that structure and describe data. The phenomenological method views data as social artifacts, that cannot be described from an absolute, objective point of view. Instead occurrences of data are studied as "'phenomena': appearances of things, or things as they appear in our experience" (Smith 2009). Phenomenology as philosophical discipline has its origins in the thinking of Husserl (1931; 1986), followed by writings of Heidegger, Merleau-Ponty, Sartre and others. According to Spiegelberg (1982, 681ff.) a phenomenological investigation can be laid out in three steps: phenomenological intuiting, phenomenological analyzing, and phenomenological describing. First, the phenomenon must be experienced "without becoming absorbed in it to the point of no longer looking critically". Second, it is examined in all of its aspects without adhering to possibly known concepts and categories. This step "trace[s] the elements and the structure of the phenomena obtained by intuiting. It does not in any sense demand dissecting them into separate parts. It comprises the distinguishing of the constituents of the phenomena as well as the exploration of their relations to and connection with adjacent phenomena." Finally, the phenomenological description "forces us to concentrate on the central and decisive characteristics of the phenomenon and to abstract from its accidentals". The description should reveal the *essence* of a phenomenon and give a "reliable guide to the listener's own actual or potential experience of the phenomena."

The phenomenon investigated in this research is the way digital data is structured and described. A detailed analysis of this phenomenon is given in chapter 3. Chapter 4 summarizes general constituents and provides a typology to talk about data. The essential description of data structuring is finally provided with chapter 5 in form of a pattern language, as explained in section 2.6. As far as I know, a combination of phenomenological method and pattern theory has not explicitly been practiced before.[3]

The research method can be justified by limitations of existing approaches. These are either theoretical, as they normatively describe how metadata *should* be structured, or empirical but limited on statistics (data mining) and automatic methods (machine learning). Both are limited in their scope. Normative data descriptions do not necessarily reflect existing data, because norms are often (mis)interpreted, ignored, and changed. In practice, data is shaped by both explicit and implicit structures. For instance every document in the extensible markup language (XML) is an ordered tree, but the nesting and order of elements might be chosen intentionally or in an arbitrary manner, just because there has to be some order. Data schemas, like those expressed in XML Schema (XSD), rarely cover all aspects, so they are extended by conventions like cataloging rules and profiles, which may only exist as

---

[3] At least a literature search for terms like "phenomenological method" or "Husserl" combined with "pattern theory" and "Alexander" led to no results. Only Palmer (2009) follows a related approach with a phenomenological analysis of meta-systems and systems engineering – among them some patterns and schemas.

conceptions. Explicit and implicit structures are intertwined on multiple levels, and both structure and describe data.

Data mining and machine learning, on the other hand, can only recognize known structures at one level of description, but they cannot automatically detect and interpret unexpected kinds of structures. In a nutshell, one cannot find out whether and how different things relate to each other by treating them all as equal. Quantitative methods only show patterns within the constraints of a fixed format. For instance data mining can find co-occurrences in data fields from a large number of records, but first one must identify what constitutes a field and a record. These entities are examples of general data patterns, which we are looking for.

The goal of this thesis is not yet another, unified 'über-model', but "another look at data" as Mealy (1967) titled his early work on data theory. Since then, information technology has created a plethora of different models, formats, languages, and methods to structure data. It is disputable whether there will ever be a final unification in addition to the universal binary code. Data integration, migration, and mapping are still useful and worth to investigate in concrete domains, but they can only provide partial solutions. The goal of this thesis is not to unify data structuring methods, but to analyze, relate, and describe them. To further locate the scope of this thesis, data is assumed to be digital, stable, and finite. Aspects of transforming non-digital or dynamic digital material into fixed sequences of bits are not dealt with, and details of implementation, such as performance and security, are only mentioned where they show how and why specific structures have evolved.

1.4. Related work

If I have not seen as far as others, it is because there were giants standing on my shoulders.
— Harold Abelson

Both, the scope of this thesis, and its method applied to the revealing of patterns in data description, independent from particular technologies, are unique. Nevertheless there are several related works to build on. These works either deal with particular technologies and parts of the problem, or they tackle the problem of data description from different points of view and with different methods. The following section gives a brief overview of related work with emphasis on concrete publications and authors. The overview begins historically with early and foundational works, followed by analyzes of patterns in particular domains, including metamodels and taxonomies. Some additional works are relevant because they share theoretical or methodological fundamentals with this thesis. In order to better find revealed aspects of data structuring I also paid particular attention to researchers that complained about established treatment of data and digital documents (Kent, Nelson, Naur, etc.). General approaches from specific disciplines and methods (mathematics, computer science, library and information science, semiotics, philosophy, and the study of patterns and pattern languages) will be dealt with in chapter 2.

Some data patterns before the advent of computer systems may be found in forms and questionnaires (page 138). Most aspects of the of history of forms, however, still have to be written, so I skipped this topic. The use of bits as most fundamental unit of data also dates back to the pre-electronic age.[4] The first foundational analyzes were created in the late 1950s until the 1960s — around the same time when distinctions between data and information were introduced (Gray 2003) and when computer science emerged as an independent discipline. These early works remain important also because they are less bound to particular technological trends and paradigms, that later emerged. For instance the "abstract formulation of data processing problems" by Young and H. K. Kent (1958) contains a clear separation between information sets (sets of possible information items belonging to the same class, from which data is drawn), and documents (collections of related information items). The concept of a "hierarchy of models" in models of data (Suppes 1962) can also help understanding general problems of data structuring, although early notions of data tend to conform to the idea of data as recorded observations (see page 42). Later the interest of researchers shifted from data to concepts like 'information' (or even 'knowledge'). Against this, Naur (1966, 1968) suggested the term 'datalogy' for "the science of the nature and use of data". As described by Sveinsdottir and Frøkjær (1988), Naur also criticized the focus of computer science curricula on formalization, disregarding social aspects, psychology of programming and applications. My application of pattern analysis instead of mathematical formalisms follows Naurs understanding of datalogy. Another foundational discussion on data is given by Mealy (1967) and a response by Chapin (1968).

Several works deal with intellectual analysis of data patterns or similar concepts *in particular domains*: Armstrong (2006) identified common patterns in Object Orientation by literature analysis and named them "quarks". The most common quarks, asserted as characterizing Object Orientation in more than every second analyzed article, are inheritance (71 of 88 articles), objects (69), classes (62), encapsulation (55), methods (50), message passing (49), polymorphism (47), and abstraction (45). Patterns in hierarchical documents, with focus on XML based languages, have been analyzed by Dattolo et al. (2007). Their basic patterns for segmentation and extraction of structural document elements, first identified by Vitali, Di Iorio, and Gubellini (2005), are: markers (with meaning depending on position), atoms (such as unstructured plain text), block and inline elements, records (sets of unordered, optional and non-repeatable elements), containers (sets of unordered, optional and repeatable elements), and tables (sequences of homogeneous elements). More collections of patterns can be found in (conceptual) data modeling literature, although their primary focus is on problems in business enterprises. The most general compilations have been collected by Hay (1995) and by L. Silverston (2001). Among other business tasks, the former contains a brief chapter on simple document modeling, and the latter provides template data models for common entities such as people,

---

[4] The binary number system is attributed to Leibniz (1703) and Boole (1854). Earlier examples of non-numerical uses of binary systems are the African Ifa divination and the Chinese I Ching hexagrams.

organizations, products, orders, and accounting.

The follow-up publications by Hay (2006) and by Len Silverston and Agnew (2009) describe more *general modeling patterns*: Silverston's Universal Data Model is an example of the many metamodeling approaches one finds in conceptual data modeling literature. Other examples include metamodels based on mathematical notations (C. M. Keet 2008c), meta-standards (Object Management Group 2009), and hypergraph models (Boyd and McBrien 2005) among other approaches. Given that even normal data modeling is not consistently applied in practice, the practical benefit of meta-modeling seems limited, and existing works tend to ivory-tower research. Nevertheless some general data patterns exist in metamodels in the same way as in other kind of data models (see section 3.8.4 on meta-modeling). More practical publications include review articles that summarize and compare specific technologies of data structuring. Examples include Kerschberg, Klug, and Tsichritzis (1976) with a taxonomy of database models, W. Kent (1983a) with a taxonomy of entity-relationship models, and Riley (2010) with a broad overview of metadata formats and technologies.

Important principles of data structuring and description are dealt with in the works of William Kent and Ted Nelson. Both criticize data structuring and description in the best sense of the term, as they show that different methods are possible. An example is given by W. Kent (1988) in a paper on the multiplicity of forms to encode a simple fact in data. In his main work W. Kent (1978) deals with the relation between data and reality. Several fundamental issues, such as normalization and identity (W. Kent 1983b, 2003) are topic of his later works. His analyzes are focused on (limitations of) data and data models in traditional databases, but he explicitly says that the topics are relevant in general. To a large degree my work confirms and updates Kent's results, also for new data technologies. Ted Nelson thought about properties and possibilities of *purely digital* documents before the invention of elaborated file systems, word processing and related technologies (Nelson 1965a). During the last decades he kept criticizing the way we deal with digital documents — a way that still resembles properties of physical media (Nelson 1981, 1986). His vision of hypertext, in contrast, is based on documents which (parts of) can be referenced, cited, and reused by deep links and transclusion (Nelson 1999). This requires knowledge about the structure of digital documents and methods to identify particular document pieces.

Related topics that partly overlap with my research include the design of information systems (Hirschheim, Klein, and Lyytinen 1995), semantic data heterogeneity (Bergman 2006; P. J. Hayes and H. Halpin 2008; Pluempitiwiriyawej and J. Hammer 2000; Sheth, Ramakrishnan, and Thomas 2005), and the creation of data standards (Meek 1995; Stamper et al. 2000). Another concept of data patterns has been developed by (Jay 1995, 2009), but his model is more related to pattern matching than design patterns. The most similar works compared to my thesis are ISO 11404 (2007) with a collection of language independent data types (Meek 1994b), and the thesis by Honig (1975) (see Honig and C. R. Carlson (1978) and appendix A). Honig conducted a survey of data structures in 21 representative programming languages and database management systems, resulting in a description model with core properties, such as homogeneity, atomicity, repeatability etc., similar to the patterns identified in this thesis. Honig's work, apparently, has neither been taken up nor updated so far. Both ISO 11404 and Honig's model are compared with the final data pattern language in section 5.6.

Chapter 2

Foundations

The phenomena to be analyzed in this thesis include all methods to structure and to describe digital data. To experience these phenomena we must first broaden our view to see where they can be found. For this reason, this chapter will first introduce the disciplines that deal with data and the description of digital documents. This introduction also includes definitions of some basic concepts and notations. These foundations are both used during collection and analysis in the proceeding chapters and they can be instances of phenomena in their own right. For instance mathematical set theory is used to define other methods of data structuring, but set theory alone can also be used for data structuring. We cannot fully avoid this circularity as every description must be formulated in some other description — basically this is the core problem of data description. Nevertheless we can show how different disciplines approach and tackle the problem. The largest part of this chapter introduces mathematics (section 2.1) and computer science (section 2.2) because these make the traditional foundations of data: mathematics has proved to be an effective tool to exactly describe structures of any kind and computer science provides the most examples, as most problems of practical data processing belong to its domain. The approach of library and information science (section 2.3) is different: it is basically concerned with the organization and description of documents. While more and more documents become digital, the discipline should more and more deal with data. The impact of philosophy is more subtle: as outlined in section 2.4 there is not much explicit philosophy of data, but philosophical issues permeate all other disciplines and philosophy helps to reveal blind spots of other points of views. Semiotics (section 2.5) is relevant to this thesis because it deals with signs and language, which all meaningful data is an instance of. Section 2.6 finally introduces the fundamental concepts of patterns and pattern languages. Both can be combined to pattern theory, which is more a practice or an art than a scientific discipline.

2.1. Mathematics

As far as the laws of mathematics refer to reality, they are not certain;
and as far as they are certain, they do not refer to reality.
— Albert Einstein

Mathematics has proved to be an effective tool to exactly describe structures of
any kind. This section introduces mathematical foundations and notations that are
referred to throughout the following chapters. It begins with mathematical logic
(section 2.1.1) and set theory (section 2.1.2). Both have been used as foundation
of mathematics and to describe data types in computer science (see section 2.2.2).
Other methods to express data in mathematical terms are based on graph theory
(section 2.1.4). Mathematics provides powerful methods of formal description and
to deductively draw conclusions from given axioms. Yet it cannot prove this basic
assumptions but only detect inconsistencies.[1] Despite the exactness of mathematics,
to make use of it we must carefully look out for which connections we draw between
abstract structures and anything outside of the domain of pure mathematics.

2.1.1. Logic

Mathematical logic has its origin in philosophy which also studied the principles
of valid reasoning. In particular the logic of Aristotle was influential until the mid-
nineteenth century, when a mathematical analysis of logic was introduced by Boole
(1847, 1854). Mathematical logic replaced natural language with formal symbols to
express truth values and logical statements. Typical notations include:

- $\perp$ or 1 for true and $\top$ or 0 for false

- $\neg$ for negation

- $\wedge$ and $\vee$ for logical conjunction and logical disjunction

- $\rightarrow$ and $\leftrightarrow$ for logical implication and logical equivalence

- symbols such as a, b, x, y for variables and individual constants, independent of
  the ontological status of their referents

Alternative visual notations of logic systems, as introduced by Euler (1768) and
Venn (1880), are dealt with in section 3.9. The basic rules how to combine and
interpret statements from these formal symbols can defined by Boolean algebra.
Figure 2.1 contains laws of Boolean algebra and resulting truth tables for the basic
operations, $\neg$, $\wedge$, $\vee$, $\rightarrow$ and $\leftrightarrow$. Law 5 to 8 could also be derived from 1 to 4 and in
total there are 16 binary boolean operations. The laws of Boolean algebra can be used

---

[1] As shown by Gödel (1931) mathematics can even prove that in a system of axioms that is complex
enough there are consistent statements which cannot be proven or disproven without additional
axioms.

1. commutativity	$x \wedge y \Leftrightarrow y \wedge x$
	$x \vee y = y \vee x$
2. distributivity	$x \wedge (y \vee z) \Leftrightarrow (x \wedge y) \vee (x \wedge z)$
	$x \vee (y \wedge z) \Leftrightarrow (x \vee y) \wedge (x \vee z)$
3. annihilation	$x \wedge 0 \Leftrightarrow 0$
	$x \vee 1 \Leftrightarrow x$
4. excluded middle	$x \wedge \neg x \Leftrightarrow 0$
	$x \vee \neg x \Leftrightarrow 1$
5. idempotence	$x \wedge x \Leftrightarrow x$
	$x \vee x \Leftrightarrow x$
6. associativity	$x \vee (y \vee z) \Leftrightarrow (x \vee y) \vee z$
	$x \wedge (y \wedge z) \Leftrightarrow (x \wedge y) \wedge z$
7. absorption	$x \wedge (x \vee y) \Leftrightarrow x \vee (x \wedge y) \Leftrightarrow x$
8. logical identity	$x \wedge 1 \Leftrightarrow x$
	$x \vee 0 \Leftrightarrow x$

x	$\neg x$		x	y	$x \wedge y$	$x \vee y$	$x \rightarrow y$	$x \leftrightarrow y$
			0	0	0	0	1	1
0	1		0	1	0	1	1	0
1	0		1	0	0	1	0	0
			1	1	1	1	1	1

Figure 2.1.: Laws of Boolean algebra and resulting truth tables

for *inference*, that is to derive new logical statements from given logical statements by deductive reasoning[2] For instance one can proof that $\neg(x \wedge y) \Leftrightarrow \neg x \vee \neg y$ and $\neg(x \vee y) \Leftrightarrow \neg x \wedge \neg y$ which is known as De Morgan's law. The logic of Boolean algebra is equivalent to *propositional logic* and to the algebra of sets (see section 2.1.2) among other descriptions. In particular, digital switching circuits can be described by Boolean algebra (C. Shannon 1938), which is the base of all digital computer systems.

Further formalization of logical statements is possible with *predicate logic*, which extends propositional logic with predicates and quantification. A logical *predicate* is an individual symbol that refers to a general statement with zero or more empty spaces. Predicates are typically written in functional syntax, for instance $f(\_,\_)$ denotes the binary predicate f and $g(a)$ denotes the unary predicate g where the space is a filled by variable a. The number of spaces is called the predicate's *arity*. Predicates are logical statements insofar as they have a truth value for each combination of individual variables. For instance $g(a)$ with predicate g and variable a is either true or false. The ontological status of predicates, however, is irrelevant to predicate logic: for instance predicated could refer to properties (e.g. $g(a) \Leftrightarrow$ 'a is blue'), concept types ($g(a) \Leftrightarrow$ 'a is a book'), relations ($f(a,b) \Leftrightarrow$ 'a is friend of b'), or

---

[2] See also figure 2.10 for methods of reasoning.

attributes ($f(a, b) \Leftrightarrow$ 'a has size b'). Normal predicate logic (also known as *first-order predicate logic*) has two fundamental kinds of quantification: universal quantification ($\forall$) to state that a logical statement is true for all possible values of variable, and existential quantification ($\exists$) to state that there is at least one value of a variable that makes a logical statement true. If predicates and/or quantifiers can be replaced by variables, predicate logic is extended to higher-order logic. Higher-order logic allows more complex statements about statements, but it is hard to verify statements even in second-order logic. A common and less complicated extension of predicate logic is the introduction of an identity predicate or identity relation, also referred to as equality. With the *equality relation* '=' one can define a *uniqueness quantifier* to denote that exactly one object exists. We write $\exists! x : \phi(x)$ to denote that there is only one x for which $\phi(x)$ is true. The equality relation can also be used to state that a statement is true for a specific number of distinct values. Further extensions and modification of propositional logic and predicate logic are possible by adding and by modification of the basic laws of Boolean algebra. For instance one can argue against the law of excluded middle (law 4 in figure 2.1) and introduce a third truth value in addition to true and false to denote 'unknown' or 'irrelevant' (ternary logic). Other so-called non-classical logic extensions include:

- an interval of possible truth values (*fuzzy logic*)

- additional quantifiers to express modality of statements (*modal logic*)

- elimination of the law of excluded middle and double negation so statements only have a truth value only if they can explicitly be inferred (*intuitionistic logic*)

- introduction of default values and exceptions (*default logic*)

- support of inconsistent statements (*paraconsistent logic*)

One example of modal logic relevant to data description is *deontic logic*, because this logic is concerned with obligation, permission, and norms (McNamara 2010). Deontic logic, however, includes several outstanding philosophical problems: the basic problem, known as Joergensen's dilemma is based on the relation of deontic values to logical truth values and (Jorgensen 1937): On the one hand norms cannot be true or false but only fulfilled or violated, but on the other hand some norms seem to follow logically from others. If one tries to formalize this implications, one may get unexpected results such as the Good Samaritan Paradox: given that a person is robbed and given that one should guard a person that is robbed, it follows that a person should be robbed, because without robbery one cannot guard anyone.

The choice of a specific logic system and how it suits the domain to be described is a philosophical question (see section 2.4). We mostly assume classical logic, but on a closer look methods to structure and describe data include non-classical elements, such as the introduction of NULL values (ternary logic) and default values (default logic), combined with annotations (higher-order logic). On the other hand, data description should be easy to compute, so even first-order predicate logic can be

	description logic	notation	predicate logic
TBox	concepts	$A, B, C \ldots$	$A(x), B(x), C(x) \ldots$ (unary predicates)
	roles	$R, Q \ldots$	$R(x, y), Q(x, y) \ldots$ (binary predicates)
	top concept	$\top$	$\forall x : \top(x)$ (predicate hold for all x)
	bottom concept	$\bot$	$\neg \exists x : \bot(x)$ (predicate holds for no x)
	concept complement	$\neg C$	$\neg C(x)$
	concept intersection	$A \sqcap B$	$A(x) \lor B(x)$
	concept union	$A \sqcup B$	$A(x) \lor B(x)$
	concept hierarchy	$A \sqsubseteq B$	$A(x) \rightarrow B(x)$
	universal restriction	$\forall R.C$	$\forall y : R(x, y) \rightarrow C(x)$
	existencial restriction	$\exists R.C$	$\exists y : R(x, y) \rightarrow C(x)$
ABox	concept assertion	$a : C$	$C(a)$
	role assertion	$(a, b) : R$	$R(a, b)$

Table 2.1.: Allowed types of logical statements in description logic $\mathcal{ALC}$

too complex — there is no automatic method to decide whether a general set of statements can be true (the problem is equivalent to the problem of *decidability* or computability described in section 2.2). For this reason, subsets of predicate logic called *description logic* are preferred, especially for knowledge representation (Baader et al. 2010). In description logic, only specific kinds of statements are allowed with up to three variables. There are unary predicates ($A, B, C \ldots$) to describe concept types, binary predicates ($R, S \ldots$) to describe relationships (also called 'roles'), and a set of possible methods to combine statements from these predicates. The statements in description logic are typically divided into statements about concepts and roles (*TBox*) and statements that make use concept and role predicates with concrete variables (*ABox*). A TBox together with an ABox are also called a knowledge base. Table 2.1 summarizes the statement types of $\mathcal{ALC}$. This *Attributive Concept Language with Complements* is used as base of other description logics, some of which go beyond predicate logic.[3] To express and exchange logic statements in data there are some standards such as ISO Common Logic (International Organization for Standardization 2007b), conceptual graphs (Sowa 1992a, 2000), and controlled natural language (Fuchs, Schwertel, and Torge 1999).

2.1.2. Set theory

Sets and properties occur in data description at least everywhere you deal with multiple objects (see the 'collections and types' paradigm in section 4.2.3). We hereby define 'naive' set theory and notation in natural language. A deeper introduction and axiomatic definition that avoid some paradoxes can be found by Jech (2003). In short, a *set* is a defined collection of objects. The objects in a set are called its *elements*

---

[3] See http://www.cs.man.ac.uk/~ezolin/dl/ for an overview of description logic variants and their computable complexity.

or *members*. We write $a \in A$ to denote that a is a *member of* the set A or *contained in* the set A and $a \notin A$ to denote that a is not a member of A. A set that contains no elements is called the *empty set* and denoted by {} or $\emptyset$. The number of members in a set A is called its *cardinality* and denoted by $|A|$. The cardinality of the set of natural numbers $\mathbb{N}$ is denoted $|\mathbb{N}| = \aleph_0$. Sets with cardinality $\aleph_0$ are called *countable infinite* in contrast to a *countable finite* set with finite number of elements. The cardinality of the continuum (the set of real numbers) is denoted $|\mathbb{R}| = \mathfrak{c}$ which is strictly greater than $\aleph_0$. If every member of a set A is also member of a set B we call A a *subset* of B and write $A \subset B$. Reciprocally if every member of B is also member of A then B is a *superset* of A or *included* in A and we write $B \supset A$. To denote that A is not a subset of B we write $A \not\subset B$ and $B \not\supset A$. If for two sets A and B both $A \subset B$ and $A \supset B$ then the sets contain the same members and are called *equal*, written as $A = B$. If A and B are not equal we write $A \neq B$. If A is a subset of B, but not equal to B, then A is also called *proper subset* of B and we write $A \supsetneq B$ and $B \subsetneq A$. A *partition* of a set A is a set of subsets of A such that every member of A is exactly in one of the subsets and none of the subsets is the empty set. Furthermore we define the following operations on sets:

- $A \cup B$ is the *union* of two sets A and B, which is the set of all objects that are members of one or both of the two sets.

- $A \cap B$ is the *intersection* of two sets A and B, which is the set of all objects that are members of both sets.

- $B \setminus A$ is the *complement* of one set A relative to another set B, which is the set of all objects that are not members of A but members of B.

- $\mathcal{P}$ is the *power set* of a set A, which is the set of all of its subsets. The set of all subsets with a given cardinality n is written as $\mathcal{P}_n(S)$.

To define particular sets, there are two methods. First, one can provide a *property* that all members of the set must satisfy. In set-builder notation we write $\{x \mid \phi(x)\}$ to denote the set of all elements that satisfy the property ϕ and ϕ is also called the sets *membership function*. For instance the set of all prime numbers could be written as $\{x \mid x \text{ is a prime}\}$. With membership functions we can give more formal definitions of operations on sets, for instance $A \cup B = \{x \mid x \in A \wedge x \in B\}$. Properties and sets can be used interchangeably: each property defines a set and each set A defines a property 'being member of set A'. Using properties to define sets, however, requires to somehow refer to a collection of all possible members, which may or may not satisfy a property. This collection is called the *universal set* $\mathcal{U}$ or a *universe* if it is limited to some specific objects. The second method to specify a set is to write down a list of its elements in curly brackets. For instance $\{\times, \triangle, \heartsuit\}$ can denote the set of a cross symbol, a triangle symbol, and a heart symbol. Note that neither the order of listed members nor any repetition of the same member is relevant — the same set could also be written as $\{\triangle, \heartsuit, \times, \triangle\}$. The identification of 'same' elements is out of the scope of set theory (unless elements are restricted to sets themselves). For instance the sets $\{+, \blacktriangle, <3\}$ and $\{\times, \triangle, \heartsuit\}$ both contains a cross symbol, a triangle symbol, and a heart symbol. Whether both sets are equal depends on whether visual differences between the symbols in both sets matter or not. Using properties such as $\{x|x$ looks like a heart symbol$\}$ neither solves the symbol grounding problem: arbitrary properties based on a general universal set lead to paradoxes such the impossible set $R = \{X|X \notin X\}$ (Russell's paradox). This set is defined to contain all sets that do not contain themselves, so R must contain itself if it does not contain itself, which is a contradiction.

To avoid such paradoxes of naive set theory there are several strategies. Zermelo-Fraenkel set theory with the axiom of choice assigns each set a *rank*, that is the smallest ordinal number greater than the ranks of its members. There is no universal set but only the set $\mathcal{V}_\alpha$ of all sets with rank α. The full cumulative hierarchy, starting with $\mathcal{V}_0 = \emptyset$, is called *von Neumann universe*. Another strategy adds *classes* or *categories* as distinct objects to sets. A class is defined in the same way as a set, but it can only have sets as members. For every property ϕ one can define the class Φ of all sets with property ϕ. Every set is also a class, but some *proper classes*, such as the class of all sets, and the paradoxical class R cannot be described as sets but only as classes. Classes and categories as abstractions of sets and other mathematical objects are also studied in category theory.

2.1.3. Tuples and relations

Tuples and relation are mathematical constructs that appear at many places in data description. They can best be defined based on set theory. A *tuple* is a finite ordered list, also known as sequence. A tuple with n elements is called an *n-tuple*. The 2-tuple is also called *ordered pair*. We use angle brackets and write $\langle x_1 \ldots x_n \rangle$ to denote the n-tuple of x_1 to x_n. Similar to sets, tuples have members, but the order of elements in a tuple is relevant ($\langle a, b \rangle \neq \langle b, a \rangle$). The same element can also occur multiple times in a tuple ($\langle a, a \rangle \neq \langle a \rangle$ but $\{a, a\} = \{a\}$). Tuples are useful for further definitions of objects with distinct members, for instance an n-ary predicate could be defined as *n-tuple*. One applications of tuples is the definition of mathematical relations.

A *relation* is a set of similar tuples. More precisely, an n-ary relation is a set of n-tuples $\langle x_1, x_2, \ldots x_n \rangle$ and a set n of sets $X_1 \ldots X_n$ where every element x_i is member of some specific set X_i. For each sequence of sets, there is a total relation, called the *cartesian product*. Every n-ary relation is a subset of a cartesian product, which is defined as:

$$X_1 \times X_2 \times \cdots \times X_n = \{\langle x_1, x_2 \ldots x_n \rangle | x_i \in X_i, i = 1 \ldots n\}$$

A *binary relation* r between two sets A and B is some set of ordered pairs $\langle a, b \rangle$, where a is element of A and b is element of B. In this case, A is called the *domain* of r and B is the *codomain* of r, and we write $r : A \longrightarrow B$ (not to be confused with the logical implication arrow $\rightarrow$). The set of all such ordered pairs is the cartesian

injective (left-unique)	$\forall \langle x_1, y_1 \rangle, \langle x_2, y_2 \rangle \in r : (y_1 = y_2) \rightarrow (x_1 = x_2)$
functional (right-unique)	$\forall \langle x_1, y_1 \rangle, \langle x_2, y_2 \rangle \in r : (x_1 = x_2) \rightarrow (y_1 = y_2)$
one-to-one	$\forall \langle x_1, y_1 \rangle, \langle x_2, y_2 \rangle \in r : (y_1 = y_2) \leftrightarrow (x_1 = x_2)$
(left-)*total*	$\forall x \in X \, \exists y \in Y : \langle x, y \rangle \in z$
surjective (right-total)	$\forall y \in Y \, \exists x \in X : \langle x, y \rangle \in z$
function or *map*	$\forall x \in X \, \exists! y \in Y : \langle x, y \rangle \in z$
bijective	$\forall x \in X \, \exists! y \in Y : \langle x, y \rangle \in z$ and
	$\forall y \in Y \, \exists! x \in X : \langle x, y \rangle \in z$
correspondence	$\forall x \in X \, \exists y \in Y : \langle x, y \rangle \in z$ (total) and
	$\forall y \in Y \, \exists x \in X : \langle x, y \rangle \in z$ (surjective)

Table 2.2.: Types of binary relations

product $A \times B = \{\langle a, b \rangle | a \in A \wedge b \in B\}$. The sets of a relation do not necessarily have to be disjoint. For instance a binary relation r over a set A is $r \subseteq A \times A$. Binary relations over sets are also studied in graph theory as these relations are isomorph to digraphs (see section 2.1.4). In data structures these relations are called recursive. Obviously one can turn any binary relation over two sets A and B into a relation over one set C with $C = A \cup B$.

Binary relations can be classified according to which kind of tuples they contain. Table 2.2 lists the most important types for a binary relation $z : X \longrightarrow Y$. Part of the terminology was originally coined by the Bourbaki group (Bourbaki 1970). For functional relations the notation $r(x)$ denotes the element from r's codomain where $\langle x, r(x) \rangle$ is in r. The *domain of definition* and *range* refer to the subset of term and codomain that actually take part in the relation, but the usage of this terms is not coherent and 'domain' implicitly refers to the domain of definition. Figure 2.2 illustrates the basic terms and types with several binary relations over two out of four sets $A = \{a_1, a_2, a_3\}$, $B = \{b_1, b_2, b_3\}$, $C = \{c_1, c_2, c_3\}$, $D = \{d_1, d_2, d_3\}$ and its subsets A', B', and D'.

A bijective relation is also injective and surjective and a one-to-one correspondence. The extension of this concept in category theory is called isomorphism, while structures that can be transformed injectively or surjectively are called monomorphism or epimorphism, respectively. Binary relations can also be combined to create new relations. The relation $g \circ f$ is defined as the set $\{\langle x, z \rangle | \exists y : \langle x, y \rangle \in f \wedge \langle y, z \rangle \in g\}$ (see figure 2.2 for an example).

2.1.4. Graph theory

Formal graphs as method of description were introduced in the late 19th century by Cayley (1857) and Sylvester (1878) for chemical structures. Among other applications, graphs can be used to model binary relations over a set of objects. Most of the following definitions can be found in any introduction to graph theory but terminology differs among authors in slight details.

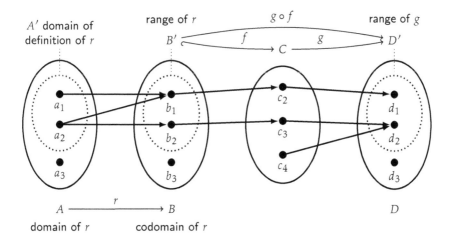

relation	domain	codomain	type of relation
r	A'	B	left-total
	A	B'	right-total (or surjective or onto)
	A'	B'	correspondence (left- and right-total)
f	B'	C	injective and partial function
	C	D	(total) function
g	C	D'	surjective and function
$g \circ f$	B'	D'	bijective
	B	D	one-to-one

Figure 2.2.: Terms and types of binary relations

A *graph* is a pair $\langle V, E \rangle$ where V is a finite set of *nodes* (or *vertices*) and E is a finite set of *edges*. Unless otherwise indicated the graph is a *simple graph*, that means edges are 2-sets without orientation and cannot connect a node with itself: $E \subseteq \mathcal{P}_2(V)$ Two nodes u, v are *adjacent* if $\{u, v\} \in V$. The *degree* of a node v is the number of adjacent nodes $\{u \mid \{u, v\} \in V\}$. A *path* is a sequence of two or more nodes $v_1, \ldots v_n$ such that v_i and v_{i+1} are adjacent for $1 \leq i < n$. Unless otherwise noted a path uses every edge at most once. A *cycle* is a path with $v_1 = v_n$. If there is a path between two nodes u and v, they are *connected* and their *distance* is the length of their shortest connecting path. A graph is said to be connected if every pair of nodes in the graph are connected. Unless otherwise noted a graph is assumed to be connected. A *planar graph* can be drawn on a plane without intersecting edges. A graph is *bipartite* if its nodes can be partitioned into two sets such that no nodes of the same set are adjacent. Unless mentioned otherwise we will use the term bipartite graph more specific for a *fixed bipartite graph* $\langle V_1, V_2, E \rangle$ with specific node partition – which is isomorph to a binary relation (see example 1).

A *directed graph* or *digraph* is a graph whose edges (also called *arcs*) are ordered

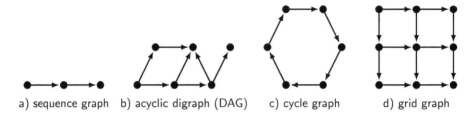

a) sequence graph   b) acyclic digraph (DAG)   c) cycle graph   d) grid graph

Figure 2.3.: Some digraph types exemplified

pairs: $E \subseteq V \times V$. An arc $\langle u,v \rangle$ is said to direct, link, or point from u to v; unless otherwise indicated a *loop*, that is an arc that pairs a node to itself ($u = v$), is not allowed. An arc $\langle u,v \rangle$ is *symmetric* if its reverse link $\langle v,u \rangle$ is also present. A simple graph can be modeled by a digraph that only holds symmetric links. In a digraph we must distinguish the number of edges pointing to a node as *indegree* and the number of edges pointing from a node as *outdegree*. A (directed) *path* is a non-empty sequence of nodes, one pointing to the next without use a link twice. A node u is *reachable* from another node v if there is a directed path from v to u. A path that starts and ends in the same node is a *cycle*. If a node u can be reached from v on two disjoint paths, the union of both paths is called a *diamond*. Adding all reverse links to a diamond results in a cycle. A digraph is *strongly connected* if every node is reachable from every other node and *weakly connected* if adding all missing symmetric links would result in a strongly connected digraph. Unless otherwise noted a digraph is assumed to be weakly connected.

Some types of directed graphs deserve special treatment: A *sequence graph* (figure 2.3 a) is a strongly connected digraph in which only one one node has indegree 0 and all other nodes have indegree 1. A (directed) *cycle graph* (c) is a digraph that consists of a single cycle. A *directed acyclic graph* (DAG) or *acyclic digraph* (b) is a directed graph containing no cycles. The edges of a (directed) *grid graph* (d) are defined by a n-tuple $\langle s_1, \ldots, s_d \rangle$ where d is the *dimension* of the graph and $s_i \in \mathbb{N}^+$ are its *sizes*.

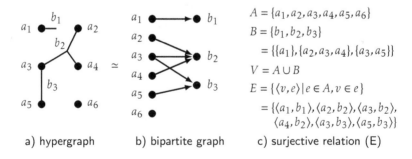

a) hypergraph   b) bipartite graph   c) surjective relation (E)

$$A = \{a_1, a_2, a_3, a_4, a_5, a_6\}$$
$$B = \{b_1, b_2, b_3\}$$
$$= \{\{a_1\}, \{a_2, a_3, a_4\}, \{a_3, a_5\}\}$$
$$V = A \cup B$$
$$E = \{\langle v, e \rangle \mid e \in A, v \in e\}$$
$$= \{\langle a_1, b_1 \rangle, \langle a_2, b_2 \rangle, \langle a_3, b_2 \rangle,$$
$$\langle a_4, b_2 \rangle, \langle a_3, b_3 \rangle, \langle a_5, b_3 \rangle\}$$

Example 1: A hypergraph and its (fixed) bipartite graph

The graph concept can be further extended: A *multigraph* is a graph in which multiple edges can exist between any two nodes. The maximum number of edges linking two nodes is called the *multiplicity* of the multigraph. A multigraph can be defined two ways: Either the edges E do not form a set but a bag; in this case multiple edges are indistinguishable. Or the two nodes that are connected by an edge are not their element but but there is an additional function $\vartheta : V \longrightarrow E \times E$ that maps edges to node-pairs. There can be simple and directed multigraphs. Unless defined otherwise edges are not ordered.

In a *hypergraph* an edge can connect any positive number of nodes. The edges of a hypergraph are also called *hyperedge*. There is an isomorphism between hypergraphs and fixed bipartite graphs that have no unconnected nodes in the second partition (example 1 **b**): Let $H = \langle A, B \rangle$ with $B \subseteq \mathcal{P}(A) \setminus \emptyset$ be a hypergraph. You can then construct a directed bipartite graph $P = \langle V, E \rangle$ as shown in example 1, or express the hypergraph as surjective relation between two disjoint sets. By lifting the disjointness constraint, one gets a *generalized hypergraph* in which edges can also connect other edges. This neutralizes the distinction between nodes and edges – if the graph is also a multigraph, one can simply view nodes as empty edges. It is easier to visualize generalized hypergraphs as directed acyclic graphs (if edges can only contain edges of smaller rank) or as general directed graphs. Nodes of the new graph correspond to edges in the hypergraph and edges represent edge containment. This representation of a generalized hypergraph is sometimes called Levi graph.

There are several forms of *graph labeling*, that is the assignment of labels, or other elements to edges, nodes, or both of a graph. We define a *property graph* as tuple $\langle V, E, P, \Phi \rangle$ with E being a finite set of edges, V being a finite set of nodes, P being a finite set of properties and $\Phi : G' \longrightarrow P$ with $G' \subseteq (V \cup E)$ a partial function that maps edges and/or nodes to properties. For $\Phi : E \longrightarrow P$ (only edges have properties) the graph is a *edge-property graph* and for $\Phi : V \longrightarrow P$ (only nodes have properties) it is a *node-property graph*. This definition makes no assumption on the nature of nodes and thus can be applied to all kinds of graphs (simple graphs, directed graphs, multigraphs, hypergraphs). There is no assumption on properties: they can be labels, types, weights, colors, identifiers, attributes, sets, tuples etc. depending on the particular property graph type. A relevant instance is a property graph where $(V \cup E)$ can be mapped via bijection to P so every node and edge can be identified uniquely by its property.

An *undirected tree* (figure 2.4 **a**) is a simple graph without cycles. Tree nodes with degree one are also called *leafs*. An unconnected tree is called a *forest*. By selecting a single tree node as *root*, one gets a *rooted tree* (**b** without the dashed lines). This selection implies a direction on every edge. The direction is typically defined pointing outwards from the root. Unless noted otherwise the term tree will be used for such rooted trees. By reversing the direction on all edges, one gets *inverted tree*. The tree nodes that are directly connected from a given node via one outgoing edge are its child node which are siblings to each other. All nodes reachable from another are its *descendants* which for a subtree. All nodes that can reach another node are its *ancestors* which form a sequence graph starting from the root. An *ordered tree* is

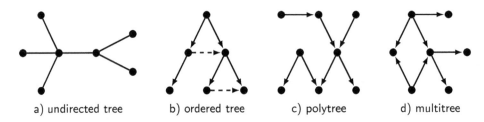

a) undirected tree   b) ordered tree   c) polytree   d) multitree

Figure 2.4.: Tree types

a tree in which the child nodes of each node are ordered. In (figure 2.4 b) ordering is indicated by dashed linkes pointing from one sibling to the next. There are two special kinds of DAGs that are also called trees: A *polytree* (c) is a directed acyclic graph containing no undirected cycles and a *multitree* (d) is directed acyclic graph without directed diamonds (Furnas and Zacks 1994). In a multitree the descendants of any node form a tree and the ancestors of any node form an inverted tree but there may be undirected diamonds. Every polytree is also a multitree and every directed tree is also a polytree.

2.2. Computer science

Any sufficiently advanced technology is indistinguishable from magic.
— Arthur C. Clarke

The following sections introduce three topics from computer science that are relevant to this thesis: *formal languages* and computation are fundamental computer science concepts to reason about sets of data (section 2.2.1). *Data types* are important to manage data structures in programming languages and in databases (section 2.2.2). Finally, *data modeling* tries to bridge the gap between some reality and its description in form of data in some information system (section 2.2.3). First the discipline should be put in context by a short overview.

In general, computer science deals with the theoretical and practical automatic processing of data or information. The first scientific computing organization was founded in 1947 with the Association for Computing Machinery (ACM). Computer science as an independent academic field was established until the 1960s. The history of the discipline, which can be located somewhere between applied mathematics and engineering, is directly connected to the development and application of computer systems. The first computers as programmable, general purpose machines were created in the 1940s for military calculations.[4] Meanwhile, computers are used in almost any aspect of daily live with an impact comparable to the industrial revolution or with the invention of the printing press. The economic weight of the so called information industry is another factor that must be beard in mind when thinking about promises and motivations of (applied) computer science.

From the beginning of computer science, there has been a tendency to describe computers not only as tools for automatic data processing, but to attribute them with human terms like 'intelligent', 'thinking', 'knowledge', 'brain', and 'semantic'.[5] The comparision of automatic systems with brain power is also drawn, if computing is viewed as a natural phenomenon, with mental activity as instances of information processing, similar to computer systems (Denning 2007).

The traditional, rationalistic paradigm of computer science is contrasted by constructivist views that stress the relativity of automatic systems as social artifacts. For Turing Award winner[6] Peter Naur, pioneer in software engineering who suggested

---

[4] The first computers include: Zuse Z3 (1941) and Z4 (1945) that were created for calculations in military aviation, as well as other early German calculating machines from this time (Lange 2006, p. 202ff.); Collosus (1944) that helped to decipher encrypted messages by British codebreakers; Harvard Mark I/ASCC (1944) and its successors that were used by the US Navy; ENIAC (1946) and EDVAC (1949) that were used by the US Army. Only the IBM SSEC (1948) also served non-military purposes until in 1949 three computers were completed at research institutions, partly with commerical support: EDSAC in Cambridge, Manchester Mark 1 in Manchester, and CSIRAC in Sydney. More about early computers can be found in the collection by Rojas and Hashagen (2000).

[5] See for instance Berkeley (1949) and the whole terminology of artificial intelligence. Even the term 'language' is misleading because programming languages and other formal languages, unlike human languages, are based on precise formalization but not on speech and communication (Naur 1992).

[6] The Turing Award, annually awarded by the ACM is the highest distinction in computer science.

the term datalogy in favour of computer science, programming is not comparable to industrial production, but an act of theory building (Naur 1985), and "the core of programming is the programmer's developing a certain kind of understanding of the matters of concern." (Naur 2007).[7] Despite the predominant practice in computer science, computing artifacts are neither objective description of reality (W. Kent 1978) nor an optimal solution of a given problem. Instead "we construct the problem as well as the solution" (Floyd 1996) and must therefore take responsibility for the thus constructed reality (Weizenbaum 1976). Having said this, computer science provides powerful theories and tools to describe and process data.

2.2.1. Formal languages and computation

The study of formal languages emerged independently during the 1950s in linguistics and in computer science: Noam Chomsky applied it to human languages, and John Backus to programming languages (Greibach 1981). The basic properties of formal grammars, languages, and computation are explained by Hopcroft and Ullman (1979). A *formal language* is a defined set of sequences of symbols. The symbols are also called the *alphabet* of the language, and the sequences are also called strings or *words*. Examples of formal languages include: the set of words that can be build as sequences of the letters A to Z; the set of roman numerals with symbols I,V,X,L,C,D,M; and the set of genome sequences with adenine, cytosine, guanine, thymine as symbols. A formal language can be defined by either listing all of its words, if the language is finite, or by specifying a membership property that all of its words must satisfy. In computer science formal languages are studied in form of their membership properties, as automata or formal grammars, which will both be described in the following.

An *automaton* is an mathematically defined method (a process or algorithm) to compute whether a string belongs to a given formal language. The automaton is said to *decide* whether a string belongs to the language, if the method is guaranteed to halt with positive or negative result after a finite amount of time. As shown first by Turing (1936) and Church (1936), there exist formal languages which are *undecidable*: that means no automatic process can compute whether a string belongs to the language or not: any algorithm at least for some strings will not halt computation in finite time.[8] The concept of decidability is based on the concept of *computation*, which is a core concept of the whole discipline of computer science. Crucial for the concept of computation is the idea of a process where all steps are precisely defined. There are several models of computation which can be grouped in classes of equivalent computational power. A model of computation that belongs to the most powerful class is said to be *Turing-complete*, and it can be used to compute all computable problems, as stated by the Church-Turing-thesis. The terms 'computable' and 'decidable' can

---

[7] See Wyssusek (2007) for a more detailed discussion of Naur's position.

[8] The proof provided by Turing (1936) is known as 'halting problem': in particular the formal language of 'all programs that will halt' is not decidable.

be used interchangeably, as all functions with enumerable domain can be expressed as formal languages with tuples as words.

A *formal grammar* is a set of rules that describe how to form words of a formal language. It consists of the alphabet of symbols A, one selected *starting symbol* $S \in A$, and a set of *production rules*, each rule of the form $\alpha \to \beta$, where α and β are sequences of symbols. The empty sequence ϵ can also be allowed, for instance to express removal of a sequence ($\alpha \to \epsilon$). To better analyze formal grammars, the alphabet is partitioned in two sets: *terminal symbols* may occur in words and *non-terminal symbols* occur only as variables, that are replaced by other sequences during the production process. Example 2 shows a formal grammar that can produce all roman numerals up to 4999, or the empty sequence. The grammar can also be written in more concise form as regular expression.[9] Regular expressions and other methods to express formal grammars will be described in section 3.7.1.

starting symbol	S
terminal symbols	I, V, X, L, C, D, M, ϵ
non-terminals	T for thousands, H for hundreds, E for hundreds from ϵ to CCC, Z for tens, Y for tens from ϵ to XXX, U for units, O for units from ϵ to III
production rules	$S \to THEU$ $T \to \epsilon$, $T \to M$, $T \to MM$, $T \to MMM$, $T \to MMMM$ $H \to E$, $H \to CM$, $H \to CD$, $H \to DE$ $E \to \epsilon$, $E \to C$, $E \to CC$, $E \to CCC$ $Z \to Y$, $Z \to XC$, $Z \to XL$, $Z \to LY$ $Y \to \epsilon$, $Y \to X$, $Y \to XX$, $Y \to XXX$ $U \to O$, $U \to IX$, $U \to IV$, $U \to VO$ $O \to \epsilon$, $O \to I$, $O \to II$, $O \to III$

The language could also be expressed by the following regular expression:
`^M{0,4}(CM|CD|D?C{0,3})(XC|XL|L?X{0,3})(IX|IV|V?I{0,3})`

Example 2: Formal grammar of roman numerals up to 4999

Unrestricted formal grammars are Turing-complete, so any computable process can also be encoded as a formal grammar. For instance Functional programming languages like Haskell make use of rewriting systems, as shown below. By putting restrictions on the general form of production rules and/or on the process of replacing sequences by applying rules, one can define subclasses of formal languages with less complexity. The most known classification is the *Chomsky hierarchy* with the following languages:

- Type-0: *recursively enumerable languages* (RE) include all languages that can be defined by any formal grammar. Rules have the form $\alpha \to \beta$ where α and β are

---

[9] grammar has been adopted from a regular expression that was kindly provided and explained by user 'paxdiablo' at `http://stackoverflow.com/questions/267399/#267405`.

unrestricted sequences of symbols.

- Type-1: *context-sensitive languages* (CSL) have production rules of the form $\alpha X \beta \rightarrow \alpha \gamma \beta$ where X is a non-terminal symbol; α, β, γ are sequences of symbols; and only α and β can be empty. In addition, a rule of the form $X \rightarrow \epsilon$ is allowed, if X does not occur at the right side of any rule. The sequences α and β specify the context in which X is replaced by another sequence.

- Type-2: *context-free languages* (CFL) have only production rules with one single non-terminal symbol at the left side ($X \rightarrow \alpha$). The context of X is not taken into consideration when it is replaced.

- Type-3: *regular languages* (REG) limit production rules to rules of the form $X \rightarrow A$, $X \rightarrow \epsilon$, and either only $X \rightarrow AY$ (right regular) or $X \rightarrow YA$ (left regular), where X and Y are non-terminal symbols and A is a terminal symbol.

Each type is a proper subset of the former, and each corresponds to a class of computational power, with type-0 being the class of Turing-complete languages. Most programming languages are Turing-complete, that means the set of valid programs can only be defined by a grammar in *RE*. In practice, many computable problems are also decidable so they could be expressed in a less powerful language type. The corresponding class of *recursive languages* (R), which can always be decided, is between *RE* and *CSL*. However, such sub-Turing programming languages are not widely used, apart from theorem provers and tools for formal software verification.

To make use of formal languages, there are two general problems: first the problem to specify a formal grammar, and second the problem to determine whether and how a word can be produced by a given grammar (*parsing*). The specification problem is related to the application of schema languages for writing down grammars (section 3.7). The most difficult part is to formalize a possibly infinite set of words from a finite set of examples and assumptions. Unfortunately there can be many grammars that define the same language and even for *CFL* it is not computable whether an arbitrary grammar is equivalent to or is a subset of another grammar. The second problem is computable at least for recursive languages, but the computation may be very complex (time-intensive),[10] and a word may be producible by multiple paths of rule application. A specific list of rule applications and intermediate symbol sequences that transform the starting symbol into some word is also called the word's *parse tree* or syntax tree. If a grammar covers words with multiple parse trees, the grammar is called *ambiguous*.

Ambiguous grammars, complexity of parsing, and other limitations of formal language types have motivated the creation of additional language classes and computation models between *REG*, *CFL*, a and *CSL*. Some relevant classes are:

---

[10] The task of determining whether a given word belongs to a given context-sensitive language may take more than *polynomial time* (P): that means there is no upper bound k so that it takes less than n^k steps to check any sufficiently large word of n symbols length. For many problems P is a limit of practical computability.

- *deterministic context free language* (DCFL) include all non-ambiguous CFL.

- *linear languages* (LINL) and *deterministic linear languages* (DLINL) are CFL with at most one non-terminal symbol at the right side of a grammar rule.

- *indexed languages* (IND) enrich each non-terminal in CFL rules with a stack of index symbols to remember what rules were applied and in which order.

- *growing context-sensitive languages* (GCSL) have rules of the form $\alpha \to \beta$ where $|\alpha| < |\beta|$ (McNaughton 1999).

- *Tree-adjoining grammars* (TAG) use ordered trees instead of sequences in its production rules. Vijay-Shanker and Weir (1994) showed that TAG express the same language types as several other formalisms for so called mildly context-sensitive languages (linear indexed grammars, head grammars, etc.).

- *conjunctive grammars* (CG) extend rules of CFL with conjunction operators. *boolean grammars* (BG) also add negation operators (Okhotin 2010). The rules of a *BG* have the form $X \to \alpha_1 \& \ldots \& \alpha_m \& \neg\beta_1 \& \ldots \& \neg\beta_n$ (without β_i for *CG*). A sequence that replaces X must satisfy all sequences α_i and none of the sequences β_i. Parsed words of a *CG* or *BG* have acyclic graphs instead of parse trees.

- *visibly pushdown languages* (VPL) or *nested words* capture linear and hierarchical structures by adding symbols for tagged *calls* and *returns* (Alur and Madhusudan 2009). Equally tagged call and return symbols hierarchically connect to nested edges that must not overlap, but may be pending. Figure 4 contains two examples of nested words with call symbols $a^\uparrow$, $b^\uparrow$, return symbols $a^\downarrow$, $b^\downarrow$, and normal symbols c, d. Ordered trees are a special case of nested words that start with a call, end with a corresponding return, and contain no pending edges.

The relations between the language classes mentioned above are summarized in figure 2.5 with arrows depicting the proper subset relationship. P and NP denote no grammar types, but important complexity classes from the theory of computation.

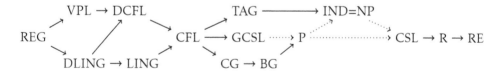

Figure 2.5.: Relations (proper containments) between classes of formal language

Formal grammars can be generalized to *rewriting systems*. A rewriting system is digraph in which nodes represent objects and edges represent a rewriting relation '$\to$'. The rewriting relation can be used as rules to replace one object by another. Suppose for instance the set $\{a, b, c\}$ and the rewriting relation $\{(a \to b), (a \to c), (c \to a), (c \to b)\}$: the system is non-ambiguous as there are several paths from a to b, either by direct replacement or by first replacing a with c and then c with b. Objects with outdegree zero act as terminal symbols (in this example b) and there may exist paths that can be followed infinitely (in this example $a \rightarrow c \rightarrow a \rightarrow c \rightarrow \cdots$).

To illustrate the general concept example 3 shows a rewriting system in which objects are build of geometric figures (visual symbols). The system consists of two rules that can be used to replace a simple triangle by a structure of two or three triangles. Starting with a simple triangle (start) one can create an infinite number of different figures by applying rule 1 or rule 2 to selected parts of the figure. However, the set of figures that can be reached from a given start symbol, is strictly defined. For instance the figure in the bottom right of example 3 is no valid figure in the given rewriting system.

Rewriting systems are of special interest, if the objects to be rewritten have some internal structure. Common types of such systems are: formal grammars as string rewriting systems, that operate on sequences of symbols; term or tree rewriting systems with applications for instance in symbolic computation, automatic theorem proving, and code optimization; and graph rewriting systems.

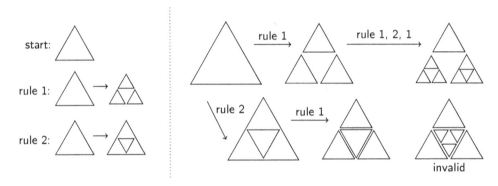

Example 3: Rewriting system on geometric figures

In summary, formal languages and rewriting systems describe structures of sequences, trees, or graphs; and how these structures can be parsed. This requires the identification of symbols or objects of same kind: for instance the size of two triangles in example 3 does not matter, but their orientation. Another often overlooked property of formal languages and rewriting systems is that they only deal with syntax although they are often used to described some semantics. If one compares example 2 and example 3, only the first has some known meaning. An intelligent reader can give meaning to some of the non-terminal symbols, but other symbols may be irrelevant artifacts, only introduced because of formal grammar limitations. To give another example, the production rule $C \rightarrow IBTCECF$ with terminals I, T, E, F and non-terminals B and C has special meaning but being a production rule. We can change the names of symbols to get the following rule in Backus-Naur-Form (see section 3.7.1 and table 3.16 for details about this syntax):

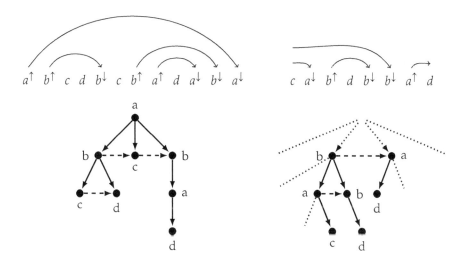

Example 4: Nested words (the left also being an ordered tree)

```
command = "if" boolean "then" command "else" command "end"
```

The meaning of this rule, however, is only added by telling that this rule is used for a construct from a programming language created for some purpose, and that it will trigger a specific action when given as input to an interpreter. Especially the name of non-terminal symbols is irrelevant as they never show up in final words of a languages. For instance the rule above could also be written as:

```
x = "if" y "then" x "else" x "end"
```

In summary, rules from formal languages can be used as base for meaningful constructs, but they do not hold meaning in its structure alone.

2.2.2. Data types

Algorithms + Data Structures = Programs
— Niklaus Wirth (1976)

Until the 1960s, programming languages only provided a limited set of predefined data types and programmers had to choose data representation close to the internal structure of memory. The influential programming language ALGOL 60 (Naur 1963) with fixed data types for integers, decimal numbers, boolean values, and arrays, introduced lexical scoping, so parts of a program could have their own private variables. Grouping data was further improved by records and other types in Pascal's precursor ALGOL W (Wirth and Hoare 1966), by object-orientation in SIMULA (Dahl and Nygaard 1966), and by *abstract data types* (Liskov and Zilles

1974). The basic idea of abstract data types is to define data objects based on how they can be used and modified by operations specific to each data type. Operations hide the representation of an object's state and only show the 'what' instead the 'how' of computing with data objects.

Programming languages and some other methods of data structuring such as schema languages (section 3.7) provide a basic set of *primitive data types* and mechanisms to create new types based on existing types. Typical primitive data types include the boolean type, character and character string types, and numeric types (see section 3.1.2) but domain-specific types such as date and time may also be primitive, depending on the language. A special primitive type in some languages is the *unit type*, which can hold no information because all unit type variables have the same value. General mechanisms to derive new data types include referencing (pointer types), aggregation, choice, and subtyping, which will be described below. Both the set of primitive data types and mechanisms to define new types differ among programming languages, so one cannot simply exchange typed data from one language to another. As most programming language features, data types are only a tool but no requirement. Some languages have no data types at all or types are not explicitly defined but only used by convention.

The main purpose of explicit typing in programming languages is to check that data object (variables) are used in a predictable way, so programmers can work with abstract data values instead of stored representations of values. Type checking can either be performed before execution of the program (static typing) or on execution (dynamic typing). Some languages also allow to infer a type from the object's properties (duck typing). Systems of primitive types together with possible rules of type derivation are studied as *type systems* in programming language theory. An important theoretical method for describing type systems are *algebraic data types*, which were introduced in functional programming languages with Hope as first (Burstall, MacQueen, and Sannella 1980) and Haskell as currently most popular instance. The theory of algebraic data types is based on mathematical type theory and category theory, which advanced in the 1990s (Pierce 2002). Extensible programming languages were another approach to better separate data structures from implementation and to facilitate definition of new data types (Balzer 1967; Schuman and Jorrand 1967; Solntseff and Yezerski 1974). Incidentally the term 'metadata' was coined by Bagley (1968) in this context. Extensible programming languages received less adoption because they made difficult code sharing, but they now receive a revival as host systems for domain specific languages.

To find common patterns in data types, it is wise not to look only at theoretic type theory but also at the actual diversity of data types and existing approaches to create mappings between type systems from different programming languages. As described by Meek (1994a,b), a working group on language independent data types created ISO 11404, which was last revised in 2007 (ISO 11404:2007). ISO 14404 influenced some type systems of data binding languages (section 3.5.1) and schema languages (section 3.7), such as the XML Schema datatypes (Biron and Malhotra 2004) described in section 3.7 IV. The standard defines a data type as "a set of

Boolean	a Boolean logic value
State	a value from an unordered list of possible values
Enumerated	a value from an ordered list of possible values
Character	a value from a set of possible characters (see section 3.1)
Ordinal	an ordinal number (1st, 2nd, 3rd...)
Date-and-Time	a value from all points in time
Integer	a number from $\mathbb{Z}$
Scaled	a fixed point number from a subset of $\mathbb{R}$
Real	a number from $\mathbb{R}$
Complex	a complex number from $\mathbb{C}$
Void	the unit type

Table 2.3.: Primitive data types defined in ISO 11404 (2007)

distinct values, characterized by properties of those values and by operations on those values" and distinguishes three notions:

- the *value space* is the set of possible values of a given data type independent from its realization in data. The value space can be finite (for instance the Boolean values 'true' and 'false') or infinite (for instance the set $\mathbb{R}$).

- the *computational model* defines a set of representable values of a given data type with some properties and operations. For instance Boolean values are not ordered but one can apply Boolean algebra. Infinite value spaces have no exact mapping from value space to computational model, as explained in section 3.1.2 on number encodings.

- the *value representation* in a given environment, for instance the two bits 0 and 1 for the values 'true' and 'false'. The value representation is also known as lexical space.

The standard further defines some primitives data types (table 2.3), general properties (types can be ordered or unordered, and ordered types may have upper and lower bounds), and methods to derive new data types with defined value spaces and computational model. The derivation methods can be classified as following:

- the value of a *pointer type* or reference refers to another typed variable. For instance an integer reference always points to an integer variable. Two pointers are equal only if they point to the same variable but not if they point to distinct variables with same value. Most pointer types allow the special value NULL to indicate that the pointer does refers to any variable. This feature can also be implemented by a choice type of a simple type and the unit type.

- a *choice types*, also known as tagged union, defines a set of possible types that each variable can choose from. For instance a variable of choice type created from integer and string could either store an integer or a string value. The particular selection of type is also called the variable's tag.

- *aggregation types* hold multiple values as members. An aggregate type can be homogeneous, if all members must belong to a single datatypes, or heterogeneous. Typical aggregation types include sets, sequences, bags, and tables, which can be defined both homogeneous and heterogeneous. Record types correspond to tuples and associative arrays (also called maps or dictionaries) correspond to finite functions. Maps store a set of key-value pairs with unique, usually homogeneous keys and homogeneous or heterogeneous values.

- *subtypes* can be defined by limiting or extending other types. Examples include simple (untagged) unions of types, upper/lower bounds on value spaces, and selections/exclusions of specific values. Beside these simple set operations one can define more complex constraints and also extend choice types and aggregation types. An important kind of subtyping in object-oriented languages is based on heterogeneous record types which are then called classes. In most type systems a derived subtype keeps most properties of its base types (inheritance) and in most context the subtype can be used as if it was the base type. If the subtype was derived from multiple base types, this feature is called polymorphism. Polymorphism is a powerful feature because it allows one thing to have different kinds at the same time, but in practice it is difficult to determine which specific base time to refer to in which context. For this reason most type systems restrict subtyping at least to some degree.

Type constructors can be combined, even recursively. For instance a tree type with labeled leaf nodes can be defined as homogeneous aggregation type with a choice type of either an element (a leaf) or a sequence of trees (child nodes). ISO 14404 further defines provisions to mark (parts of) types as mandatory, optional, recommended etc. Optional parts can also be viewed as choice types with a base type as one option (element given) and the unit type as the other (element not given). Similar derivation methods as described above exist with differing main focus in programming languages and other type systems.

2.2.3. Data modeling

In general *data modeling* is a set of activities required to design a database or data format. The basic terms of this process have been introduced by (Association for Computing Machinery 1971; Steel, Jr. 1975) and standardized in (International Organization for Standardization 1987). As surveyed by Simsion (2007, p. 34ff.) the data modeling terminology differs, especially between academic and practitioners, but also within communities. Nevertheless there is a rough consensus to differentiate *i)* three "realms of interest" which are the real world; ideas about the real world existing in the minds of men; and symbols on some storage medium representing these ideas (Steel, Jr. 1975, p. II-1) *ii)* several stages in database design process

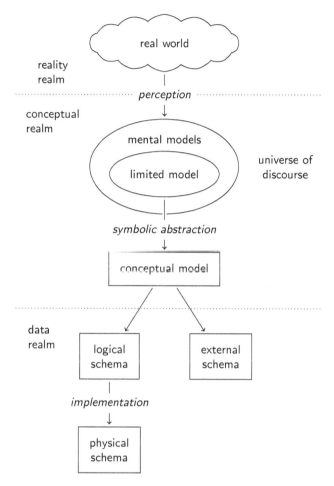

reality
realm

conceptual
realm

universe of
discourse

data
realm

Figure 2.6.: Summarized view of the data modeling process

from one realm of interest to the next, possibly with sub-steps (Simsion 2007, ch. 3.1) *iii)* several levels of description for different stages and applications (W. Kent 1978, ch. 2.2.2). Figure 2.6 shows a synthesis of data modeling process frameworks from across the data modeling literature. It is mainly based on (Simsion 2007, fig. 3-1) who gives an in-depth review of literature and on (Jr. 1975, fig. 2).[11] A common model of reality that exists in our minds, shared between individuals via any language, is called *universe of discourse*. We can only express a limited model and try to formally capture it as *conceptual schema* in a *conceptual model*. Conceptual models are also called 'domain models' or 'semantic data models' (Hull and King

---

[11] Jr. (1975, fig. 2) has a better view of Steel, Jr. (1975, fig. VIII 5.1). Most later works combine realm of reality and conceptual realm into the conceptual model and concentrate on data realm.

1987; Peckham and Maryanski 1988) and come with a graphical notation for better understandability. Most conceptual modeling techniques are based on or influenced by the *Entity-Relationship Model* (ERM) (C. Chen, Song, and Zhu 2007). This thesis uses the *Object Role Modeling* (ORM) notation as laid out below and in section 3.8.2. The terms 'model' and 'schema' are often used synonymously with connotation on expression for schemas or on meaning for models. A conceptual model can be expressed as *logical schema* in a data description language. It is also called *external schema* if it only covers parts of a conceptual model (as 'views' to the full model) or if it is not primarily meant for storing data. Both logical and external schema must be implemented in a *physical schema* to actually hold data. If data is stored as database, a *database management system* (DBMS) typically implements the physical level so users can work on the logical level. External models can also be realized as data formats and formal ontologies. Examples of languages to express logical and external schemas are SQL, XSD, and RDFS.

It is important to recognize that each step includes a feedback loop to the prior level of description: constraints of physical schemas influence logical schemas, logical schemas affect conceptual models, and reality is perceived and changed to better fit existing mental models, as language affects the way we think (Whorf 1956). Modelers and architects of information systems often ignore these feedbacks, although it can even cascade through multiple levels. If something cannot be expressed within the artificial boundaries of a system, we often mistakenly assume that is does not exist. In practice data is often created and shaped without a clean, explicit data modeling process. Instead of reflecting mental models, data modeling then starts with a conceptual model or even directly with a logical schema or implementation (Simsion 2007). One can therefore simplify the data modeling process in four levels: mind (reality and mental models), model (conceptual model), schema (logical and external schemas), and implementation (physical schemas) as shown in figure 6.1 at page 223.

Data modeling is only one part of the design process of information systems. It may be part of *software engineering* if the goal is to create an application, or part of *information engineering* if the goal is not a single application but an integrated set of tasks and techniques for business communication within an enterprise.[12] As argued by Brooks (1987) from in software engineering there is no 'silver bullet' – no single technology or management technique can provide increase in performance orders of magnitude higher compared to other good techniques. Instead programming is a creative design process and great differences can only be made by great designers. This should also apply to data modeling.

Example 5: Object Role Modeling

Throughout this thesis Object Role Modeling (ORM) is used as conceptual modeling language in its modern graphical notation ORM2. ORM is further described by T. Halpin and Morgan (2008) and in section 3.8.2. Figure 2.7 shows an annotated example of a very simple conceptual model in ORM2. The example depicts a model with two *object types*: one *entity type* Work and one *value type* Title. This means, in our conceptual domain there are works and titles, but only the latter can be written down as concrete values. The two object types are connected by a *predicate* (or relationship), that consists of two *roles*. In a particular relationship between one work and one title, the role signified is played by the work, and the role signifier is played by the title. Each predicate has a label, which can be used to verbalize concrete relationships. If some work w is connected to some title t, we can say that 'w is titled t'. Predicates with more than two roles have slots for each role in their label. For instance we could have a predicate with three roles, verbalized as 'w was translated into l by p'. The basic support of n-ary predicates is one feature of ORM which not exists for instance in RDF based modeling languages.

Basic ORM is grounded in predicate logic, so two particular objects can only be connected once by a given predicate: either w is titled t or w is not titled t. Additional constraints and integrity rules can be expressed by natural language and by a variety of ORM constraint types. In the given model from figure 2.7 each Title must play the signifier role in at least one is titled predicate (mandatory role constraint, marked by a dot), and each Work can play the signified role in at most one is titled predicate (uniqueness role constraint, marked by a bar). The conceptual model can be used to identify and discuss the universe of discourse, for instance whether works can have multiple titles, without having to deal with details of implementation in a concrete data structuring language. An example of a simple ORM model implemented in a logical schema is included in section 4.2.1 with example 29.

---

[12] The term information engineering was popularized by James Martin and Clive Finkelstein in the 1980s. It also denotes the ERM notation variant that they described in (Martin 1990).

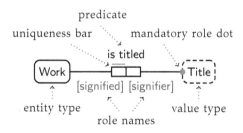

Figure 2.7.: Basic elements of ORM2 notation

2.3. Library and information science

The following section gives a short overview of library and information science and some of its core concepts relevant to this thesis. The two disciplines library science and information science are deeply connected and often combined. A major reason for their split up is a lack of attention to technical aspects by librarians and library scientists — a blind spot that only begins to diminish since the 1970s (Buckland 1998a). Actually both disciplines deal with digital documents and metadata from slightly different viewpoints, so I will treat them as one discipline.

2.3.1. Background of the discipline

One could argue that library science has been practiced since the first great ancient libraries, but as serious disciplines it originates in the 19th century. The first explicit *library science* textbook was published by Martin Schrettinger (1808), followed by others during the next decades. At the turn of the century, the development of library science was most advanced by two men: Melvil Dewey created the decimal classification system (1876), and promoted the card catalog. Shiyali Ramamrita Ranganathan is best known for his five laws of library science (1931) and his invention of facetted classification.[13] *Information science* evolved in parallel with the creation of scientific indexes. Up to the 18th century, bibliographies and catalogues mostly included single books, but no scientific journals or articles. As described by Kronick (1962) the primary function of scientific journals was that of providing a vehicle for the dissemination of information rather than a repository for the storage of new scientific ideas. When libraries concerned themselves with preservation, organization and access to physical holdings, scientists organized the overview of research on their own.[14] As in the 19th century the number of articles in scientific and technical journals increased, abstracts journals were created to summarize and review new articles and facts. Starting with the 'Pharmaceutisches Centralblatt' in 1830, dozens of periodical indexes cataloged scientific literature in their subfields. In contrast to library catalogues, these indexes not only included single articles, but they also collected references to documents independent from physical access and ownership. The most ambitious indexing project was the *Universal Bibliographic Repertory*, founded in 1895 by Paul Otlet and Henri La Fontaine. Influenced by works of Dewey, they created the first universal bibliographic database, and founded modern information science, which was then called *documentation* (Rayward 1997). The works and ideas of Otlet are remarkable in several ways: As described by Rayward (1994), Otlet anticipated later ideas of knowledge organization, such as those of Wells (1938), Bush (1945), Engelbart (1963), Nelson (1965a, 1981), and Berners-Lee (2001; 1989). After World War I, and with rise of English as predominant scientific language, most

---

[13] Ideas of facets can also be found earlier, for instance Schrettinger consideres a theoretical system of parallel classifications in his work's second volume (Schrettinger 1829, p. 85).

[14] This schema repeats regularly: for instance the first digital repositories were not created by librarians.

of the works of Otlet, Ostwald and other researchers fell into oblivion. Two aspects of Otlet's work have stayed characteristic for documentation and later information science: the proactive use of technology, and the central role of document concepts.

While libraries regularly hesitate to use new technologies, information science at best is actively involved in development, and propagation of technology to ease and automize the organization of information. Otlet systematically used reproducible index cards (predating digital records), pioneered the use of microfilm, and envisioned networked multi-media machines decades before their electronic realization (Otlet 1934, 1990). In the 1950s and 1960s *information retrieval* evolved as major branch of information science with important contributions from Calvin Mooers, Eugene Garfield, and Gerard Salton, among others. The development was driven by the exponential growth of publications (Solla Price 1963) and motivated by computerized automatization, which promises to speed up and improve the process of finding relevant information. However, automatic systems tend to ignore human factors, such as motivation and ethics[15] A closer look on computer science paradigmas, especially artificial intelligence and its recurrences, also reveals suprisingly positivist images of knowledge. Meanwhile information science has lead to more specialized but interdisciplinary sub-disciplines like information systems, information architecture, and information ethics. The core concept of information — see Capurro and Hjørland (2003) and Ma (2012) for analysis — still has impact on the transformation of library and information science. For instance in 2006 the newest faculty at University of Berkeley, originating in library and information science, was simply renamed the 'School of Information'.[16]

2.3.2. Documents

Despite the trend on information, the roots of library and information science are located in the organization of collected *documents*. Since the 1990s one can identify a renaissance of the document approach with independent schools of though. The Kopenhagen school of document theory can be found in contributions by Lund (2009), Hjørland (2007), Ørom (2007) and other papers collected by Skare, Vårheim, and Lund (2007).[17] The French school of thought is most visible by publications of Roger T. Pédauque (2003; 2006; 2007; 2011), a group of scholars publishing under common pseudonym. English introductions to their discource have been given by Truex and F. Rowe (2007) and Gradmann and Meister (2008). Despite the importance of documents as core concept of library and information science, there is no commonly agreed upon definition. While libraries tend to defined documents based on physical entities — the most prominent instance of a document is a book

---

[15] This can be exemplified by Mooers' law, in which Calvin Mooers (1960) observes that "many people may not want information, and they will avoid using a system precisely because it gives them information [...] not having and not using information can often lead to less trouble and pain than having and using it". For other neglected aspects see the works of Joseph Weizenbaum (e.g. 1976).

[16] See http://www.ischool.berkeley.edu/about/.

[17] See also http://thedocumentacademy.org.

— information science tends to abstract documents from their form. This focus results from research on aspects of preservation and access to original documents on the one hand compared to research on aspects of document descriptions and connections on the other. With the shift to digital documents it is more difficult to use form as defining criterion because traditional concepts such as 'page' and 'edition' loose meaning. For this reason Buckland (1997, 1998b) argues to define documents in terms of function rather than form. This idea had already been brough up by Briet (1951) before the advent of digital documents. Eventually any entity — that is any sequence of bits in the digital world — can act as document. To be a document it must be "conservé ou enregistré, aux fins de représenter, de reconstituer ou de prouver un phénomène ou physique ou intellectuel" (Briet 1951, p. 7).[18] This implies two important properties of documents: first document must be recorded, and second they must refer to something. The document's referent is also called its *content*.[19] As described by Yeo (2010), the content is not necessarily fixed and known, but it highly depends on context. The property of being recorded distinguishes digital documents in library and information science from more general data objects, for instance databases: digital documents do not change. Even "dynamic documents" are fixed as soon as you package them in some form suitable for storage. A. H. Renear and Wickett (2009) have carried this argument to the extreme: either a change constitutes a new document or it is not relevant enough to be recorded. A document is created to persist as fixed snapshot, while other data objects can also be created to capture the current state of a dynamic system. This distinction can be exemplified by a library information system that manages both, stable digital documents, and dynamic data about users and access to documents.

The traditional role of a library is the collection of separated documents. With increase in aggregated documents which combine independent smaller parts, such as encyclopaedia and journals that hold single articles, library institutions need to divide documents into separate conceptual units. For this purpose Paul Otlet introduced the *monographic principle* in 1918 and applied this new document concept in the Universal Bibliographic Repertory (Otlet 1990; Rayward 1994):[20] the idea was to "detach what the book amalgamates, to reduce all that is complex to its elements and to devote a page to each." (Otlet 1918, cited and translated by Rayward). The monographic principle requires methods to extract individual pieces of information from documents which can then be used to create new documents. With hypertext and new document types like blog articles and tweets, the creation of monographic documents experiences a revival. In the Semantic Web community the idea is beeing reinvented as 'nano-publications' (Groth, Gibson, and Velterop 2010; Mons and Velterop 2009).

---

[18] Translated by Buckland (1997) as "preserved or recorded, intended to represent, to reconstruct, or to demonstrate a physical or conceptual phenomenon".

[19] From a semiotic point of view the relation between a document and its referent is more complex. See section 2.5 and Brier (2006, 2008) for details.

[20] As summarized by Hapke (1999) the monographic principle can also be traced back to the project "Die Brücke" founded in 1911 by Wilhelm Ostwald.

2.3.3. Metadata

More than documents as such, library and information science is interested in their description, that is bibliography (from the Greek βιβλιογραφία for '[de]scription of books'). Applied to digital documents, all bibliographic data is *metadata*. This term became popular in library and information science, during the 1990s. Meanwhile, metadata subsumes any information about digital and non-digital content, including traditional library catalogs.[21] Before this, the term metadata had been introduced in computing by Bagley (1968)[22] but it was only used casually for management data in databases and programming languages. With rise of the Web, its meaning shifted from data about data sets and computer files to data about online resources. Finally, metadata became popular with the creation and promotion of the Dublin Core Metadata Element Set (DCMES).

Similar to documents, metadata can best be defined based on its function. Coyle (2010) describes metadata as something constructed, constructive and actionable. As a result, there is no strict distinction between data and metadata but the use of data as metadata depends on context: a digital record can both be a plain data object, a digital document, and a piece of metadata, even with different content in different usage scenarios. The relevance of usage for metadata distinguishes metadata from traditional cataloguing, as described by Gradmann (1998): traditional bibliographic records were created mainly to describe a document with a very limited context of usage. Gradmann argues that metadata "are intended to be part of a usage context different than that of cataloguing records, and that they are technically linked to this context to a very high degree." The important role of a technical infrastructure which metadata is used in, requires an analysis of the infrastructure as carried out in chapter 3 of this thesis.

A major application of metadata and a growing branch of library and information science is the (long-term) preservation of digital documents. Long-term preservation provides two general strategies to cope with the rapid change and decay of technologies: either you need to emulate the environment of digital objects or you must regularly migrate them to other environments and formats. Both strategies require good descriptions of the data and environment to be archived. When time passes, the descriptions themselves become subject of preservation. By this, digital documents may get buried in nested layers of metadata or they may become migrations of migrations as shadows of the original documents. Knowledge of general patterns in data

---

[21] Shelley and Johnson (1995) according to Caplan (2003) state NASA's Directory Interchange Format (DIF) as the first standard that defines metadata in its modern sense (NASA 1988, F-10). The definition in this standard includes any information describing a data set, including user guides and schemas. One of the first specifications named metadata was the Content Standard for Digital Spatial Metadata (CSDSM) (FGDC 1994).

[22] Solntseff and Yezerski (1974) refer to "The notion of 'metadata' introduced by Bagley", citing Bagley (1968), but I could not get a copy of his report because of copyright restrictions. Philip Bagley is among the forgotten forefathers of library and information science, also because he created the very first analysis of possibles uses of an existing computer, the *Whirlwind I*, for document retrieval (Bagley 1951).

and metadata could help to reveal data by "data archaeology" also when long-term preservation has failed (see section 6.2.1 in the outlook). In other applications but preservation, metadata is difficult to work with, because it is aggregated from heterogeneous sources with different structures than expected (Tennant 2004; Thomale 2010). Nevertheless, existing metadata research provides useful some guidelines and tools to achieve interoperability even among applicatons with different usage context: Metadata registries collect and describe standards, metadata crosswalks provide mappings, and metadata application profiles allow for customization without loosing a general consensus how data should be structured. The vast diversity of metadata standards and formats, which are defined and evaluated in library and information science, shows both the need for metadata and its complexity. A broad overview of the large number of metadata formats and specifications in the cultural heritage sector is provided by Riley (2010).

2.4. Philosophy

Philosophy is the principal field of research, which all other scientific disciplines originate from. It typically adresses questions, that are ignored by other fields, including itself and its own methods. Philosophy critically examines beliefs and finds problems, that are difficult to answer within the limited scope of one domain. Such examinations are not always welcome, or regarded as somehow interesting but essentially irrelevant. Philosophy often deals with 'blind spots' like hidden assumptions and foundations. Such blind spots also exist in library and information science and in computer science in regard to the description of digital documents. This section summarizes some existing philosophical approaches and questions about documents and data, that may unhide these hidden assumptions.

2.4.1. Philosophy of Information

Connections between philosophy and library and information science (LIS) with emphasis on the concept of information have been drawn by Floridi (2002a) and by Capurro and Hjørland (2003).[23] Floridi argues that philosophy of information (PI) is the philosophical discipline that can best provide the conceptual foundations for LIS. The main question of PI, as coined by Floridi (2002b), is "What is information?". How does this question relate to the description of documents and data? Floridi (2002a) defines LIS as applied PI, which in his words is "concerned with documents, their life cycles and the procedures, techniques and devices by which these are implemented, managed and regulated." By this it "does not cover all PI's ground" but "information [...] in the weaker and more specific sense of recorded data or *documents*". This definition ignores objects of LIS, that are not primarily focused on documents, such as information literacy. Cornelius (2004) in his response to Floridi (2002a) argues that LIS "has reconstructed itself away from an overwhelming concern with information materials (documents) and their organizational systems to an equal concern with the behavior of individual people who use libraries, and documents." Documents alone do not make a library, if they are not put in a cultural and social context. Unless you share the positivist view, in which documents hold an objective and stable meaning, you cannot separate documents from their description.

Current research in PI, as summarized in Floridi (2009), does not deeply deal with concepts like documents and recorded data. More specific questions like "What is a document?", "What is a data?", and "What does it mean to be recorded?" better capture the philosophical foundations of digital documents. But they are rarely asked in PI, although they refer to the fundamentals of this discipline: In particular, the *General Definition of Information* (GDI), which defines information as is well-formed, meaningful data, has widely been accepted.[24] Data however, is "intuitively described

---

[23] The intellectual exchange between this philosophers, however, is suprisingly low. I found no explicit reference from Floridi to Capurro, one rejection of Floridis position by Capurro (2008), an overview by Compton (2006) and a comparision of both in Persian (Khandan 2009).

[24] Floridi (2005) adds that (semantic) information must also be veridical, but we can ignore this aspect.

as uninterpreted differences (symbols or signals)." (Floridi 2009). The terms data and symbols are even used synonym when Floridi refers to the *Symbol Grounding Problem* (SGP) as "data grounding problem". The data/symbol grounding problem is one of the open problems in philosophy of information (Harnad 2007; Taddeo and Floridi 2005).[25] In short SGP asks, how symbols aquire their meaning. The question was raised by Stevan Harnad, inspired by Searle's *Chinese Room Argument*. The latter shows that manipulation of formal symbols (as defined in terms of formal languages) is not by itself constitutive of, nor sufficient for, thinking. So how can symbols inside an autonomous system be connected to their referents in the external world, without the mediation of an external interpreter? I disagree with the view that "data constituting information can be meaningful independent of an informee" (Floridi 2010, p. 22). SGP cannot be solved, because symbols always require some mediation. Data are not "uninterpreted differences (symbols or signals)", but you already require interpretation to draw distinctions, which are needed to constitute symbols. Apparently we need a deeper philosophical look at data, not simply derived from concepts like information and meaning.

2.4.2. Philosophy of Data

The concept of *data* is rarely studied as main topic of philosophical investigation, but mostly mixed with the discussion of information, knowledge, and meaning. Even in disciplines that use data as a central concept, there is no single, commonly accepted definition of data. Gray (2003) has shown for the early field of information systems, that until the 1960s authors made no clear distinction between data and information. The same can also be observed in othere areas and in more recent literature.

Data is often assumed as 'something given', as signified by the latin root *datum*. The latin term originates from a translation of Euklid's work Δεδοενα from the 4th century BC, in which he deals with geometric problems. Later the term was mainly used to discuss epistomological question in philosophy of perception — for instance Bertrand Russel's concept of *sense-data* — and in philosophy of science. In order to assess existing philosophical understandings of data, Ballsun-Stanton (2010, 2012) used methods of experimental philosophy.[26] He found three general types of data: data as communicated bits, data as hard numbers of objective facts, and data as recorded but subjective observations. Independent of this conceptions, some people distinguish raw data, and derived data, which origins from raw data by automatic calculations. The philosophy of *data as bits* considers computers as only arbiter of data, and of only data. To transform data into information and knowledge, humans need to analyse and interprete the input and output of computed actions. The philosophy of *data as hard numbers* views data as product of objective, reproducible, and unambiguous measurements. This data requires a set of precisely understood

---

[25] We will ignore positions like those of Steels (2007) and Taddeo and Floridi (2007), which argue, that the symbol grounding problem had been solved.

[26] Experimental philosophy supplements analytical philosophy with empirical methods like surveys to discover how people ordinarily think about concepts.

philosophy of data	data as
data as hard numbers	objective observation
data as recorded observations	subjective observation
data as bits	creation instead of observation

Table 2.4.: General philosophies of data, based on Ballsun-Stanton

metadata, which itself does not count as data. Data as hard numbers are mostly used in scientific contexts, where statistical data analysis is the main method to derive data from other data. The philosophy of *data as recorded observations* understands data from an engineering perspective, as recorded product of observations. Everything produces data and our knowledge is needed to select relevant instances. Data can be turned into information and knowledge by contextualization against other data, information, and knowledge in a hierarchical process or in feedback cycles. A summary of these different philosophies is given in table 2.4. In the following we will ignore the positivist view of data as hard numbers — most digitital docments do not simply origin from subjective or objective observations, but from designed creations.

In philosophy of information the concept of data is only covered briefly to define information. A serious treatment of the term 'metada' in particular does not exist. Floridi (2005, 2010) refers to the *diaphoric definition of data*, and gives a simple classification with five, non mutually exclusive types of data (primary data, secondary data, metadata, operational data, and derivative data) In his definition data is

> x being distinct from y, where x and y are two uninterpreted variables and the relation of 'being distinct', as well as the domain, are left open to further interpretation.
> — Floridi (2010, p. 23)

More formally, a set of data can be described as $\{(\neq, x, y) | x \neq y\}$, where '$\neq$' denotes a lack of uniformity between x and y. This definition is linked to the problem of identity, which has a much longer philosophical history. The general five types of data are vaguely defined with direct reference to the information that they convey: *primary data* is the general form of data, as stored in a technical system. *Secondary data* is constituted by the absence of primary data. Floridi argues, that the absence of information is also information. The conclusion, that the absence of (primary) data should be secondary data, is less clear. *Metadata*, to fully quote his words, "are indications about the nature of some other (usually primary) data. They describe properties such as location, format, updating, availability, usage restrictions, and so forth.". *Operational data* regard the operations of data systems. In contrast to metadata, which describe properties of data, operational data describe properties of systems that processes data. Finally *derivative data* are data that can be extracted from other data whenever the latter are used as clues about other things than directly adressed by the data themselves. In other words, operational data is data that conveys different information, if put in another context than originally intended.

primary data	
secondary data	derivative data
operational data	metadata

type	distinction among
de re	existing things
de signo	percieved signals
de dicto	interpreted symbols

Table 2.5.: Types of data, based on Floridi

Floridi further describes three applications of the diaphoric definition of data: pure data or proto-epistemic data 'de re', that is a lack of uniformity before any interpretation or cognitive processing; data 'de signo' as lack of uniformity between (the perception of) physical states or signals; and data 'de dicto' as lack of uniformity between symbols, for example between the letters A and B. Without further critique of this typology, we can limit analysis on data 'de dicto', namely the bits, that each digital document is made of. A summary of Floridi's types of data is given in table 2.5.

2.4.3. Philosophy of Technology and Design

Another path to advance philosophy of data, metadata, and digital documents, can be found in philosophy of technology and design. Following the view of data as bits or as other symbols, data is not observed, but created. More precisely it is intentionally created and shaped for automatic processing by technical systems. This property differentiates data from natural language. In philosophy the discussion of technical system is still quite new. Apart from brief statements in ancient literature, philosophy of technology has emerged in the last two centuries. After a long domination of methaphysical and ethical questions, some philosophers turn from the discussion of the impact of technology on society, to analytical philosophy of technology, which is more concerned with technology itself (Franssen, Lokhorst, and Poel 2009). A central term in this field is the *design process* as intentional practice to create and control technology. Design is applied not to find out how the world is, as in science, but to bring the world closer to how it should be. Technology always serves, or is intended to serve, a particular purpose by executing a specific function. By this, technology is normative, so philosophy of technology is directly connected to philosophy of norms (Vaesen 2008). The products of technological design processes are called *artifacts*. Artificats are not limited to physical objects, but they can also be repeatable operations, for instance computer programms. Most works in philosophy of technology, however focus on physical artifacts or on the implication of artifacts to the physical world.[27] A philosophical analysis of the design and function of data as technological artifacts has yet to be written.

---

[27] An exception is the discussion of virtual reality, which was popular for some years.

2.5. Semiotics

Modern semiotics and linguistics were established in the early 20th century, mainly influenced by Charles Sanders Peirce and by Ferdinand de Saussure (also named as 'semiology'). Influences of both researchers still exist as independent scholarly traditions. For introductions to semiotics see Eco (1976, 1977, 1984), Chandler (2007), and Trabant (1996). The discipline is related to linguistics, literary studies, philosophy, cognitive science, and communication science, among other fields. Some authors have investigated connections between semiotics and library and information science (Brier 2006, 2008; Huang 2006; Mai 2001; Raber and Budd 2003; Warner 1990). The following section briefly introduces to the sign as central concept, justifies its application to data and digital documents, and highlights some semiotic results that will assist the phenomenological description of data structuring and description.

I. Digital documents as signs

The *sign* as core concept of semiotics is most relevant to this thesis. The classical definition of a sign is often referred to as "aliquid stat pro aliquo" (something stands for something), but this definition has always been just one component of the function of a sign, even in medieval semiotics (Meier-Oeser 2011). More precisely, according to Peirce (1931a, paragraph 2.228) a sign is "something which stands to somebody for something in some respect or capacity". The triadic form of Peirce's model of signs is further described below. For Saussure (1916) a sign consists of a form (signifier) and a mental concept (signified) which both cannot be separated (see figure 2.9). As explained by Taverniers (2008), this dyadic model has been refined by Hjelmslev (1953) as relation between expression and content, both having substance, form and purport among other dimensions. In the European tradition the focus of semiotics/semiology later shifted from signs to signification with researchers such as Roland Barthes (1967), Algirdas Julien Greimas (1966), and Umberto Eco (1984).

Despite some semiotic focus on linguistic signs (especially words), signs can also be images, sounds, gestures and other objects, as long as they are interpreted. Most related to the structuring of description of data there are approaches to analyse signs in form of diagrams (Bertin 2011), human-computer interaction (Souza 2012), and information (Brier 2008; Huang 2006; Raber and Budd 2003), but there is no semiotics of data so far. This thesis includes at least a preliminary semiology of data. From a semiotic point of view, a digital document is a sign as soon as it is created or perceived as document. In particular it is impossible to create a document that does not act as some sign, as it is impossible not to communicate (Watzlawick, Helmick-Beavin, and Jackson 1967). Even an empty file or a random sequence of binary data can communicate something, for instance the fact that something went wrong.

II. Signs are more than signals

The semiotic view to data as sign reveals some important aspects that are less visible from other disciplines. First of all, data — at least if it is given as some digital document — is more than a simple signal in the 'mathematical theory of communication'. In this model (C. E. Shannon 1948) information from a source is encoded as signal by a sender. The signal is then transmitted to a receiver and decoded to a destination (see figure 2.8 above and figure A2 with an illustration of the theory of communication adopted for diagrams). The information can fully be reconstructed unless the signal is altered during transmission by noise. In practical data processing systems this process is nested in chains of encodings and decodings (figure 2.8). This model is limited at least for two reasons. First, the mathematical theory of communication explicitly excludes all aspects of meaning and it only deals with limited sets of predefined signals:

> The fundamental problem of communication is that of reproducing at one point either exactly or approximately a message *selected* at another point. Frequently the messages have meaning; that is they refer to or are correlated according to some system with certain physical or conceptual entities. *These semantic aspects of communication are irrelevant* to the engineering problem. The significant aspect is that the actual message is *one selected from a set* of possible messages.
> — C. E. Shannon (1948), emphasis not included in the original

Second, transmitter and receiver are part of the sign. Not only can signals be changed or interrupted by noise between each encoding and decoding. Also choice and application of encodings and decoding operations comprises risk of errors. If data is seen as sign which involves more than simple encoding and decoding, we can describe nesting by a process of "unlimited semiosis" (Eco 1979). In short, a semiotic sign is not limited to syntax, neither should be digital documents.

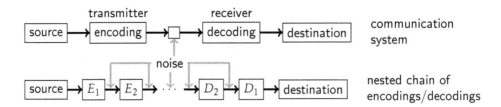

Figure 2.8.: Shannon's model of a communication system extended by nesting

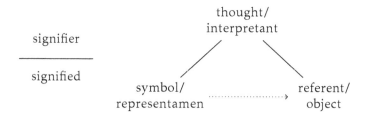

Figure 2.9.: Dyadic and triadic models of a sign

III. Signs are interpreted

According to de Saussure, the relationship between signifier and signified is an arbitrary result of social convention, which is difficult to change. The social aspect of signs is relevant also for data: for instance hyphen, dash, or similar characters can be found to indicate missing values or not applicable fields, independent from the particular data description language, but just because of social convention. Data specifications try to formalize the use of data fields, but all specifications require some social grounding.

To better understand how signs are interpreted, it helps to look at Charles Sanders Peirce's triadic model of a sign (figure 2.9, right). In this model, a sign is part of an interaction, which Peirce refers to as *semiosis*. Semiosis involves three components: the form of a sign (*representamen*), a mental effect or thought (*interpretant*), and the thing for which it stands (*object*).[28] This trichotomy can be traced back to Aristotle and it is also known as *semiotic triangle* with different names for each of the three components. Crucial in the semiotic triangle is the lack of a direct connection between symbol/representamen and referent/object. A symbol does not stand for a referent, but it is "used by someone to stand for a referent" (Ogden and Richards 1923, p. 11). In practice, the triadic interaction is embedded in a chain of unlimited semiosis (Eco 1979): every thought again is a sign in the mind of a person, interpreted with another thought, and so forth.

The arbitrariness of the connection between signifier and signified, based on social convention, is important to understand that there is no 'natural' or 'true' relation between expression and content and that the relation cannot be derived automatically. Nevertheless the relation is not random. In addition to fully arbitrary *symbolic signs*, Peirce distinguishes *iconic signs* with some similarity between symbol and thought (for instance a metaphor or parts of diagrams as described in section 3.9), and *indexical signs* that are directly connected to their thought (for instance physical traces). This distinction can help at least to explain some use of data, for instance brackets for grouping and annotation. The impossibility of automatic derivation

---

[28] Peirce writes "The thing having this character I term a *representamen*, the mental effect, or thought, its *interpretant*, the thing for which it stands, its *object*" in a in a revised version of a paper from 1867 (Peirce 1931b, paragraph 564). I have not found the original publication of this revision yet.

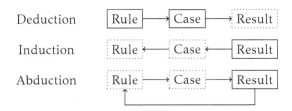

Deduction

Induction

Abduction

Figure 2.10.: Methods of reasoning, as illustrated by Eco (1984)

neither prevents interpretation of unknown signs. According to Eco (1984, section 1.11) signs are interpreted by *abduction*. Figure 2.10 compares abduction with other methods of logical reasoning: solid boxes indicate known propositions and dotted boxes indicate tentative propositions produced in the process of reasoning. Only *deduction* can automatically infere new results by application of formal logic: for instance if all objects of type A have some property B (rule) and a is of type A (case) then a must also have property B (result). Inductive reasoning reconstructs the meaning of a sign through repeated experiences. If objects are experienced to have property B every time they are of type A, one may conclude a general rule from these examples. Abduction, in contrast, directly concludes a rule from a result. In the case of signs, the content is concluded as as hypothesis from the expression. For instance if a has some property B, one may presume some type A that is responsible for having B. The abductive diagnosis is often exemplified by detectives which work with indications.[29] As such, the interpretation of signs is always tentative and it carries the danger of fallacies: the form of abductive reasoning is equal to the logical fallacy 'post hoc ergo propter hoc' that takes temporal sequence with casuality.

IV. Signs are not isolated

The third result from semiology consists of the fact that signs rarely occur alone. Instead they are used in a system together with other signs. This system as described by Peirce is a language ('langue'), in contrast to the actual use of a sign in communication ('parole'). The term language should not be limited to formal languages as they are described in section 2.2.1. Applied to data as signs, digital objects do not occur alone, but they are collected and combined with other digital objects. This collection and combination again is a method of data structuring. Based on e Saussure, Hjelmslev (1953) identified syntagm and paradigm as two fundamental relations by which elements of a language can be connected.

A *syntagmatic* relation consists between elements which occur together. An example of syntagmatically connected data elements are file name, file type, and file extension. Syntagm also provides context in form of a structure in which elements

---

[29] The name of William of Baskerville, Eco's main protagonist in 'The name of the Rose', is an allusion to the famous fictional detective Sherlock Holmes.

can be embedded, but syntagm is not limited to syntax and grammar. Similar elements that can be embedded in same places are connected by *paradigmatic* relations. Examples of data elements connected by a paradigmatic relation are arrays and lists, and the different RDF nodes types which can all be used as object in an RDF triple (see table 3.11). The final collection of data patterns (chapter 5) also includes paradigmatic links between patterns (as 'alternative patterns') and syntagmatic links between patterns (as 'implied', 'specialized' and 'related patterns').

V. Further insights

More insights from semiotics and linguistics may be possible if we take into account the acts of communication which signs are used in. The usual classification of communication studies includes aspects of *syntax* (relationships among signs, without reference to their meaning), *semantics* (relationships between signs and meanings), and *pragmatics* (relationships between signs and their use). Detailed models of communication are given for instance by Jakobson (1963), in the theory of *speech acts* (Austin 1962; Searle 1969), and in discourse analysis (Foucault 1969). For the following analysis, however, details of communication are ignored because our focus is not the situation in which data is used but the way it is structured and described. Neither does this thesis include the diachronous nature of data, that is the temporal context in which it changes. The difference between synchrony and diachrony has also been introduced by de Saussure, an introduction to this opposition with application to information as sign is given by Raber and Budd (2003).

In summary, semiotics provides fruitfull insights to the nature of data, even with limitation to immutable properties. Taking into account the full nature of signs, there are many issues left for further research in data semiotics.

2.6. Patterns and pattern languages

Design and programming are human activities; forget that and all is lost.
— Bjarne Stroustrup (1997)

The novel approach of this thesis is to use *patterns* for data description, independent from particular structuring methods and technologies. This section will first introduce the notion of patterns, then summarize existing works that deal with patterns in data structuring and finally give an example.

Patterns as systematic tools for describing good design practice were first introduced by Christopher Alexander, Sarah Ishikawa, and Murray Silverstein 1977. They identified 253 existing architectural patterns from entire regions and cities to buildings, rooms, and furniture. In Alexander's original definition 1977, p. x "each pattern describes a problem which occurs over and over again in our environment, and then describes the core of the solution to that problem, in such a way that you can use this solution a million times over, without ever doing it the same way twice." Patterns can be found by observing current practice and then looking for commonalities in solutions to a problem. In contrast to simple rules or best practice guidelines, a pattern, however, does not solve the problem by providing a particular solution, but by showing benefits and consequences. Each pattern provides a solution and each solution has some tradeoffs. The pattern description guides designers in their decisions of particular solutions for particular applications. Each pattern is given a name, which can be used to refer to one pattern from another. The full potential of patterns unfolds if a set of patterns is collected and combined in a *pattern language*. In Alexander's words "a pattern language is a network of patterns that call upon one another. Patterns help us remember insights and knowledge about design and can be used in combination to create solutions." A pattern language for writing patterns was presented by Meszaros and Doble (1997).

The pattern language approach with its application in architecture has been adopted in other fields of engineering, especially in software engineering (Beck and Cunningham 1987). Erich Gamma, Richard Helm, Ralph Johnson, and John Vlissides (the so-called 'gang of four') published an influental book on *design patterns* in object oriented programming (Gamma et al. 1994). In 1995 Ward Cunningham created the Portland Pattern Repository (Cunningham 1995), accompanied by WikiWikiWeb, which was the world's first wiki.[30]

Although these design patterns are used for the creation of computer programs, they do not reflect problems and solutions of data structuring as analyzed in this thesis. Design patterns refer to dynamic processes, while digital documents are static. General patterns in description and structuring of data must also be separated from *pattern recognition*, as practiced in data mining and other statistical methods of machine learning. These quantitative methods can only recognize structures within the boundaries of a fixed method of data description (for instance statistical patterns

---

[30] The Portland Pattern Repository and WikiWikiWeb are still active at http://c2.com/.

in lists of numbers without questioning the nature of numbers and lists). A general limitation of existing approaches is the focus to one specific formalization method. This practical limitation blocks the view to more general data patterns, independent from a particular encoding, and it conceals blind spots and weaknesses of a chosen formalism. Some works about patterns in particular data description languages have been mentioned in section 1.4.

Example 6: One data element, many patterns

The following example shall illustrate the application of patterns in data description. The patterns mentioned here anticipate members of the final pattern language summarized in chapter 5. A more complex example is given in appendix D.

Given the following sequence of twelve bytes:

$$44\ 75\ 62\ 6c\ 69\ 6e\ 2c\ 20\ 4f\ 68\ 69\ 6f$$

How can this particular piece of data be structured and described? To start with, we need at least some context or indication. Let's assume each byte corresponds to one character. This kind of correspondence can be summarizes as *encoding* pattern. Given ASCII or Unicode encoding, the sequence is:

```
Dublin, Ohio
```

Several patterns provide obvious solutions to further description:

- The data may be a list of two elements, **Dublin** and **Ohio** (*sequence* pattern).

- It may consist of two elements as part of an unsorted collection (*container* pattern), so **Ohio, Dublin** should be equal to **Dublin, Ohio**.

- It may just refer to the name "Dublin, Ohio" without any relevant structure (*label* pattern).

- It may consist of two words, one of which (**Ohio**) being used as qualifier for the other (**Dublin**).

Given the last interpretation, a *qualifier* may be a pattern in its own right or it may be an example of a more general *flag* pattern to indicate the interpretation of one element (**Dublin**) by another (**Ohio**).

One can further deconstruct the structure of a data element to parts, a typical process of description (*schema* pattern):

```
Dublin  ,  Ohio
```
   1   2   3

The third part is attached as additional element to the first (*dependence* pattern), and it may unambiguously refer into a registry of allowed qualification values (*identifier* pattern). The second part acts as connection or delimiter (*separator* pattern). Even its two bytes (,) can have structure: the whitespace character is often used as filling without significance (*garbage* pattern).

In summary one can identify several typical structuring methods in the twelve bytes given above. The interpretation, however, does not need to be right — depending on context the sequence could mean virtually anything — but patterns help to reveal interpretations that were most likely intended when creating the data.

Chapter 3

Methods of data structuring

This chapter holds the main empirical part of my thesis. Based on intensive review of literature and standards, I give a comprehensive analysis of methods and systems for structuring and describing data. The summary focuses on conceptual properties: details of implementation such as performance and security, are only mentioned briefly, if they show why specific techniques have evolved. The goal of this analysis is to later find patterns and paradigms independent from particular methods. For this reason I followed Meek (1995) whose trick to become language-independent was "to develop a healthy disrespect for all languages, and look for faults in them all the time." The division of methods in sections partly anticipates a more detailed typology that will be developed in detail in chapter 4. The survey starts with character encodings (section 3.1) that are needed to express any textual data. Identifiers (section 3.2) are used as part of all other methods as as well. The most basic method to store and manage digital data are files (section 3.3) followed by databases (section 3.4). The analysis does not consider concrete database systems, but general database models which Database Management Systems (DBMS) can be classified into. Data structuring or serialization languages (section 3.5) organize data in general forms for storage and exchange; popular examples include XML, CSV, and RDF. There is some overlap with markup languages (section 3.6), which mainly apply to text and similar sequential data. Schema languages (section 3.7) express logical schemas as data formats. Conceptual modeling languages (3.8) are used to capture a part of reality in formal language. They are often combined with a graphical notation which is a strict form of a conceptual diagram (section 3.9). Query languages (section 3.10) can define or be part of an Application programming Interface (API) to select or identify a specific piece of data.

3.1. Character and number encodings

```
Breakdowns : portrait of the artist as a young %@[squiggle][star]!
```
— Unknown library cataloger, titling a book by Art Spiegelman

All data must be written down in some form. At least a standardized set of base symbols (*characters*) is needed together with a set of conventions how to meaningfully combine these symbols. We call this two sets a *writing system* or notation. The connection of data and writing systems is not an invention of the digital age: Cuneiform script on clay tablets, the earliest known records of a writing system from the 4th millennium BC, was first used exclusively for accounting and record keeping, thus for capturing data. The simplest writing system can only write down sequences of binary data. It consists of two distinct symbols (usually called zero and one), and the convention of concatenating these symbols to sequences. More complex writing systems involve more characters. A *character encoding* maps characters and their combination rules to a writing system on symbols that can easier be stored and communicated. Examples of character encodings include Morse code, Braille, the American Standard Code for Information Interchange (ASCII), and Unicode. Digital character encodings map characters to a sequence of bits. Before Unicode became the dominant character encoding standard (starting in the early 1990s), there were many alternative encodings for different sets of characters. Table 3.1 lists some pre-Unicode encodings and their mappings of the capital letter Å:

encoding	hexadecimal	binary
US-ASCII	—	—
ISO 646 DK/NO/SE	5D	1011101
EBCDIC CP37 etc.	67	01100111
Mac OS Roman	81	10000001
Allegro-DOS/IBM437	8F	10001111
NeXTSTEP	86	10000110
ISO 8859-1	C5	11000101
ANSEL (MARC-8) combining ° + A	EA 41	11101010 01000001

Table 3.1.: Various character encodings of the capital letter Å

3.1.1. Unicode

Unicode aims at unifying all binary character encodings by covering all characters for all writing systems of the world, modern and ancient (The Unicode Consortium 2011). The standard includes graphemes and grapheme-like units like punctuations, technical symbols, and many other characters used in writing text. The Unicode standard defines a *grapheme* as "a minimally distinctive unit of writing in the context of a particular writing system." or "what a user thinks of as a character". For instance the lines in example 7 consist of equal sequences of graphemes in Unicode because typographic differences do not matter.

Lorem Ipsum

Lorem Ipsum

Lorem Ipsum

Lorem Ipsum

Lorem Ipsum

Example 7: Equal sequences of graphemes (if encoded in Unicode)

In contrast to earlier systems, Unicode also covers multiple combination rules, such as combining diacritics, bidirectional text, line and paragraph separators etc. Unicode even included language tags — special characters to identify text as belonging to a particular language — but this practice has been marked as deprecated in favor of markup languages. The following analysis of character encodings focuses on Unicode. It is referenced in many other standards, and most characters of any other other relevant digital character encoding are also located at some place in Unicode. Unicode is explicitly designed as open, evolving standard. New versions do not remove or change characters, but only add new characters and possibly change character properties after careful deliberation. That explicitly makes any possible abstract character a potential candidate for inclusion in the Unicode standard. To do so, one can define character mappings in private use areas, but there is no standard way to tell external applications about appearance and other properties of the corresponding graphemes. For this reason the use of Unicode is limited to symbols that are officially accepted as graphems in the standard — for instance written sign language (Sutton 2002) and other two-dimensional notations are not included. The set of characters encoded in Unicode is called the *Universal character set* (UCS) and the set of symbols, which is a subset of the integer values, is called the *Unicode code points* (codepoint) in table 3.2). All Unicode code points are located in the range 0x00 to 0x10FFFF which theoretically makes 1,114,112 possible values, expressible in 21 bit. A Unicode code points is referred to in documentation by writing 'U+' before its value in hexadecimal notation. By now, most code points are not assigned[1] and 2,114 values are explicitly excluded: the surrogates U+D800 to U+DFFF and 66 special noncharacter codes are permanently reserved for internal use. They are forbidden for use as character code point in UCS and in open interchange of Unicode text data (table 3.2).

Unicode characters are not directly mapped to binary sequences. Instead the standard defines a number of encodings such as UTF-8, UTF-16 etc. to map ustring to sequences of Bytes. The mapping is neither injective, nor surjective or functional. Table 3.3 lists several schemes that all encode the capital letter Å. The abbreviations

---

[1] As of Unicode 6.0.0 there are 109,449 assigned graphical characters, 207 special purpose characters for control and formatting, and 142,999 reserved for private use.

```
codepoint     = [#x00-#x10FFFF]
surrogate     = [#xD800-#xDFFF]
ustring       = ( codepoint - surrogate )*
noncharacter  = [#xFDD0-#xFDEF] | #xFFFE |#xFFFF |#x1FFFE|#x1FFFF|
    #x2FFFE|#x2FFFF|#x3FFFE|#x3FFFF|#x4FFFE|#x4FFFF|#x5FFFE|#x5FFFF|
    #x6FFFE|#x6FFFF|#x7FFFE|#x7FFFF|#x8FFFE|#x8FFFF|#x9FFFE|#x9FFFF|
    #xAFFFE|#xAFFFF|#xBFFFE|#xBFFFF|#xCFFFE|#xCFFFF|#xDFFFE|#xDFFFF|
    #xEFFFE|#xEFFFF|#xFFFFE|#xFFFFF|#x10FFFE|#x10FFFF
```

Table 3.2.: Symbol ranges in Unicode

'LE' and 'BE' indicate the byte order little-endian (default) and big-endian. Different combinations of UTF-8, UTF-16, UTF-32, or UTF-EBCDIC[2] with BE or LE define alternative transformation formats. They can easily be mapped to each other as isomomorphic encodings of UCS. A full breakdown of the encoding of the composed character is provided with example 34 in section 4.2.5.

Unicode encoding scheme	hexadecimal	binary
UTF-16, LE: Ångström sign	21 2B	00100001 00101011
UTF-16, BE: Ångström sign	2B 21	00101011 00100001
UTF-16, LE: Å	00 C5	00000000 11000101
UTF-8, LE: Å	C3 85	11000011 10000101
UTF-16, LE: A + combining °	00 41 03 0A	00000000 01000001 00000011 00001010
UTF-8, LE: A + combining °	41 CC 8A	01000001 11001100 10001010

Table 3.3.: Various Unicode encoding schemes encoding the capital letter Å

As described by Davis (2010), Unicode does not directly encode characters in UCS but it encodes graphemes, which may be combined to grapheme clusters as user-perceived characters. In general each graphem should be assigned to exactly one Unicode code point. For historical reasons there are some exceptions, like U+00C5 (latin capital letter a with ring above) and U+212B (angstrom sign). One may argue that both are different characters, if used in different context, but as they both map to the same visible grapheme, the difference is difficult to sustain. Some same grapheme clusters can be created by multiple sequences of codepoints. For this reason the Unicode standard defines two kinds of equivalence between code point sequences: *canonical equivalence* and *compatible equivalence*. Canonical equivalence is based on character composition, that is the process of combining multiple char-

---

[2] UTF-EBCDIC was defined to better support mainframe EBCDIC computers, which nowadays may only be found in archaic systems, like nuclear power plants.

acters to one — the reverse process is called decomposition. A combined character sequence and its canonical equivalent precomposed character should always have the same visual appearance and behaviour. Compatible equivalence is based on minor visual differences, that may be significant in some contexts only. Examples of compatible equivalences are font variants, ligatures, and digraphs. Composition and decomposition are mappings that ground on character properties of the Unicode character database. Given these mappings, there are four official normalization forms (Davis, Whistler, and Dürst 2009): http://unicode.org/reports/tr15/ Normalization Form D (NFD) transforms a string by mapping each character to its canonical decomposition. Normalization Form C (NFC) first decomposes all characters with NFD and then transforms the resulting string by canonical composition. For instance a string that contains the letter Å in any of the forms U+212B, U+C5, and U+41 followed by U+038A will only contain it as U+C5 after NFC. Normalization Form KD (NFKD) transforms a string by compatible decomposition and Normalization Form KC (NFKC) adds canonical (sic!) composition after compatible decomposition. NFKD subsumes NFD and NFKC subsumes NFC. Normalization also provides a unique order for combining marks, so it can be used to determine string equivalence. Once normalized, a string should not change when normalized again with the same operation.[3] None of the normalization forms is bijective (fully reversible) because each maps the set ustring to a smaller subset.

On a closer look, Unicode contains many inconsistencies and exceptions in respect to character properties and normalization. For example Chinese characters are composed of strokes, but there is no decomposition mapping to the set of strokes which form a given chinese character. Some icons, ligatures and digraphs are included in UCS but others are rejected, even if used as distinct graphemes.[4] Said that, one must keep in mind that the aim of Unicode is not to create an objective model of all human writing systems but to ensure compatibility in exchange of character strings. In addition to composition properties, the character database contains a large number of attributes to describe relevant characteristics and relations like character type, case, order etc. (Whistler and Freytag 2009). However this metadata is relatively static and excludes many aspects like historical relations and visual similarities. Based on character properties, applications can define custom normalization forms, for instance NFKD followed by lowercase case-folding and removal of all diacritics.

While Unicode is the dominant standard for character encoding on the level of

---

[3] This implies that equivalence mappings of a given character cannot be changed in future versions of Unicode. The stability guarantee on normalization only applies to assigned characters in UCS.

[4] For instance one method of writing the Māori language in the early 20th century contained a special 'wh' ligature as distinct character. Although there are printed books that use this letter, it was rejected for inclusion in Unicode. See http://unicode.org/faq/ligature_digraph.html for the objections of Unicode Consortium in ligatures and digraphs. Icons and pictograms are reluctantly included as well, but Unicode version 6.0 introduced several hundred Emoji icons for animals, clothes, vehicles, food and other random artifacts. The history including the capital sharp s, rejected in 2004 but included as U+1E9E in Unicode version 5.1.0 after a second proposal, reveals some interesting insight into the process of standardization.

byte sequences, there are other methods that express characters as sequences of other characters or symbols (see table 3.4). Some encodings are not reversible because they map multiple characters to the same symbols. Problems frequently arise, if data include symbols without known character encoding or if different creators and users of data do not agree on a common character encoding and interpretation.

encoding	symbols
named HTML entity	`&Aring;`
XML character entity	`&#xc5;`, `&#xC5;`, `&#197;`, `A&#x030A;` ...
Swedish 6 dot Braille	⠡ pattern P16 (Unicode `U+2821`)
Eurobraille 8 dot	⡼ pattern P34567 (Unicode `U+287C`)
Transcription	Aa
Morse code (å = à, no case)	· - - · ·

Table 3.4.: Additional character encodings of Å

3.1.2. Number encodings

A typical misconception about computers is that they deal with numbers, but they only deal with bits. Sequences of bits are used to encode numbers, just like character encodings encode characters. In contrast to arbitrary characters, the value space of numbers includes a mathematical model, that defines algebraic operations for calculation (see section 2.2.2). Digital number encodings should support these operations on representations of numbers, but they are typically defined on a limited computational model. First of all, most number systems are infinite while most number encodings limit each number to a fixed number of bits. The most prominent types of number encodings are integers, floating point numbers, and possibly boolean data types which map one bit to one boolean value (true or false).

Integer data types represent (a subset of) the integer numbers $\mathbb{Z} = \{\ldots -2, -1, 0, 1 \ldots\}$. One can encode $\mathbb{Z}$ (up to limits of memory) by using a variable size encoding like used for instance in the Protocol Buffers data binding language (Varda 2008). In practice most integer data types have some fixed size of n bits that store an integer value in binary numeral system. The range that can be encoded with n bit is -2^{n-1} to $2^{n-1} - 1$ for signed integers (Int_n) and 0 to $2^n - 1$ for unsigned integers (UInt_n).

There are several encodings for subsets of the real numbers $\mathbb{R}$ with *floating point* data types as most common method. The basic idea of floating point numbers is to represent a real number r as the result $r = m \cdot b^x$ with two integer components, exponent $x \in \mathbb{Z}$, and mantissa $m \in \mathbb{Z}$, and a base b. For example with base $b = 10$ the number 374.2 could be represented as $3742 \cdot 10^{-1}$. The mapping allows for multiple encodings of the same number, for instance 374.2 is also $37420 \cdot 10^{-2}$. For this reason floating point numbers are typically stored in normalized form where the mantissa must be in a specific range. In digital encoding, the base of most floating point encodings is $b = 2$. The exponent is typically stored as unsigned integer with a fixed bias value and one can save the first bit of the mantissa by assuming that it must always be 1 for normalized numbers. Calculation with floating point numbers is tricky because there are several ways in which the result of a calculation may not be part of the selected subset of $\mathbb{R}$. This can also happen in integer encodings but floating point encodings often support special values for this cases, such as signed zeroes (−0 and +0 are encoded as different values), infinities (+inf and −inf are allowed), and "not a number" values (NaN). IEEE 754 (Institute of Electrical Electronics Engineers 2008), the most popular floating point encoding, distinguishes between two kinds of NaN, quiet NaN and signaling NaN. However, there is no portable way to assign the second as data value because either it is converted to a quiet NaN or an exception is raised. Furthermore IEEE 754 and related standards still allow for some variations in implementations that can led to different results, depending on the computer platform (Monniaux 2008).[5] In summary one must take care which specific floating encoding one deals with or better avoid floating point values in favor of other encodings like decimal notation with arbitrary precision or symbolic notation.

3.2. Identifiers

What's in a name? that which we call a rose by any other name would smell as sweet.
— William Shakespeare: Romeo and Juliet

While character and number encodings are used as base of data structuring, identifiers virtually pervade systems to structure and describe data on all levels. This section first introduces basic identifier principles (section 3.2.1) followed by properties of namespaces and qualifiers (section 3.2.2) which identify the context of association between identifier and referred thing. Identifier systems (section 3.2.3) provide an infrastructure in which identifiers are assigned, managed, and used. Part 3.2.4 on descriptive identifiers and section 3.2.5 on ordered identifiers highlight two important but often overlooked properties of identifiers on a more theoretical level. Finally hash codes as special kind of distributed identifier systems are explained in section 3.2.6. A summarized overview of designated identifier properties is given in table 3.6.

3.2.1. Basic principles

In its most general form, a digital identifier is a piece of data (string, number, letter, symbol, etc.) that refers to an object. This makes identifiers a special type of metadata which more generally describe objects. In contrast to general metadata, an identifier should be unique (no homonyms), persistent and short, at least in some context.

---

[5] Under specific circumstances a floating point variable may even change its encoding without an assignment to it.

Distinct objects must have distinct identifiers to avoid ambiguity, and the number of identifiers that refer to the same object (synonyms) should be low for practical reasons. The following analysis is limited to digital identifiers in their general form as finite sequences of characters. Examples of identifiers from the previous section include number encodings that refer to the mathematical concepts of numbers, byte sequences that refer to Unicode code points, and Unicode code points that refer to characters. It is shown that this forms – also known as names, labels, locators, codes, or pointers – only make the visible part of an identifier. The concluding example of Pica format field identifiers will then illustrate some basic properties of data identifiers.

Most literature on identifiers deals with selected types of identifiers or with special aspects, such as identifier persistence. More general discussions are provided by Eriksson and Ågerfalk (2010), Campbell (2007) Coyle (2006), Vitiello (2004), Lynch (1997), and W. Kent (1991). The authors define identifiers as data objects that "refer to", "reference", "represent", or "serve as surrogate for" other objects, but the general idea is the same: a relatively short piece of data is associated with another (data) object. Campbell (2007) provides a more detailed deconstructions of identifiers in six parts:

1. a "thing" that is referenced

2. a "symbol" that references the thing. Unless otherwise indicated, this symbol in particular is meant by the word "identifier"

3. an "association" between the symbol and the thing

4. a "context" that the association occurs within

5. an "agent" that states the association and context

6. a "record" of the association, context, and ideally also the agent

In the following the same terminology will be used. Symbol, thing, and association are typically found as "symbol", "referent", and "thought" or under different names in the semiotic triangle (Ogden and Richards 1923) as described in section 2.5. The important aspect for the analysis of identifiers is that there is no direct connection between symbol (signifier) and thing (signified). It requires an association that always depends on some context, is established by an agent, and may or may not be recorded.

Following the philosophical position of radical constructivism (Glasersfeld 1990), one can even neglect the thing, as there is no direct access to real-world objects by language. This also applies to digital identifiers about things in the reality realm (in terms of data modeling). However, digital identifiers about digital objects can be compared with their referents, because both are recorded in data. In fact digital records of identifiers and their referents are common practice in many data structures and known as *lookup tables*. In some cases one can even swap symbol and referent, because both are unique on their side of the table (see table 3.5 for an example).

Unambiguity (each identifier must refer to only one object) and uniqueness (for each object there should be only one identifier) of often combined as *uniqueness* as most important requirement for an identifier. Other properties frequently cited as important qualities are *persistence* (identifiers should not change over time), *scope* (the context of an identifier should be broad or even 'global'), *readability* (identifiers should be easy to remember or contain information), and *actionability* (given an identifier one should be able to do something with it, for instance access the identified object). A summary of these and more designated identifier properties is given in table 3.6. To ensure the required properties it needs an identifier system as controlled mechanism or convention for creating, managing, and using identifiers (see part 3.2.3). When we analyze general data, identifier properties can also indicate whether some piece of data is actually used as identifier or not: being an identifier is nothing inherently inscribed in data, but it is an example of a popular data pattern, that is used all all over systems to structure and describe data.

Example 8: Field identifiers in PICA format

description	year	title	edition	place and publisher	DDC
Pica3 tag	1100	4000	4020	4030	5010
Pica+ tag	011@	021A	032@	033A	045F
repeatable	no	no	no	yes	yes

Table 3.5.: Some fields of Pica record format

The bibliographic record format *Pica* consists of a simple field-subfield-structure, similar to MARC (compare with figure A5). Each field can be identified by a so called Pica3 tag or by a Pica+ tag. Figure 3.5 lists a lookup table for some fields with their tags and a repeatability flag from the cataloging rules of the GBV library network (GBV 2010). Assuming that the fields somehow refer to things in the reality realm, we cannot directly map from tags to these things. Fields like "place and publisher" also indicate that the referent can be quite artificial: most people know places and maybe publishers, but what kind of ontological status has their combination? Beside the intangible referent of such artificial identifiers, textual descriptions make no good identifiers, because one can write them in several forms (the original descriptions are given in German) and because there may be different fields with same description. Tags in contrast can at least identify field descriptions and tags of the other kind (Pica3 to Pica+ and vice versa), because they all exist in the data realm. The repeatability flag finally identifies a thing from the conceptual realm, namely the set of fields, that are repeatable (**yes**) or not repeatable (**no**). In practice one must always take in mind, in which context an identifier is used. A Pica3 tag like **5010** may refer to the corresponding Pica+ flag **045F**, to a concrete set of field value, or to the abstract concept of the field. In data structuring we often deal with cascaded identifiers that only link to the reality realm in a last step. For instance 045F refers to the "DDC" field, which in a bibliographic records contains a notation from the Dewey Decimal Classification (DDC), which by itself is another identifier.

3.2.2. Namespaces and qualifiers

Namespaces and *qualifiers* are both used to avoid the problem of homonymy. In addition they can provide context and refer to authority through a hierarchy of identifiers. A possible term to describe both is *qualified identifier*. Qualified identifiers are used in formal systems like programming languages and knowledge organization systems (thesauri, classifications, authority files etc.) where a name must always refer to one distinct object. A defined syntax in a formal language is needed to separate the namespace or qualifier part and the local part of a qualified identifier. Otherwise it would be ambiguous for instance whether 'band-spectrum' refers to a 'band' of radio communication frequencies, or to the Australia band 'spectrum' which formed in 1969, or whether the minus sign does not indicate the existence of a namespace qualifier at all. Namespaces are typically prepended to the local identifier and qualifiers are added in parentheses (see example 9). If the context is known as by definition of a *default namespace*, one may also omit the qualifier or namespace.

identifier	local	qualifier	syntax	description
Frankfurt/Main	Frankfurt	Main	L/Q	city name
Dublin, Ohio	Dublin	Ohio	L, Q	city name
US-OH	OH	US	$Q\text{-}L$	ISO 3166-2 area code
std::set	set	std	$Q\text{::}L$	C++ identifier
rdf:type	type	rdf	$Q\text{:}L$	URI reference in RDF
10.1000/182	1000/182	10	$Q.L$	DOI as specific Handle
sgn-US	US	sgn	$Q\text{-}L$	IANA language & subtag

Example 9: Qualified identifiers with local part (L) and qualifier (Q)

For some prefixed types of namespaces, the qualifier is not fixed, but can be replaced by another prefix for the same namespace. For instance http://dx.doi.org/ and other known resolver addresses are actually used as prefix for the namespace of *document object identifiers* (DOI) but one could also use the DOI as *Uniform Resource Identifier* (URI) with prefix info:uri/. Another example is a prefixed element name in the Extensible markup language (XML, see section 3.5.5): some XML applications ignore the prefix and respect a locally defined namespace, some ignore the prefix, and some need both to identify an element (see example 14 at page 104). Finally, there are systems in which a namespace is just an abbreviation that can be defined and expanded as needed (see the @prefix statement from Notation3 as described in section 3.5.6 and table 3.12).

Qualifiers, more often than namespaces, may also encode a special meaning, especially when they are used for syntactic indexing in knowledge organization languages. For instance the identifier Marx, Karl, 1818-1883 from the Library of Congress name authority file include the qualifier 1818-1883. This qualifier specifies the years of birth and death of the identified person.[6] In other cases the primary role of a qualifier is to disambiguate, so one is more free to choose, for instance Paris (city) and Paris (mythology), Paris (place) and Paris (person), or just Paris (1) and Paris (2) for two distinct concepts. A general problem of meaningful qualifiers is the limitation to one aspect. For instance there are multiple early computers referred to as "Mark I". One can either use their location as qualifier (Mark I (Harvard) and Mark I (Manchester)) or their year of completion (Mark I (1944) and Mark I (1949)). Combining multiple aspects quickly gets complicated, similar to nesting of multiple namespaces in one mono-hierarchical system, as described in the next part.

Above all, namespaces and qualifiers do not solve the general problem of identification but they only shift it to another domain, level, or authority. Namespaces and qualifiers only draw aside avoid homonymy and provide context in some known identifier system and both are identifiers in their own right. To avoid an infinite chain of qualified identifiers one hasto start at some authority as root context, which is also known as the global namespace.

3.2.3. Identifier Systems

> URIs don't change. People change them.
> — Tim Berners-Lee (1998)

All identifiers are artificially created — either explicit by naming or implicit by providing a mechanism that creates identifiers. An *identifier system* defines which identifiers exist (registry); or how identifiers are created and managed (assignment politics); how recorded associations between identifier and referent can be looked up (resolving); which syntax rules as naming conventions apply (grammar); or which relations to other identifier systems exist. Popular digital identifier system covered as examples in the following are: Uniform Resource Identifier (URI), its counterpart Internationalized Resource Identifier (IRI), Uniform Resource Locator (URL), Uniform Resource Name (URN), Domain Name System (DNS), Internet Protocol (IP), International Standard Book Number (ISBN), and European Article Number (EAN). Relations between these systems, together with their character encodings are illustrated in figure 3.1.

In general any sequence of bits or other digital symbols can act as digital identifier. To define a possible set of sequences, an identifier system includes a formal language

---

[6] The first part of the identifier (Marx) may also be seen as a namespace of all people's identifier with this surname, and the local part Karl signifies a given personal name, so in this example all parts encode some meaning if one takes person names as meaningful.

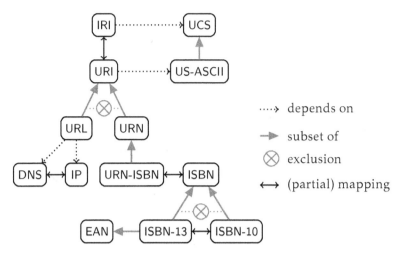

Figure 3.1.: Relations between several identifier systems

(see 2.2.1) as identifier syntax (see section 2.2.1). Every identifier symbols must conform to this syntax, so its grammar rules help to discover and use identifiers: with a well-defined syntax one does not need to resolve each string to check whether it is an identifier, but one can validate possible identifiers based on their shape. Often only parts of the grammar are defined in a schema language (see section 3.7.1), and there may be additional informal agreements to exclude some sets of characters and sequences. For instance whitespace characters are less used in identifiers: even if allowed, at least multiple consecutive whitespace characters are not encountered in practice. If identifier system depend or reuse each other, for instance as namespaces and qualifiers (see the dotted relations in figure 3.1), there can be difficulties to embed one identifier within the syntax of the other. If such an embedding may lead to disallowed character sequences or to syntax ambiguities, the host identifier system usually defines a method to escape the embedded identifier. A typical escaping mechanism, is *percent-encoding*. A character code of one byte in percent encoding is replaced by the percent character "%" followed by the two hexadecimal digits representing that byte's numeric value (T. Berners-Lee, R. Fielding, and Masinter 2005, section 2.1). However, the question when and which parts of an identifier must be encoded, is a frequent source of confusion. Quite often an identifier reuses another identifier that already includes an embedding, so one ends up with a complex hierarchy of dependencies and nested encodings.

If readability is no primary requirement, digital identifiers can be plain numbers or sequences of bits (see part 3.2.5). An example are IP addresses, which can be mapped to more readable DNS names. But even a very simple identifier syntaxes such as number ranges can cause problems: in 2011 the IP system version 4 ran out of identifiers because it was limited to 2^{32} distinct numbers. The update to IP version 6 takes several years, because version 4 is used in many other specifications and implementations that must also be updated accordingly. A similar but less extensive update of an identifier system was the extension of International Standard Book Numbers from ten digits (nine plus one check digit) to thirteen (nine plus bookland namespace and check digit). The assignment of ISBN identifiers is delegated to national agencies who then delegate it to publishers. Therefore the system is not always used as intended: in theory an ISBN can never be reused and every edition of a title must have a new ISBN. In practice new editions often reuse the ISBN of the previous edition and some publishers even assign existing ISBNs to totally different books.[7] The update from ISBN-10 to ISBN-13 was based on an already existing encoding of ISBN-10 in the European Article Number (EAN). Nevertheless, it required a lot of marketing and modifications in library systems (Halm 2005). Among other things difficulties resulted from different syntaxes to express equivalent ISBNs (example 10). I fact all syntaxes (except ISBN-13 with bookland namespace 979) can be mapped to each other, so it is an arbitrary decision, which form to take as the 'real' ISBN. Similar problems of synonymy are also present in other identifier systems.

ISBN-10 with hyphen	1-4909-3186-4
ISBN-10 with space	1 4909 3186 4
plain ISBN-10	1490931864
EAN	9781490931869
EAN barcode aligned	9 78149 093186 9
ISBN-13 with hyphen	978-1-4909-3186-9
plain ISBN-13	9781490931869
URN-ISBN	URN:ISBN:1-4909-3186-4

Example 10: Different syntaxes that express equivalent ISBNs

Today the most used identifier systems, apart from character encodings, are *Uniform Resource Location* (URL) (referred to as web addresses in common speech), *Uniform Resource Identifier* (URI), and *Uniform Resource Name* (URN). These systems are often confused because they all evolved together with the *World Wide Web* (WWW) and the *Hypertext Transfer protocol* (HTTP). The WWW was introduced by Tim Berners-Lee in 1990. His first design includes considerations on document naming as "probably the most crucial aspect of design and standardization in an open hypertext system". Tim Berners-Lee (1991) discusses addressing, naming, and uniqueness as three different properties and introduces URL to cover the addressing as part of a global naming system. HTTP as defined by Tim Berners-Lee (1992) allowed for use of different types of "Universal Resource Identifiers", but only listed URL and other addressing schemes (FTP, gopher, etc.) as examples.[8] In 1992

---

[7] For instance ISBN 3-453-52013-0 was used for two unrelated books by Heyne-Verlag in 1974 and 2004 and ISBN 3-257-21097-3 was assigned to every single work of B. Traven published by Diogenes-Verlag.

[8] An exception was the *Content-ID* (cid) scheme which did not include a server as physical address. cid was later specified as "URL scheme" (sic!) with RFC 2111 (1997) and RFC 2392 (1998) but it

an URI working group was formed to define other types of "Uniform Resource Identifiers" (Emtage 1992) but it was difficult to come to consensus. The working group concluded in 1995 with several recommendations after Tim Berners-Lee (1994) had published his vision of the URI system with subtypes URL for addresses and URN for persistent names. Tim Berners-Lee, Masinter, and McCahill (1994) first describe the aim of URI as "[encoding] the names and addresses of objects on the Internet". In the same document they broaden the scope to a more universal identifier system as they write: "in order to abstract the idea of a generic object, the web needs the concepts of the universal set of objects, and of the universal set of names or addresses of objects." After several years and revisions the current version of URI is specified together with URL by T. Berners-Lee, R. Fielding, and Masinter (2005). The standard defines a hierarchical namespace architecture with URI schemes on the global namespace level. This common identifier system is useful because it provides a common formal language that other identifier systems can be embedded into with schemes as namespaces Embedded identifier systems, however, do not need to define normalization rules, so equivalent identifiers such as listed in example 10 are quite common and impossible to detect for general URIs. The system neither solves the conflict between addressing and lookup as one purpose of an identifier and persistent identification as another. Most URIs are used primarily to retrieve documents, either directly via HTTP or by embedding other URI types in an URL.[9] For this reason the identifiers actually identify a location, that may hold different objects, but not an object, that may be available at different locations. The example of ambiguous house numbers at page 68 shows that confusing location and located object can lead to unexpected results.

Several suggestions have been made to clarify the distinction between access and reference as independent functions of an URI, for instance by Mealling and Denenberg (2001). Some of these developments even further complicated the use of URI as global identifier system. For instance the Resource Description Framework (see section 3.5.6) claims to build on URI but instead introduces its own concept 'URI reference' that slightly differs from URI.[10] Similar problems exist with the *Internationalized Resource Identifier* (IRI) system. Contrary to popular belief, IRI as defined with RFC 3987 by Duerst and Suignard (2005) is not a superset of URI, but a complement that is defined in UCS character sequences instead of ASCII character sequences. The misleading statement "every URI is by definition an IRI" that can be found in section 3.1 of RFC 3987 only means that if one tries to convert an URI with the defined IRI-to-URI mapping, the original URI is not modified. Instead there is

---

never got fully adopted in practice. However, it is a good example of a mapping between an identifier system and a key-value structure: for instance the identifier `cid:foo` corresponds to the MIME header `Content-ID: <foo>` with field name `Content-ID` and field value `foo`.

[9] Originally, HTTP was designed to retrieve information about resources identified by any kind of URI, possibly mediated via proxy servers. This property was partly removed, beginning with dropping of URI-related header fields in the HTTP specification drafts between August 3rd and 13th, 1995.

[10] In particular, URI references may contain characters that are disallowed in an URI. For details see page I, Klyne and Carroll (2004, section 6.4), and P. Hayes and McBride (2004, section 1.2).

unambiguous	each identifier must have only one referent
unique	each referent must be associated with only one identifier
global	identifiers should not require a specific context
persistent	associations do not change or expire
readable	identifiers are easy to read and remember
structured	identifiers are described by a formal grammar
uniform	identifiers are uniformly distributed
performant	identifiers are easy to compute and to validate
descriptive	identifiers contain information about the referent or association
actionable	identifier can be used, for instance to retrieve the referent
distributed	identifiers do not require a central institution
ordered	identifiers have a known strict and total order

Table 3.6.: Summary of designated identifier properties

a conversion algorithm that maps URI to IRI. If URI was a subset of IRI, no such mapping would be needed. Both mappings use UTF-8 as intermediate format and percent-encoding of special characters.

The ongoing problems of URI and related identifier systems have multiple reasons. For instance the assumption of an "universal set of objects" leads to paradoxes because real world objects and identifiers have no rank or category in terms of set theory. With the `data:` URI scheme one can even convert any piece of data into an identifier (Masinter 1998).

Above all, many goals of an identifier system cannot be solved on a purely technical level. The *domain name system* (DNS) gives examples how politics and social power structures shape identifier systems (Rood 2000). Identifier systems can also be implemented and interpreted differently by different users. As noted by Tim Berners-Lee (1998a), people change identifiers, by purpose or by accident. Like all social constructs, identifier systems can also become outdated: for instance the URI scheme `info:` was launched in 2003 but closed in 2010 in favor of URL (OCLC 2010; Sompel et al. 2006). Last but no least identifier systems often try to solve problems that cannot be solved together: Wilcox-O'Hearn (2001) showed that an identifier system cannot provide securely unique, memorable (readable), and decentralized (distributed) identifiers at the same time but only two of these properties can be combined: local identifier systems can generate readable and distributed identifiers but they are not globally unique, centralized systems such as DNS can globally unique and readable identifiers, and cryptographic hashes are distributed and unique but not readable. Partial solutions to "Zooko's triangle" (Stiegler 2005) involve multiple layers of identifier systems, which is another example of the importance to study relationships in combined identifier systems such as depicted in figure 3.1.

3.2.4. Descriptive identifiers

In general the association between an identifier as symbol and the thing it refers to is rather arbitrary unless the thing already has a natural identifier. *Descriptive identifiers* circumvent this limitation by defining a general and independent association for all possible things, by which one can derive an identifier from its referent. In a broader sense descriptive identifiers subsume so-called natural, smart, or intelligent keys from database and information systems and hash codes which are described in part 3.2.6. In a narrower sense a descriptive identifier symbol must reveal some information about the object it references.

If one knows the method by which descriptive identifiers are created, an identifier tells something about the object it refer to. For instance one could define a descriptive identifier for bibliographic resources by concatenating the first author's surname and the year of publication, so one already knows this attributes by looking at the identifier. Descriptive identifiers are easy to remember and they do not require a central registry as identifier system. However two distinct objects may share the same attribute values, so they accidently get the same identifier. For this reason, a descriptive identifier often identifies something else than originally intended – in this example the set of all publications from a given year and a given surname. Another example is a descriptive identifier for a houses, based on its postcode, street name, and house number. This decriptive identifier actually identifies one or more addresses as locations, but not necessarily a house: some houses have multiple numbers, so one only identifies a part of a house, and some house numbers refer to a complex of multiple buildings. A third example is taken from Eriksson and Ågerfalk (2010): the Swedish person identification number contains of ten digits where digit one to six represent a person's day of birth (`YYMMDD`) and the tenth position is a check number that can be calculated from the digit one to nine. This implies that one cannot derive the full day of birth, because the century is not included (2005 and 1905 both become 05). To distinguish people born at the same day (without century), digit seven to nine of the identifier contain a unique sequence number that is only partial descriptive. The ninth position is odd if the number identifies a man and even if it identifies a woman. To be more precice, the ninth position can only describe the assumed sex of a person at the time when the identifier was created, because for some people the sex may have changed during their life. Furthermore some attributes may be unknown: when more and more immigrants with unknown birthdate got a Swedish person identification number, the first of January or the first of July was recorded instead and the identifier system ran out of numbers (Eriksson and Ågerfalk 2010). Such problems are always possible if an identifier is not based on inherent properties but on properties that are attributed to an object.[11] To summarize, descriptive identifiers are problematic, if the attributes that they base on are not unique, not always known, or subject to changes. This reasons are

---

[11] The difference between attributed and inherent is not obvious. For instance most people would see gender as given while others as purely artificial (Butler 1990). However most identifier conflicts origin from different interpretations what kind of object the referent actually is.

arguments for "meaningless identifiers" or "surrogate keys" as proposed Kimball (1998) and Wieringa and Jonge (1991) among others.

3.2.5. Ordered identifiers

The possibility to arrange identifier symbols in a meaningful way is seldom cited as important to digital identifiers, allthough the basic form of digital data is an ordered sequence of bits. *Ordered identifiers* can be defined as any identifiers that have a strict and total order. Simple examples in data include memory addresses and line numbers. Ordered identifiers have several usefull properties: First, one can sort objects by their identifiers, so every set of objects with distinct identifiers has a normalized form, and second, one can specify ranges of identifiers. Sorted ranges further allow efficient searching based on binary search. The range CA to CI, for instance, specifies the range of all notations from the Regensburg Classification Scheme RVK.[12] In practice however, collation is often not simply determined by the order of characters that the identifier is build from. For instance the identifier 9X could be sorted after the identifier 10Y if the first character is given most importance ($9 > 1$), but it could also be reverse if the identifiers are interpreted as starting with numbers ($9 < 10$). The more structured identifiers are, the more complex it can be to compare them. Sorting rules for ordering personal names, for instance, depend on language and culture and on the ability to break a name into given name, surname, and other parts.

   Ordered identifiers are easy to implement if there is a finite number of items or if new items are added sequentially. For instance in the *numerus currens* system of library shelving books get signatures (and locations) in order of their acquisition. Another examples are bates numbers that are used to assign consecutive numbers with a stamp. The order implies a mapping from identifier symbols to the natural numbers $\mathbb{N} = \{1, 2, 3, ...\}$,[13] or to a subset of $\mathbb{N}$. In many applications the natural numbers are directly used as identifier symbols without any mapping function in between. However, for many ordered identifiers no specific mapping to $\mathbb{N}$ (or to a subset $\mathbb{N}_m = \{x \in \mathbb{N} | x \le m\}$) is known. A meaningful mapping may also be injective instead of bijective with gaps of numbers that no identifier is mapped to. A known bijective mapping without gaps is useful because it adds some properties to ordered identifiers: first, the last identifier gives the total number if objects, and second, one can always tell the number of objects in a given range of identifiers. The latter is usefull especially because it allows to calculate with identifiers like coordinates.

3.2.6. Hash codes

A *hash function* is a computable function that maps arbitray large sequences of bits into smaller bit sequences of fixed length (figure 3.2). The output of a hash function

---

[12] See http://rvk.uni-regensburg.de/ for more information about the classification.
[13] or $\mathbb{N} = \{0, 1, 2, ...\}$ depending on personal preferrence.

is called *hash code*, hash key, digest, or just hash and the input is also called message especially for cryptographic hash functions. A good hash funtion should be easy to compute[14] and it should map typical input values to uniformly distributed hash codes, so every code is generated with the same probability. Distinct input values that are mapped to the same hash code are called a *collision*. Depending on properties of a hash function and its application, collisions either imply equivalent input values or they are so unlikely that in practice hash codes are virtually unique. Thus, hash codes can be used as compact and distributed identifiers, either of equivalent or of unique digital objects. The main applications of hash functions are storage, duplicate detection, and cryptography. Hash functions for storage in hash tables or data caches utilize the uniform distribution of hash codes but they may allow some collisions. This makes them rather identifiers of addresses computed from data objects than identifiers of data objects. Hash functions for duplicate detection neither directly identify digital objects but sets of objects that are assumed to be equivalent based on their content. In contrast to hash functions for the other two types of applications, hash functions for duplicate detection highly depend on the type of input values as they only take into account a significant part of the input. For instance the bibliographic hashkey for bibliographic records in the social cataloging platform BibSonomy only uses specific parts of the fields of author, editor, title, and year (Voß, Andreas, and Robert 2009). The quality of a hash function for duplicate detection depends on the ability to define which object properties count as significant and when two objects should be treated as equal - a problem that is far from trivial (A. H. Renear and Wickett 2009; Yeo 2010). If the function is not choosen good enough, it can better be described as heuristic or classifier with error rate of false positives and false negatives instead of a kind of identifier.

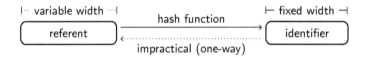

Figure 3.2.: (Cryptographic) hash function

Cryptographic hash functions treat the whole input as significant part: any change of an input value must result in a different hash code, so attackers cannot modify messages without modifying the message digest. In addition the function should fullfill the following properties: First, the hash code should not reveal more information about the input that its own expression.[15] Second, the hash function must be a *one-way function*: given a hash code it must be very hard to find a message that is

---

[14] Some hash algorithms allow the hash of a composite object to be computed from the hashes of its constituent parts. For instance the Rabin fingerprint f of a concatenation $A.B$ of two strings A and B can be computed via the equality $f(A.B) = f(f(A).B))$ (Broder 1993).

[15] In a broader sense, all hash functions are descriptive because their hash codes are defined based on the full digital content as property of the identified object. In a narrower sense cryptographic hash keys are not descriptive because they only describe the hash code as property of the object's content.

mapped to this digest. This property is also needed to prevent creating a message as collision of another given message. Third, an even more strict requirement used to evaluate the strength of cryptographic hash functions is the lack of a method to find any collisions. Given that the number of possible input values is much large than the number of possible hash codes, there always exist collisions, but it is very difficult to find them. For instance the cryptographic hash function SHA1 (D. Eastlake and Jones 2001) has codes of 160 bit length, so there are 2^{160} different SHA1 hash codes. According to rules of probability the expected number of hashes that can be generated before an accidental collision ("birthday paradox") is 2^{80}. The sun will expand in around 5 billion years (less than 2^{58} seconds from now), making life on earth impossible. Until then one can generate 2^{22} (4 million) hashes per second and collisions are still unlikely. With systematic crypographic attacks the number can be smaller but it is still much larger than other sources of error.

3.3. File systems

A file is the most basic method to store and manage digital data. Other methods are build on files by one means or another. A *file system* is a method of storing, organizing and retrieving files on all sorts of storage devices, such as a hard disk, flash drive, and magnetic tape. Provided as core part of the operating system, the file system abstracts from underlying storage media. Thus application can work on files without having to bother where and how their content is physically stored. Operating systems may also provide file systems as interface to read and write from and to devices and programs.[16] In the following we will limit a *file* to an object that holds a (possibly empty) finite stream of sequent bytes. Issues of performance and security – the main driving force behind file system development – will be ignored as well as any relation to physical storage media. General introductions to file systems are given by Tanenbaum (2008), Reimer (2008), and Giampaolo (1999).

3.3.1. Origins and evolution

Despite all variety, basic properties of file systems have not changed much since their introduction in the early 1960s. Compared to other trends in computing the evolution of file systems is very slow, because they are deep-rooted in operating systems and bound to properties of storage media. The basic layout of todays file systems evolved parallel to the change from storage devices with sequential access (piles of punched cards or magnetic tapes) to disks that allowed random access. The next shift may take place today with techniques like cloud computing and solid state drives (SSD), that blur the borders between local and external storage, and between random-access main memory and hard disk drives (see section 3.4.6).

In most early operating systems such as Multics (1969), CP/M (1975), and Apple DOS (1978) there was only one 'native' file system which could not be separated from the operating system. Later systems such as SunOS 2.0 (1985), System V (Release 3 in 1986) and Linux (in 1992) introduced a virtual file system as abstraction layer to access multiple file systems in a uniform way. However a clear separation between operating system and file system is still difficult because the operating system may impose additional restrictions on files.

To overcome incompatibilities between different Unix dialects, the Portable Operating System Interface (POSIX) was standardized in 1988 (Institute of Electrical Electronics Engineers 1988). POSIX defines a common set of utilities and programming interfaces, among them an API to access different file systems in a consistent way. Most modern file systems conform to POSIX. This is good for interoperability but limits the conceptual evolution of file systems to a least common denominator. Nelson (1965a), in his first influental talk about "hypertext",[17] asserted that "there

---

[16] This design principle is brought to a head in Plan 9: this successor to the Unix operating system represents every object as file.

[17] Actually, he had already given a talk about hypertext at the conference of the International Federation for Information and Documentation (FID), in the same year (Nelson 1965b). The abstract is reprinted

are probably various possible file structures that will be useful in aiding creative thought". Regularly he complained about "The tyranny of the file" and hierarchical directory structures (Nelson 1986).[18] His article was referenced in the specification of Multics file system (Daley and Neumann 1965) but never really picked up among file system developers, so today POSIX remains the standard way of thinking about files.

3.3.2. Components and properties

Operating systems provide methods to access a file system by 'mounting' it from a specific disk or other location. Files can then be accessed independent of their location by APIs such as POSIX. *Virtual file systems* combine and wrap multiple file systems into one. In general we can call every mountable storage system a file system. This also includes revision control systems, HTTP (especially with WebDAV), and archive files (see section 3.3.3). The following analysis of general file system components and properties abstracts from different access methods. Therefore file name prefixes such as protocol, host name, device, disc, volume, port etc. are not included — these namespace identifiers should not be treated as part of a file system and its file names, but as part of an API for file access. The following description is organized chronologically as most properties are based on historic trends that date back to the origins of computer systems.

I. Files and file names

The first commercial disk drive, the IBM 350 was announced in 1956 and stored 5 million 6-bit-characters (4 megabytes). The drives had the size of a wardrobe and were also called "files", leading to the modern usage of the term. The file concept gained importance with time-sharing operating systems that allowed user to directly interact with a computer. Before this data was primarily exchanged in form of physical storage media. In the early 1960s the Compatible Time-Sharing System (CTSS) introduced the concept of user files:

> These are files of information which a user wishes to store away for future reference. They may consist of programs, data for programs, or any other information the user desires. They are kept on the disk indefinitely and allow a user to retrieve a program several weeks after he wrote it. Thus, the disk replaces the decks of cards and reels of magnetic tape usually associated with a large computer installation.
> — Saltzer (1965, p. 3)

---

in Nelson (2010, p. 154). Nelson later revised his proposed design of the "evolutionary list files" to the Xanadu project and the Zzstructure.

[18] Everyone who ever tried to use a shared network folder in a cooperation should know that monohierarchies just do not work. However file system characteristics are so deep-rooted in (our perception of) computer systems that we can hardly imagine alternatives. See the video 'Ted Nelson on Software' at http://www.youtube.com/watch?v=zumdnI4EG14 for a short overview (8 minutes) of his critique on traditional file systems and their impact.

File systems normally do not restrict the content of files, even files of zero byte length are allowed. The maximum file size, the maximum number of files, and the maximum sum of file sizes may be limited in a given context. To uniquely identity files, each file should have a *file name*. This simple assumption is complicated by operating systems and file systems which impose different restrictions on file names. In its most general form a file name is a non-empty sequence of bytes. All systems exclude at least the NUL byte 0x00. File systems also limit the length of a file name to a maximum number of bytes and/or Unicode characters. Modern file systems (NTFS, HFS+, ZFS etc.) only accept valid Unicode characters, so file names are (possibly normalized) Unicode strings. Nevertheless there is a strong tradition in the Unix community to view file names sequences of as raw bytes. Some file systems are case sensitive (one can have two distinct file names A and a), some are case insensitive, and some are case insensitive but case preserving (A and a refer to the same file but its name can be named either of them). Moreover each system disallows some special characters or bytes, for instance the directory separator / or \. Other special characters include quotes (" and '), brackets (<, >, [,]), dot (.), colon (:), vertical bar (|), asterisk (*), and question mark (?).

II. Extensions and types

In the first CTSS system, files were composed of two parts, each with up to six characters. The first part was used as descriptive name and the second indicated the file's type. Many operating systems followed this convention and supported or required *file extensions*. However the extension may not reflect a well-defined type or a file may not have an extension at all. Therefore many programs treat the extension as one of multiple indicators to determine file type. Depending on the context file(name) extensions are part of the the file name or additional metadata of the file.

III. Versions

Versioning files is not common in todays file systems although it was already supported in early time sharing system systems such as ITS (D. E. Eastlake 1972) and TENEX (Bobrow et al. 1972). The ITS system simply treated numeric file extensions as version numbers. The user could select to read a file with the highest version number of a given name or to increment the highest version number and create a new version for writing. In TENEX and its successors (TOPS-20 and OpenVMS) the version number is an additional part of the file name. Today versioning is rarely implemented in the file system but on top of it in applications, for instance in revision control systems (Subversion, git, mercurial, etc.), or in storage services that can be accesed like a file system such as Amazon S3 (Amazon 2010). Other file system features like cloning or snapshots as provided in ZFS and NTFS can emulate versioning to some extend. Just like file extensions version numbers can be considered as part of the file name or as special kind of additional metadata. However version numbers allow multiple versions to share the same file name, and they define a strict order between all versions of a files (or a partial order in revision control systems that allow branches and merges). The version number itself does not have to be a simple integer but can also be a timestamp.

IV. Directories and hierarchies

Directories are a common method to group files. In CTSS each user had a private directory and there were common directories for sharing. A directory acts like a namespace for file names (see section 3.2.2): different files in different directories can share the same name. From a conceptual point of view there is little difference between simple directories and other file system prefixes such as volume or disk: both hold simply a set of file names. In a broader context each directory must have a unique name just like a file. Hierarchical file system as introduced with Multics typically apply the same rules to file names and directory names while flat file systems such as Apple DOS and Amazon S3 have different rules for directory names and file names. In addition the maximum number of files per directory can be limited.

In the mid-1960s *hierarchies* were introduced in the Multics project that led to the development of Unix after Bell Labs pulled out of Multics in 1969 (Ritchie 1979). In Multics a directory is a special kind of file and the file structure is a tree of files, some of which are directories (Daley and Neumann 1965). The user is considered to be operating in one directory at any one time, called his 'working directory'. File names must only be unique with respect to the directory in which it occurs. For every file and directory one can define a unique name by prepending the chain of directory names required to reach the file from the root. This chain is called absolute path ('tree name' in Multics). One can also construct a relative path starting from a given working directory. Pathes require a special character as directory separator that must not occur in file names. It should be noted that POSIX does not require a file system to form a tree. The first Unix file system had the shape of a general directed graph (Ritchie 1979). However the requirement to have unique pathes was more important. For this reson other hierarchies but trees such as directed (acyclic) graphs, or polytrees are forbidden by the file system or operating system. Other restrictions can be put on the maximum depth directory nesting and the maximum length of a path.

V. Links

In simple file systems each file is identified by its name. Multics and Unix changed this one-to-one relationship by seperating files and directory entries (hard links) and by adding pointers to file names (symbolic links). Both kinds of links are included in POSIX and supported by most modern file systems today.[19]

A *hard link* is a equipollent name of a file. Internally each file is identified by a unique number (inode number in POSIX) that all names link to. In reverse, the inode only stores a link count telling how many hard links point to it. The file is only deleted if the last hard link is removed (or even later if the file is held open by a running program). Usually all hard links to one file must lie on the same physical disk. Moreover hard links are restricted to normal files to avoid breaking the directory hierarchy. The operating system defines two unchangeable exceptions: each directory contains a file named '.' (dot) as hard link to itself and a file named '..' as hard link to the parent directory (or to itself in case of the root directory).

Symbolic links are special types of files that consist of a pointer to another file or directory. The pointer is stored literally as relative or absolute path. Symbolic links, in contrast to hard links, can span different file systems and point to non existing targets. For most applications, the use of symbolic links is transparent: opening a symbolic link opens the target file for reading or writing. NTFS supports similar links named junction points.

Both hard links and symbolic links are unidirectional: There is no simple lookup table to get all names a file is known under. One can think of alternative link mechanisms but few are implemented in the file or operating system. One example is the Linking file system (LiFS) proposed by Ames et al. (2005) that introduces arbitrary links between files. Each link holds a set of attributes that express the nature of the relationship. The containment of a file within a directory is simply one relationship among many that can be expressed with these links.

In addition to hard links and symbolic links, there are link types such as 'alias' in Mac OS, Windows shortcurts, desktop icons in KDE or GNOME. These links cannot be used on the file system level but require additional APIs.

VI. Attributes

File attributes contain additional metadata about, or associated with a file. POSIX defines a fixed set of attributes for file type (regular file, symbolic link, or directory), file size, access permissions, and the times of creation, last modification, and last access. The set and purpose of this so called regular attributes is fixed and defined by the operating system. Their content and effect cannot freely be chosen by the user, some attributes (such as the file size) are even automatically derived from other properties. Therefore one must carefully ponder whether a given attribute is part of the conceptual level or only a technical artifact.

In addition to regular attributes, most file systems support *extented file attributes* that can be choosen by the user. A file's extended attributes consist of a map between names and values. Both may be arbitrary sequences of bytes or Unicode characters depending in the specific system. Typically the size and number of attribute names and values per file is limited. A fork is a special kind of extended file attribute

---

[19] Symbolic links were available in Multics from the beginning but they were ported to Unix not until the Berkeley Fast File System implemented them in the BSD-branch of Unix in 1983.

introduced in the Macintosh File System (MFS) in 1984. Unlike other attributes the fork can be a byte sequence of arbitrary size just like the file content. Forks are available in Apple's successor file systems HFS/HFS+ and as Alternate Data Streams in Microsoft's NTFS (1993).

From a conceptual point of view the file content can be treated as one attribute or fork of the file among others. In practice extended attributes are rarely used beyond system applications because of limited support in user interfaces. The BeOS file system supported typed attributes (string, time, double, float, int, boolean, raw, and image) and indexing, searching, and sorting by any attribute field similar to a databases (Giampaolo 1999). A query to all files with specific attribute properties could also be used as "virtual directories" similar to views in a database.

3.3.3. Wrapping file systems

File system instances can also be embedded in a single file of another file system. The container file is called *archive file* or *disk image* depeding on the main purpose. Archive files are used to package and transfer files that otherwise may get corrupted or split up when directly copied from one system to another. In addition one can apply compression and encryption to the set of contained files. Two of the most used archive formats are TAR (Free Software Foundation 2009) and ZIP (PKWARE 2007). The archive format defines the conceptual properties of its file system. For instance extended attributes or forks are not always included and older versions of TAR imposed more rigid restrictions on size and names of contained files (Free Software Foundation 2009, section 8). In contrast to most file systems, files in a TAR archive have an order and are permitted to have more than one member with the same name – both cannot losslessly be mapped to most other file systems. Properties of the ZIP format have also changed, for instance to support plain UTF-8 file names since version 6.3.2 (PKWARE 2007). Other extensions of ZIP such as file comments and extra fields cannot directly be mapped to other file systems without additional agreements. Archive files are also used as wrappers for more specialized file formats, for instance OpenDocument (OASIS 2012) and Java Archives (`.jar`) are ZIP files, and Debian software packages (`.deb`) are `.ar` archive files that each contains two TAR archives (thus two file systems wrapped in a file system wrapped in a file). Other file formats use non-standard archive file systems like the Compound Document format which many Microsoft products are based on[20] A remarkable curiosity of compressed archives is the possibility to create an infinite chain of archives. Cox (2010) created a "self-reproducing zip file". It contains one file that is identical to the original. Each file contains another ZIP file so there is always one level more inside. See section 4.2.3 for more about the question whether this file contains itself or not.

Disk images store a file system's underlying raw stream of bytes in one file. Having access to the storage media one can transform every file system into an archive file.[21]

---

[20] The Apache POI project reverse-engineered and implemented this format and named it POIFS (Poor Obfuscation Implementation File System).

[21] On Unix one can copy a whole disk partition with its file system to a file on another partition and

3 Methods of data structuring

The program or location to mount a given disk image is also called virtual drive. Virtual drives are common to abstract from storage media, for instance when one emulates another computer system in a virtual machine. Mounting specific archive files is also possible but less common.[22] Another way of abstracting a file system is to route all file system API calls through another API that wraps the underlying file system – this is how virtual file systems like GnomeFS/GVfs/gio[23] and KIO[24] are implemented.

---

mount the resulting disk image this way:
```
dd if=/dev/partition of=/mnt/otherpartition/image
mount -o loop image /mnt/image
```
[22] See http://code.google.com/p/fuse-zip/ for a file system that mounts ZIP files.
[23] http://library.gnome.org/devel/gio/
[24] http://api.kde.org/4.x-api/kdelibs-apidocs/kio/html/

3.4. Databases

Historically, data base systems evolved as generalized access methods [...] As a result,
most data base systems emphasize the question of how data may be stored or accessed,
but they ignore the question of what the data means to the people who use it.
— John F. Sowa 1976: *Conceptual Graphs for a Data Base Interface*

A *database* is a managed collection of data with some common structure. The general
form of a database is shaped by its *database model*, which is implied by the particular
implementation of a *database management system* (DBMS). Overviews of database
models can be found in Silberschatz, Korth, and Sudarshan (2010); Elmasri and
S. Navathe (2010); S. B. Navathe (1992); and Kerschberg, Klug, and Tsichritzis (1976).
Although you can identify some general model types, the exact definitions of specific
database models differ. As pointed out by W. Kent (1978, chapter 9), comparisons
should not confuse data models and concrete implementations. Database models
rarely occur as such, but only as abstractions of DBMS implementations. The model
can be derived from an explicit specification, from the DBMS' schema language (see
section 3.7.4), and from its query API (see section 3.10).

The development of database systems and models is not a logical chain of improvements, but driven by trends and products. In the 1960s the difference between file
systems, as described in the previous section, and database systems was still small —
for instance IBM marketed a series of mainframe DBMSes 'Formatted File System'.
Simple databases were (and still are) build of plain records and tables without any
elaborated model (section 3.4.1). The hierarchical model (section 3.4.2) and the
network model (section 3.4.3) were designed close to properties of the underlying
storage media. A better separation between logical level and physical level was
introduced with the relational model (section 3.4.4). Since the 1970s (in database
research) and the 1980s (in commercial products), it has become the preferred
database model, at least in its interpretation by SQL. In the 1980s object oriented
databases (section 3.4.5) and graph databases appeared. Object orientation had
impact on relational databases, which partly evolved to object-relational databases.
Graph databases experience some revival since the late 2000s in connection with the
NoSQL movement (section 3.4.6).

So called 'semantic database models' (Hull and King 1987; Peckham and Maryanski 1988) will be described as conceptual data models in section 3.8. Other more
specialized databases models not covered here are spatial, temporal, and spatio-
temporal databases, and multidimensional databases. The former add better support
of space, time, and versioning (C. X. Chen 2001). The latter are used to efficiently
summarize and analyze large amounts of data (Vassiliadis and Sellis 1999).

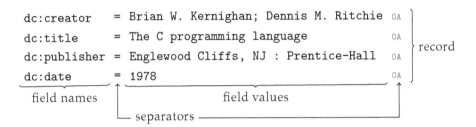

Figure 3.3.: Dublin Core record (field names included)

3.4.1. Record databases

The *record model* dates back to pre-electronic data processing with punched cards. A database was a set of punched cards that each stored one record.[25] Records are usually stored in databases or files. Although records are still the most used form of structuring data, the record model is not often described in database textbooks and research. A detailed critique is given in W. Kent (1979) and W. Kent (1978, ch. 8). Internally data may be structured in different ways, but the most prominent medium to enter, edit, and display data is the form, which usually is shaped as a record.

In its most general sense the term *record* is used for any collection of related data, storage devices, files, documents and more, equal to the general term of a digital 'document'. In a more strict sense, a record is a grouped unit of data elements, that are called its *fields* or its *attributes*. The fields may be ordered in a sequence and identified by *field names* or indices. Field names often act as a mnemonic aid to human users. In most databases they are not part of the record, but included with field descriptions in the specification of a *record type* or *record schema* which records conform to. To map data elements of a given record to fields, the elements must be separated and identifyable. There are three methods to fulfill this requirement:

- the record type defines a fixed set of fields with fixed length and position

- the record type defines a fixed set of fields with fixed order

- field name are included in the record

With the first two methods, the record type strictly defines, which fields must occur in which order. Fields may further be described by a data type or domain, that values of the field in each record must conform to. This corresponds to the classical notion of records as described by W. Kent (1978, ch. 8), and as used in other database models. Both methods impose a restriction on field values, either on their length, or on the set of symbols allowed to represent field values. The second method needs at least one special symbol to separate field values (table 3.7; other popular symbols are comma, semicolon, and space). If the field separator symbol occurs in

---

[25] See McGee (1981) on database history and the quote about 'files' (Saltzer 1965, p. 3), also at page 74.

field values, it must be escaped. The second method is favoured in database theory, because it directly maps to the mathematical concept of a tuple and you can list multiple record in a table (figure 11). However single records are not self-describing and do not allow exceptions or repeated fields. In practice, they lead to the invention of special NULL-values to denote 'not applicable' or 'unknown' field values and to ad-hoc formatted lists of values, packed in one field.[26] The third method is more flexible, but it also needs some separators between field names and field values. An example of a self-describing[27] record is shown in figure 3.3. It contains a Dublin Core (DCMES) record, encoded with the special characters '=' (U+3D) and line break (U+0A). Another example with numbers and characters as field names is given in appendix D.

The inclusion of field names in records is also known as markup, which is described in more detail in section 3.6. Markup allows you to freely omit, repeat, and order fields. Such records do not even need a record schema but can consist of a simple list of field names and field values, such as in INI files (see section 3.5.2). These schema-free records have been avoided in most databases the last decades, but they are getting popular again with NoSQL databases. If fields are unordered and they can only occur once per record, the record model corresponds to the concepts of associative arrays, maps, hashtables, or dictionaries from type theory and programming languages. If stored or sent as sequence of bytes, however, the record does not show, whether fields are ordered and which fields have been omitted. Given the record in figure 3.3, you need background knowledge about the record type Dublin Core Metadata Element Set (DCMES) to know, that the order dc:creator, dc:title, dc:publisher, dc:date is not relevant, and that there are eleven other possible fields defined in DCMES. Other interpretations of DCMES allow repeating the dc:creator field to express lists of creators, which requires field order to be preserved. The limitation of fields of a record to non-repeatable, atomic values – also known as first normal form – is often assumed implicitly. But as described by Fotache (2006), the notion of atomicity depends on context. For instance in figure 3.3 you could split the dc:publisher field value into the publisher's name (Prentice-Hall), place (Englewood Cliffs), and state (NJ). dc:title could be split in words and characters, and dc:date in century, decade, and year of the decade. The inclusion of field names in records increases flexibility, but it still selects a specific set of fields, that may be quite different in another context.

Some record models, for instance the MultiValue/PICK database and MARC records, allow fields to be repeated or split up into subfields. If you allow arbitrary nesting of records in fields, subfields, sub-subfields and so on, you end up with a hierarchical database. If you restrict the number of levels to a fixed value n you can represent an ordered, flat file database structure with n special separator elements that must not occur in (sub)field values. ASCII defines four such control characters

---

[26] See the list of names, the creator field in figure 3.3.

[27] The term 'self-describing' is used with similar carelessness as the term 'semantic'. In most cases, the only 'description' of self-describing data is a simple mapping of data elements to their field names.

Code	ASCII name	Unicode name	MARC name
U+1C	File Separator (FS)	INF. SEPARATOR FOUR	–
U+1D	Group Separator (GS)	INF. SEPARATOR THREE	Record Separator
U+1E	Record Separator (RS)	INF. SEPARATOR TWO	Field Separator
U+1F	Unit Separator (US)	INF. SEPARATOR ONE	Subfield Delimiter

Table 3.7.: Separator control characters in ASCII, Unicode, and MARC

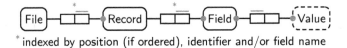

*indexed by position (if ordered), identifier and/or field name

Figure 3.4.: Flat file database model

that were used in many binary flat file formats (example 3.7).

Records are used as building blocks in many data structuring methods. The database model of a plain record store is also known as *flat file database model*. Records in a flat file database are typically stored and accessed sequentially, which enforces an order on all records and fields, no matter if this order is relevant or not. Figure 3.4 shows the model of a flat file database with atomic fields: Each file may have zero or more records, which each must belong to exactly one file. Each record may contain zero or more fields, which each must belong to exactly one record, and have exactly one field value. To refer to a particular record or field, it must be *indexed*. A record index is also called *record identifier*. If records and/or fields are ordered, their position can be used as one index. Field names are the usual index for fields, but only for non-repeatable fields. Selected field values, or combinations of multiple field values, can be used as record identifier; but only if every record happens to contain the selected fields, and if their values uniquely identify the records. Such additional constraints are not part of the record model, but fundamental in the relational model.

A *table of records* is the usual method to manage files of records, if all records share the same fixed set of fields (figure 11). The first row contains the record schema by listing its field names, and each following row contains one record. The table header can be omitted, if fields are indexed by their position. Single records are also indexed by their position, so record identifiers are neither part of the record.

The lack of a clear definition of record identifiers is one drawback of the record model. Without record identifiers as link target you cannot express relations that span multiple records. On the other hand there are implicit relationships between the fields of one record, but some relationships within a record cannot be described (W. Kent 1978, ch. 8.4f). It even depends on context, whether a record represent an entity or a relationship. In summary, records lack a clear method to express relationships while struggling with a rich variety of representational alternatives (W. Kent 1988). Nevertheless the record concept is useful in grouping data elements,

author	title	year
Kerninghan and Ritchie	The C programming language	1978
Bjarne Stroustrup	The C++ programming language	1985

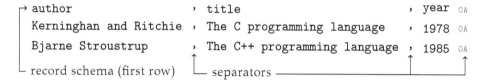

Example 11: Table of records as formatted table and as CSV

and can be found on various levels — you must only take care which variant of the record model you deal with in a particular application.

3.4.2. Hierarchical databases

Hierarchical databases are among the oldest and longest running database systems. The first hierarchical DBMS – IBM's Information Management System (IMS) – was developed in 1966-1968 and is still used today by a large number of banks, insurance companies and similar organizations.[28] Popular specialized storage systems using the hierarchical model are file systems (section 3.3), directory services such as LDAP (Lightweight Directory Access Protocol), and the Domain Name System (section 3.2.3).

In a hierarchical database the data is organized into mathematical tree structure. Records may be typed and may contain data in typed field values (attributes). There is one special type to connect records via 1:m parent-child relationships. Each record can only have one parent node (unless it is the root node that has no parent) and may have one or more child nodes. A database can be described as a set of trees, each having the same structure (you can also have multiple parallel tree structures by adding a virtual root node). Managing data in a hierarchical database is comfortable as long as the information to be stored is also hierarchic in nature. Other structures require additional arrangements as shown in the following example:

Figure 3.5 at the left shows a hierarchical database to store information about libraries and their publications. Each library has one catalog. A publication in the catalog may be assigned to one topic or more. Topics can be arranged into a hierarchy. We assume that topics follow the mono-hierarchy of a classification but not the poly-hierarchy of a thesaurus. Each time the library acquires an item, the vendor and the publication are stored. As there are only 1:n relationships, the hierarchic database cannot ensure that each library has only one catalog (1). Relations only span two records, therefore the ternary relationship between library, vendor, and

---

[28] See Blackman (1998), http://www.ibm.com/software/data/ims/, and (Silberschatz, Korth, and Sudarshan 2010, appendix E).

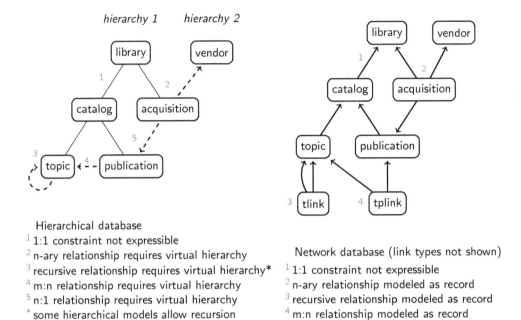

hierarchy 1   hierarchy 2

Hierarchical database
[1] 1:1 constraint not expressible
[2] n-ary relationship requires virtual hierarchy
[3] recursive relationship requires virtual hierarchy*
[4] m:n relationship requires virtual hierarchy
[5] n:1 relationship requires virtual hierarchy
[*] some hierarchical models allow recursion

Network database (link types not shown)
[1] 1:1 constraint not expressible
[2] n-ary relationship modeled as record
[3] recursive relationship modeled as record
[4] m:n relationship modeled as record

Figure 3.5.: Hierarchical and a network database with its limitations

publication must be expressed as record (2). This also requires a virtual hierarchy (called "logical" in contrast to "physical" in IMS) between vendor and acquisition and between publication and acquisition. The n:1 relationship between acquisition and publication also requires a virtual hierarchy (5). The n:m relationship between publications and topics (4) and the recursive 1:n relationship between topics and subtopics (3) are also modeled by virtual hierarchies but the monohierarchy cannot be expressed.

Virtual hierarchy pointers can be used to circumvent some of the hierarchic model's limitations, similar to symbolic links in file systems (section V). Yet in practice they are less efficient and their integrity is not ensured by the DBMS. Other hierarchic DBMS, for instance native XML databases share similar limitations.

3.4.3. Network databases

The *network database model* evolved in the 1960s from the Integrated Data Store (IDS) DBMS. Under the guidance of Charles Bachman and the Database Task Group (DBTG) within the Conference of Data Systems and Languages (CODASYL), it resulted in the first database standard specification (Association for Computing Machinery 1971; Data Description Language Committee 1978). Many basic concepts of database terminology were introduced by the DBTG, including the difference between a data description language (DDL) to define the database schema and a data manipulation language (DML) to query and modify the content of a database. The DBTG model can be described as a partly ordered graph with typed *records* as nodes and typed *links* as edges. Records can have attributes as described in section 3.4.1. Similar to the hierarchical model, links are limited to 1:n relationships. In the DBTG model a relationship is called *set* with the relationship type as *set type*, one record as *owner* and zero or more records as *member* of the set. The DDL statement "`insertion is automatic; retention is mandatory`" can mark a set type as required for the member record. Other features of the DBTG model include unique key attributes, ordering sets by a selected record attribute, and singular sets.

In contrast to the hierarchical model there is no separation between hierarchical links and virtual pointers. A record can be a member of multiple owners, as long as each membership takes place in a different set type. Other limitations of the hierarchical model are also present in the network model: there is no separation between 1:n and 1:1 relationships ((1) in fig. 3.5 on the right) and relationships with more then two members must be modeled by records ((2)). Such additional *junction records* are also used to model recursive relationships (3) and n:m relationships (4).

Later extensions of the network database model evolved to the *role data model*. It was planned as generalization of the network and the relational model, similar to object databases, but never got really adopted (Bachman and Daya 1977; Steimann 2007).

3.4.4. Relational databases

The *relational database model* was introduced by Codd (1970) as superior alternative to hierarchical and network database models. It overcomes data dependency on ordering, indexing, and access paths, and it highlights the separation between logical level and physical level. Together with the relational model, Codd introduced the idea of database normalization to avoid redundancy and inconsistencies. Based on set theory and predicate logic, the relational model gave database research a highly stimulating, mathematical foundation. However its properties are often confused with those of the structured query language (SQL), and the conceptual entity-relationship model (ERM). Both are influenced from the relational model, but with deviation from its original design, and both had far more impact on implementations. These implementations are now known as *relational database management system* (RDBMS).

In the relational database model, you declare data and queries as logic predicates in form of *n*-ary *relations*, while the DBMS takes care of storing and retrieving the data. Similar to the mathematical sense of a relation, database relations are defined as subset of the cartesian product $S_1 \times \cdots \times S_n$ over n sets $S_1, \ldots, S_n$. The sets S_i ($i = 1, \ldots, n$; the sets need not be distinct) are indexed by unique names for each relation, and called its *columns*. In contrast to mathematical relations, the rows of a database relation have no order. The relation's tuples, which are called its *rows* are also unordered. In short, a relation in the relational model is a set of distinct records, like in the record database model, with a fixed set of fields, which are indexed by names. Each fields can be restricted to a given data type, that is called its *domain*. The collection of fields, field names, and domains of a relation are sometimes called its *(record) type*. The relational model defines a *relational algebra* based on relations and types, with the basic operators selection, projection, cross join, relational set union, relational set difference, and rename.

I. SQL and its impact

Originally, Codd did not specifiy a query language for the relational model, but required that any relational query language must be based on relational algebra. Chamberlin and Boyce (1974) presented such a query language, that later evolved to SQL. Current dialects of SQL include numerous extensions, and only share basic ideas with the original relational model. As explained by Darwen and Date (1995), SQL violates the relational model in several ways, especially by using simple tables of records, which allow duplicated rows instead of set-based relations, and by inclusion of NULL values. Atkinson et al. (1989) point to SQL as the "classical, and unfortunate, pattern in the computer field that an early product becomes the *de facto* standard and never disappears". At the same time there is no consensus on what SQL really is. Only between 1987 and 1996, the National Institute of Standards and Technology (NIST) provided a test suite for SQL, which RDBMS vendors had to conform to, to get used in governmental funded projects.[29] Meanwhile each RDBMS has its own restrictions and extensions. The SQL standard, as specified by ISO, has grown in complexity and size with each new version, and no product fully implements each detail. Moreover, the specification is not freely available, which makes it hard to check, whether a specific language construct or implementation conforms to standard SQL. Despite its divergence from the relational model, and its lack of a reliable, vendor-independent specification, which deserves that appellation, SQL is perceived as lingua franca of DBMS in general. This dominance also takes into account for the dominance of the relational database model.[30] Critics from database research, such as Stonebraker, Madden, et al. (2007) and Darwen and Date (1995) therefore often argue against SQL and RDBMS, but less against the relational model as introduced by Codd.

II. Normalization

The concept of *database normalization* was a basic part of the relational model from the beginning. Similar to relational model in its original form, normalization is not fully applied in practice (Fotache 2006). Beginning with the first normal form (1NF), normalization techniques were soon extended by the second normal form (2NF) and

---

[29] The latest test suite from 1996, testing SQL, as specified in ANSI X3.135-1992 (SQL-92) is available at `http://www.itl.nist.gov/div897/ctg/sql_form.htm`.

[30] In short, the relation model had a lot of impact, especially spoiled and misinterpreted by SQL, which also had a lot of impact, especially spoiled and misinterpreted by its differing implementations.

the third normal form (3NF) (Codd 1971), the Boyce-Codd normal form (BCNF) (Codd 1974), the fourth normal form (4NF) (Fagin 1977), and more forms. The general objective of normalization is to map relations and dependencies information to database relations, without introducing possible redundancy and inconsistencies. Single facts should only be stored once, and facts, that can be derived from other facts, should not be stored at all. As a result, no queries are favoured at the expense of others. Any complex query can be build by joining multiple tables, that share fields of the same domain. To speed up specific queries, indexes and views, that act as caches of query results, can be created. In practice, some parts of the database are not normalized on purpose for performance reasons — in this case, the database user must take care of database integrity.[31]

Leaving performance issues aside, normalization is also useful independent from relational databases. *1NF* deals with uniformity and atomicity: all rows of a record type must contain the same number of fields, and field values must not be decomposable into smaller data items (subfields). First normal form is often assumed implicitly, but silently ignored at the same time. For instance a table of publications and authors must contain exactly one author for each single publication to fulfill 1NF. To express publications without author, we must either introduce a new table of all publications, or a virtual 'anonymous' author as NULL value. Lists of authors (like "Kerningham and Ritchie" in figure 11) can be allowed by either adding another table with author-list and list-member, or by allowing lists as atomic data types. The latter solution has been favoured by advocates of object-relational models such as Darwen and Date (1995), as the notion of atomicity depends on context (Fotache 2006). However, the ad-hoc introduction of NULL values and lists without any strict definition of their meaning does neither align with 1NF nor with any other database formalism.[32]

Second and third normal forms ground on the concepts of *database key*s and *functional dependencies*. Both can also be applied to other types of databases. A key is a set of one or more fields (or table columns), which in their relation (or table) uniquely identify a record. If relations are sets, every table has an implicit key, build of all their columns. Generally, keys should be short, to be used as reference (also known as foreign keys) in other tables. Under 2NF and 3NF, all non-key fields must functionally depend on the combination of all key fields. That means, the mathematical binary relations between all key-fields and any non-key field must be a total function (totality is enforced by exclusion of NULL values with 1NF). In example 12, publications are listed in table a with country, author, year, title, publisher, and place. If we choose the set {author, year} as database key (red uniqueness overline in 12), each combination of author and year must uniquely identify a publication's country, title, publisher, and place. Obviously, an author can create multiple titles per year, so we must modify the key. For instance, each

---

[31] A popular example of denormalized databases are data cubes in Online Analytical Processing (OLAP).

[32] In practice, NULL values often cover a fuzzy bunch of meanings, and lists are encoded by introduction of separators (for instance the string ' and '), that are not part of any database definition known to the DBMS.

publication can get a letter suffix between 'a' to 'z'.[33] Such additions of artificial identifiers are common, although they do not represent a given fact about the publication.

The extended table b now allows multiple publications per author and year, but it may violate 2NF. This is the case, if a non-key field depends on a subset of a key. If the non-key field country denotes the country, an author origins from,[34] it should be split up in another table, with {author, country} as key (example 12, c).

3NF is violated when a non-key field depends on another non-key field. For instance, if place denotes the place of a publisher, and if places do not change over the years, the table should be decomposed as shown in example 12 d.

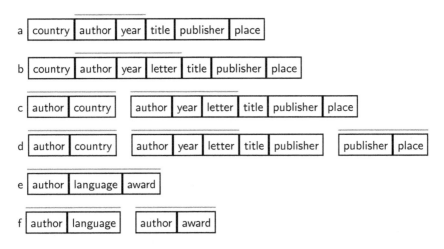

Example 12: Normalization of relational database tables

4NF and additional normal forms attempt to minimize the number of fields involved in a key. Let us assume we want to store information about the popularity of authors. Table e in example 12 list languages, that authors have been published in, and awards, that authors have received. Under forth normal form, the implicit key {author, language, award} should be split in two independent keys (tables f), because languages and awards are independent from each other. If the awards and languages are properties of publications, a normalized database should not contain tables e and f at all, because their content can be derived by relational algebra as view from other tables.

Despite the theoretical importance of database normalization, it has failed to become an ultimate aid for database designers. At most, they use normalization for validation after creation of databases based on intuition. Fotache (2006) gives some reasons for this gap: popular textbooks on database design often describe and exemplify normalization poorly or even incorrectly. Most literature on normalization

---

[33] Note that this only extends the number of publications per author and year from one to 26.
[34] For some reasons, nationalists and library classifications try to uniquely group authors under countries.

focuses on rigor and sober mathematics and uses artificial examples, instead of real world applications. There is a lack of graphical diagramming tools for functional dependencies, and other graphical modeling languages such as ERM (section 3.8.1) base on different philosophies. Another problem, also raised by W. Kent (1983b), is the dependency on uniquely identified entities. If fields contain different values for the same object, for instance different spellings of names, speaking about keys and dependencies is futile. However normalization only reveals the difference between rigor data and fuzzy reality, that would also exist without it.

3.4.5. Object database

Object Orientation (OO) was introduced during the 1960s by Ole-Johan Dahl and Kristen Nygaard with creation of the Simula programming language (Holmevik 1994). *Object Oriented Programming* (OOP) was further popularized by Alan Kay's Smalltalk and had large impact on many following programming languages. Core concepts of different OO systems have been identified retrospectively by Armstrong (2006). The main idea is to bundle data and interactions in objects. An *object* is a structure with data fields, attributes, or properties; and methods to invoke a specific behaviour. Both are combined in a *class* that, like a record type, acts as blueprint to create objects, which then are *instance*s of the class. In addition, the properties and methods of a class may be included or used as basis for another class via *inheritance*. Details of implementation are concealed by the object via *encapsulation*.

When OOP became widespread in the 1980s, the mismatch between object-oriented programs and relational databases led to the development of object(-oriented) databases. The classical definition of an *object oriented database management systems* (OODBMS) in the 'Object-Oriented Database System Manifesto' (Atkinson et al. 1989). It identifies thirteen OODBMS requirements, five of which hold for DBMS in general (persistence, secondary storage management, concurrency, recovery, ad-hoc query facility), and eight of which are specific for object-oriented systems.

- objects must be identifiable independent of their values. This implies two samenesses: same valued objects (equivalence), and same objects (identity).

- objects are defined only by which operations they can be modified and interact with. Internal representations are hidden (encapsulation).

- objects must have classes or types that define their characteristics.

- objects can be build from some basic types (integers, floats, characters, byte strings, booleans, etc.) and some object constructors (at least set, list, and tuple), that can be applied to any object, independent from its type.

- there is no distinction in usage between predefined basic types and newly constructed types.

- there are at least four types of inheritance for a class T and a subclass S: substitution (instances of S can substitute instances of T),[35] specialization (instances of S contain more information than instances of T), inclusion, and constraint (every instance of S is also instance of T if it satisfies a given constraint).

- names can denote different operations for different object types.

- the data manipulation language must be a Turing-complete computational programming language.

In summary, the characteristics of object databases are *i)* object identity, *ii)* classes and types, and *iii)* inheritance. It must be said that, 'object oriented', like many terms in computing, is also used as marketing buzzword, or to indicate a rough direction, rather then specifying a final list of features. The list of requirements given above is rarely fulfilled in existing OODBMS. Stonebraker, L. A. Rowe, et al. (1990), in response to Atkinson et al. (1989), published the 'Third-Generation Database System Manifesto' and argued that OO can be added to relational systems with keeping SQL as common database language. Some OODBMS concepts were incorporated into RDBMS, which led to *object-relational databases* (ORDBMS). However the predominance of relational databases persisted and therefore developers created *Object-relational mappings* to combine OOP and RDBMS. This error-prone task has been described by Neward (2006) as 'Vietnam of Computer Science': it "starts well, gets more complicated as time passes, and before long entraps its users in a commitment that has no clear demarcation point, no clear win conditions, and no clear exit strategy." Above all, migration to and from object databases is costly because the dominance of SQL and the lack of an accepted query language for object databases, independent from type systems of specific programming languages. A unification of the relational model and the object orientation has been proposed by Darwen and Date (1995) in a 'Third Manifesto'. They made clear that progress is hindered by adherence to the SQL database language, which is not even truly relational, but their proposed alternative *Tutorial D* (Date and Darwen 2006) had little impact on concrete implementations. Today the NoSQL movement shares some of the critics on SQL and object databases are sometimes subsumed under the NoSQL approach. Maybe the most effective impact of OO to data modeling is the Unified Modeling Language (UML) (see section 3.8.3). It is mostly used to model object oriented software but also for databases.

3.4.6. NoSQL databases

During the first decade of 21st century several providers of large web applications (Google, Amazon, Facebook, Yahoo, etc.) had started to develop their own non-relational data stores. Database researcher Stonebraker, Madden, et al. (2007)

---

[35] This type of inheritance has formally been refined by Liskov (1987) and is known as Liskov substitution principle. It states that all provable properties of instances of T must also be true for instances of S. Thus any algorithm designed for T instances of will behave exactly the same if used with S instances.

declared the relational DBMS obsolete, because of changed hardware limitations and data processing needs.

When more new non-relational open source DBMSes were available in 2009 last.fm employee Johan Oskarsson organized an event called NOSQL (for 'not SQL'), which can be seen as baptism of the following NoSQL movement. NoSQL has brought a new momentum into the development of database systems by questioning some general properties of RDBMS, such as secondary storage management, concurrency, recovery, schemas, and ad-hoc query facility. The term refers to no common database model but compasses all non-relational or 'structured storage' data stores, which may also subsume file systems. Beside object databases the following types can be distinguished:

key-value stores provide a simple dictionary where keys are mapped to arbitrary values. These systems are more comparable with flat file systems that have no data types and may only put restrictions on keys. An exception is redis,[36] a DBMS that supports strings (sequences of bytes), sequences, sets, and ordered sets of strings. Other examples of key-value stores are Amazon S3 (Amazon 2010), Berkeley DB[37], and Project Voldemort.[38]

document databases or document stores manage values as 'documents' in a specific data structuring language (mostly JSON or XML). In general, documents are not constrained by a schema, and they may be versioned. Popular examples of document databases are CouchDB,[39] MongoDB,[40] and RavenDB.[41] Native XML databases, such as eXist[42] are less often mentioned, but also fall into this category.

graph databases allow storing arbitrary graph structures with nodes, edges, and properties. In most cases, graphs are schema-free without distinction between different structural kinds of relationships (1:n, 1:1, m:n, mandatory, recursive, unique, etc.). The specific graph model depends on the particular graph DBMS (Angles and Gutiérrez 2008; Rodriguez and Neubauer 2010). Popular instances are based on the RDF graph model for triple stores (see 3.5.6) or on property graphs, but there also exist other models, for instance hypergraphs.[43] Network databases can be seen as a restricted subset of graph databases. Examples of general graph databases include Neo4J,[44] and InfoGrid.[45]

---

[36] http://code.google.com/p/redis/
[37] http://www.oracle.com/database/berkeley-db/
[38] http://project-voldemort.com/
[39] http://couchdb.apache.org/
[40] http://www.mongodb.org/
[41] http://ravendb.net/
[42] http://www.exist-db.org/
[43] See http://www.kobrix.com/hgdb.jsp for a Hypergraph DBMS.
[44] http://www.neo4j.org/
[45] http://www.infogrid.org/

column databases are table-based databases, which seperately store each column of all relation (or each field of all records), instead of keeping together rows or records. Column databases provide good performance especially for processing of sparse data. The most prominent column DBMS is Google's BigTable (Chang et al. 2006) (also supporting versioning), another instance is Cassandra (Facebook, now Apache)[46]. Similar column data-structures are also used in databases and other software for statistical analysis of large data sets.

---

[46] http://cassandra.apache.org/

3.5. Data structuring languages

Data structuring languages (DSL) or *data serialization languages* are used to express, exchange, and store data structured in general forms such as records, lists, sets, and tables. Similar to most file systems (3.3) and databases (3.4), and unlike specific markup languages (3.6) the elements of a DSL do not hold special semantics but general patterns and constraints. These constraints may further be tightened by schemas (3.7) that define concrete formats based on a particular DSL. Data that is only structured by a DSL, but not by a more specific schema is often denoted as *semi-structured data*.

Each DSL defines a simple type system and at least one syntax to serialize data in form of a stream of characters or bytes. The type system can be seen as (conceptual) data model of the DSL and the syntax as logical model of the DSL. Some DSLs provide a syntax and a clear definition of its data model (XML, RDF, YAML). Others only define a syntax, that implies a model (JSON) or they do not define a strict standard at all (INI, CSV, S-EXP structuring languages with focus on their underlying data model. CSV and INI (3.5.2), JSON (3.5.3), YAML (3.5.4), and XML (3.5.5) all provide a syntax that is also human-readable to some degree. The focus of RDF (3.5.6) is more communication between machines. Depending on what one considers as core part of RDF, it can also be seen as simple conceptual modeling language (section 3.8). If one removes all executable parts from a programming language, its type system can also be seen as DSL – a popular example is JSON that evolved as subset of JavaScript. Data binding languages (3.5.1) provide a compact and abstract form of a type system independent from a specific programming language . Some programming languages even structure data and programs in the same way: that means every program is semi-structured data in the programming language's own type system. Rules of the programming language act like a schema that restricts the DSL to valid, executable code. A typical example of such a data-oriented programming language is Lisp, which is purely based on S-Expressions (S-EXP).

3.5.1. Data binding languages

A special form of data structuring languages are language-specific *serialization formats*. These are used to convert data structures in programming languages into byte streams and vice versa, a process that is also called marshalling or deflating (structures to bytes); and unmarshalling, deserialization, or inflating (bytes to structures). The general application of a serialization format is also called *data binding* because several application can be 'bound together' by exchanging data in a common serialization format. Table 3.8 lists several languages that have been developed for data binding. Some binding languages come with a more general interface description language to specify APIs and with data definition languages (DDL) to specify more concrete formats (see section 3.7). The absence of a DDL does not mean one cannot specify concrete formats based on the particular DSL, but there is no common and defined language to express these formats.

DSL	first defined	DDL
Abstract Syntax Notation One (ASN.1)	1984 by ISO	Encoding Control Notation (ECN)
External Data Representation (XDR)	1987 by Sun (RFC 1014)	–
CORBA Common Data Representation (CDR)	1991 by OMG	Interface Description Language (IDL)
Structured Data eXchange Format (SDXF)	2001 as RFC 3072	–
Hessian	2004 by Caucho	–
Fast Infoset	2007 by ISO	same as for XML (see 3.7.2)
Thrift	2007 by Facebook	–
Protocol Buffers	2008 by Google	.proto files
Etch	2008 by Cisco	–
MGraph	2008 by Microsoft	MSchema/MGrammar
BSON	2010 by MongoDB	–

Table 3.8.: Data structuring languages developed for data binding

Example 13: Protocol Buffers

Protocol Buffers is a serialization format with associated schema language developed by Google. It was first introduced for remote procedure calls and now is used for storing and interchanging all kinds of structured data (the Protocol Buffers developer Guide names it as "Google's lingua franca for data") (Varda 2008). The format's serialization is binary and thereby much smaller and quicker to parse then XML. Schemas (see section 3.7.5) are defined in .proto files that can be used to automatically generate parsers and serializers in many programming languages. The underlying data model is hierarchical: The basic data type of Protocol Buffers is the "message", that is a multimap with unique, unsorted keys, and repeatable, sorted values. Values can be other messages or instances of 16 scalar core data types (table 3.9). An earlier version of Protocol Buffers also included a group data type which is now deprecated. Some types only differ in the way they are serialized (for instance int32 and sint32) but encode the same values.

3.5.2. INI, CSV, and S-Expressions

Comma-separated values (CSV), *initialization files* (INI), and *S-expressions* (S-EXP) exist as DSL in several variants. Despite the lack of a strict and commonly agreed specification, these languages are used because of their simplicity in a wide range of applications. Descriptions of the most used variants of each language can be found in Shafranovich (2005) and Repici (2010) for CSV, in Wikipedia (2010) for INI, and

Type(s)	in XML	in Java	Content
int32, sint32	int32	int	signed 32-bit integer
uint32, fixed32	uint32	int	unsigned 32-bit integer
int64, sint64	int64	long	signed 64-bit integer
uint64, fixed64	uint64	long	unsigned 64-bit integer
float	float	float	32 bit floating point (IEEE 754)
double	double	double	64 bit floating point (IEEE 754)
bool	bool	boolean	true of false
string	string	String	Unicode or 7-bit ASCII string
bytes	string	ByteString	sequence of bytes
enum	enum	enum	choice from a set of given values
message	class	class	multimap with unique, unsorted keys repeatable, sorted fields (possibly constraint by a schema)

Table 3.9.: Core data types of Protocol Buffers

in Rivest (1997) for S-EXP. Each language uses a tiny set of data types with strings or byte sequences as the only atomic type. Syntaxes of INI, CSV, and S-EXP are mainly defined as context-free language in Backus-Naur Form with some additional constraints.

We will now show underlying models for each of these languages. INI is primarily used for configuration files. In its most basic form, it is just a key-value structure with field names (Field) and values (Value). Some INI files may have a second level (Section). Section names should be unique per file and field names should be unique per section, but both constraints depend on the particular variant of INI. A general model is shown in figure 3.6. In summary, INI files are a special instance of the record database model as described in section 3.4.1 (see see flat file database model in figure 3.4).

CSV is popular to exchange simple lists of database records. An example is given in figure 11. CSV is based on a tabular model (figure 3.7) where data is stored in cells (Cell) that form a grid of rows (Row) and columns (Column). In general, all rows must have the same set of columns, or they are automatically unified by adding missing cells with a default value.

S-EXP originates in the Lisp programming languages and it is also used in some data exchange protocols. The model of S-EXP is a rooted, ordered tree with strings or empty lists as leafs (figure 3.8). There is not one standard but several dialects. A canonical subset of S-EXP with binary form has been proposed by Rivest (1997).

The Value of a Field, Cell, or String in INI, CSV, or S-EXP respectively can hold arbitrary byte sequences or character strings, depending on the specific language variant. Some byte or character sequences may be disallowed, especially for names of sections, fields, and columns in INI and in CSV.

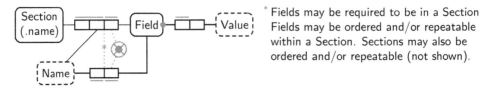

Figure 3.6.: Model of INI with variants

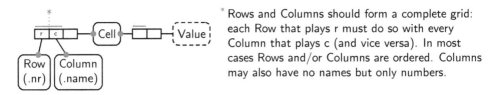

Figure 3.7.: Model of CSV with variants

3.5.3. JSON

JavaScript Object Notation (JSON) is based on notations of the JavaScript programming language. First specified by Crockford (2002) and later standardized as RFC (Crockford 2006) it soon became a widespread language to exchange structured data between web applications, serving as an alternative to XML. JSON was first published in form of a railroad diagram (see section 3.7.1) and later expressed in a variant of Backus-Naur Form. Figure 3.9 shows a full BNF grammar of JSON. In a nutshell JSON is based on data model with five atomic value types (**String**, **Number**, **Boolean**, and **Null**), and two composite types **Array** and **Object**. Strings can hold any Unicode codepoint, but most application will limit codepoints to allowed Unicode characters. Numbers include integer values and floating point values without limit in length and precision.[47] An **Array** holds a (possibly empty) list of values, and a **Object** holds a (possibly empty) map from strings as keys to data elements as member values.

The definition of JSON syntax as context-free language imposes the mathematical structure of a partly-ordered tree on models of JSON. In such a model, nodes are values but atomic types must be leaf nodes and the root node must be a composite.

---

[47] Special numbers like −0, NaN, and Inf are not allowed.

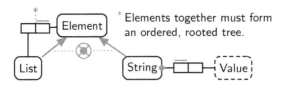

Figure 3.8.: Model of S-EXP

```
Composite  = s* ( Object | Array ) s*
Object     = "{" ( Member ( "," Member )* )? "}"
Array      = "[" ( Value ( s* "," s* Value )* )? "]"
Member     = Key ":" s* Value s*
Key        = s* String s*
Value      = Composite | String | Number | Boolean | Null
String     = '"' ( char - ( '"' | '\' ) | charref )* '"'
 charref   = '\' ( ["\/bfnrt] | [0-9A-F][0-9A-F][0-9A-F][0-9A-F] )+
Number     = "-"? ( "0" | [1-9] [0-9]* ) ( "." [0-9]+ )?
             ( ( "e" | "E" ) ( "+" | "-" )? [0-9]+ )?
Boolean    = "true" | "false"
Null       = "null"
s          = ( #x20 | #x9 | #xA | #xD )
```

Figure 3.9.: Formal grammar of JSON

Similar structures to JSON are found in many programming languages, for instance *JavaScript* and *Perl* but they may contain pointers that go beyond the tree structure. In addition, virtually all implementations add uniqueness constraint on objects keys,[48] limit maximum size of text, numbers, and nesting level, and restrict **String** to the Unicode character set.[49] With the rise of NoSQL (see 3.4.6) JSON is also used more and more to store data in databases. Most JSON databases put additional restrictions on special object keys ("", _id, id, $ref...) that are used for uniquely identifying and linking JSON documents or parts of it. Other extensions such as Binary JSON (BSON) restrict atomic types and/or add data types that are not part of the JSON specification.[50] There are some proposals for schema languages for JSON (JSON Schema,[51], Kwalify,[52] JSONR[53]...), and for query languages to select a subsets of a given JSON document (JPath,[54] JSONPath[55]...) but none of them is widely accepted. Manipulation of JSON data is usually done directly in programming languages or via custom database APIs.

The clear and simple definition of JSON has made it a popular data structuring language not only for web applications but also for ad-hoc tasks in structuring, storing, and exchanging data. Proplems may result from differences in compatibility of atomic types (especially keys and numbers) and from data that does not fit into

---

[48] repeated object keys (like {"a":1,"a":2}) are allowed in theory.
[49] Unicode codepoints outside of UCS are allowed but not supported by all implementations.
[50] BSON extends some parts of JSON but is does not support numbers of arbitrary length
[51] see http://json-schema.org
[52] see http://www.kuwata-lab.com/kwalify/
[53] see http://web.archive.org/web/20070824050006/http://laurentszyster.be/jsonr/
[54] see http://bluelinecity.com/software/jpath/ and http://bitcheese.net/wiki/code/hjpath for two different JSON path languages
[55] see http://goessner.net/articles/JsonPath/

the tree-model of JSON.

3.5.4. YAML

YAML (YAML Ain't Markup Language) was developed as human-readable alternative to XML and first published by Clark Evans in 2001 (Ben-Kiki, Evans, and Ingerson 2009). Unlike most other DSL it can natively express hierarchical and non-hierarchical structures. In contrast to most other data serialization languages, the YAML specification defines in one document: a syntax, a conceptual model, and an abstract serialization to map between syntax in model.

YAML syntax is very flexible: it allows multiple alternatives to express complex structures in a simple, human readable way as stream of Unicode characters. Some examples of language constructs are given in figure 3.10. Apart from repeatable object keys and Unicode **Surrogate** codepoints, which are not allowed in YAML, the syntax is a superset of JSON syntax. Other similarities exist with the semistructured data expression syntax (ssd) used by Abiteboul, Buneman, and Suciu (2000). The abstract serialization of YAML is called its *serialization tree*. The serialization tree can be be traversed as sequence of parsing/serializing events, similar to the event-driven Simple API for XML (SAX) (see page 3.5.5). The conceptual model of YAML is called its *representation graph*. It is defined by the specification as "rooted, connected, directed graph of tagged nodes". Eventually this is a special multi-property graph with possible loops and three disjoint kinds of nodes. Figure 3.10 gives a partial model of the representation graph in ORM2 notation:[56] **Sequence** nodes impose on order on outgoing edges, and **Mapping** nodes have their outgoing edges indexed by node values, as described below. Nodes of outdegree zero can also be of the **Scalar** kind, which each holds a Unicode string as value. Mapping keys can be arbitrary nodes, which makes the structure rather complex – but in practice most YAML instances represent simple hierarchies. Each node in a YAML representation graph has exactly one **Tag** as node type.

Tags can be either identified by an URI (**GlobalTag**) or by a simple string (**LocalTag**). A *YAML schema* is a set of tags. Each tag is defined by an URI, an expected node kind (scalar, sequence, or mapping) and a mechanism for converting its node's values to a canonical form.[57] Furthermore, a tag may provide additional information such as the set of allowed values for validation and the schema may provide a mechanism for automatically resolving values to tags. For instance a schema could automatically tag the string **true** as boolean value instead of a literal string. Normalization of node values to their canonical form is important for node comparision. Keys of a mapping node must not only be different but unequal. Two nodes are equal if they have the same tag and the same canonical content. Equality of sequences and mappings is defined recursively.[58] The YAML specification lists some possible types

---

[56] Roots, scalar values, (local) tag names and URIs are not included.

[57] See http://yaml.org/type/ for a registry of known tags.

[58] Note that recursive equality checks may require determining whether the subgraphs used as keys are isomorphic – a problem that is not solvable in polynomial time in worst case.

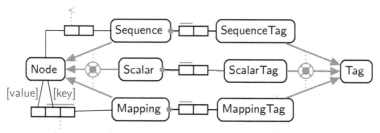

Figure 3.10.: YAML data model (partial)

&x foo	Scalar node with link anchor x and value "foo"
[*x, bar]	Sequence node with previously defined node x and another scalar node with value "bar" as members
{ key1: foo, key2: bar }	Mapping node with two key-value pairs
{!!str 42}	"42" tagged as string (instead of number)
!point {x: 12, y: 4}	Mapping node with local tag point
? [a, b] : [1, 2, 3]	Mappping node with one sequence as key and another sequence as value
&n [*n, *n]	Sequence node that contains itself twice
&m { *m : *m }	Mapping node that maps itself to itself

Table 3.10.: Examples of YAML syntax, including some edge cases

and schemas but their support depends on particular implementations of YAML parsers. YAML neither defines a standard how to express types and schemas in a machine-readable way so their defintion is only adressed to implementors and users. Support of additional collection types such as sets and ordered mappings also depends on additional conventions.

In summary the data structuring philosophies behind YAML are very sophisticated but too complex for most applications. Especially the support of arbitrary nodes as array keys has little practical value but complicates the construction of a full YAML model.

3.5.5. XML

XML has succeeded beyond the wildest expectations as a convenient format for encoding information in an open and easily computable fashion. But it is just a format, and the difficult work of analysis and modeling information has not and will never go away.
— Wilde and Glushko (2008)

The *Extensible Markup Language* (XML) was designed between 1996 and 1998 as simplified subset of the Standard Generalized Markup Language (SGML) for the Web (Bray, J. P. Paoli, and Sperberg-McQueen 1998). Its origin in SGML (see section 3.6 about SGML and markup languages in general) gave XML strong support for marked up text documents, but also some features, that for most applications only add unnecessary complexity. Beginning from the late 1990s, more and more domain specific data formats were created based on XML, or they migrated to XML from SGML. XML 1.0 was first published as W3C recommendation in February 1998. Soon it was accompanied by numerous extensions and revisions, such as the Document Object Model (DOM) in late 1998, XML Namespaces (1999), XPath (1999), XSLT (Clark 1999), XML Schema (XSD) (2001), Canonical XML (2001), XML Base (2001), XML Infoset (2001), and XInclude (2004). XML 1.1 was introduced in 2004 as successor to XML 1.0 (Bray, J. Paoli, et al. 2004), but it never got widely adopted. The listed extensions define slightly different models of XML, and the degree of their support varies among applications, what complicates an exact definition of XML documents (Dodds 2002). However, all definitions share a common subset, that can be described as an ordered tree with Unicode strings and key-value-pairs as node-properties. Beginning with XML 1.0, we will first describe the most common parts of XML syntax, then discuss aspects of XML processing and differences between models of the XML family of standards, and finally give an overview and review of the most common XML structures.

XML 1.0 is defined based on a context-free grammar over a sequence of Unicode characters with some additional *well-formedness* constraints. The grammar is given in a variant of Backus-Naur-Form. Figure 3.11 shows a slightly adopted subset of the grammar rules: A document starts with an optional prolog, followed by a mandatory root element, and optional comment, processing-instructions (pi), and whitespaces (s). The prolog usually contains an XML declaration, that among other information can specify the character encoding, a standalone flag, and a document type definition (DTD). An element in XML syntax either consist of a starttag and an endtag with the same name[59] and some content in between, or it is an emptytag. Start tags and empty tags can have a list of attribute , which are key-value-pairs with unique name per attribute list.[60] A content may contain other elements, resulting in the general tree of XML documents (see example 15 for a document).

Textual data (text) in XML can be any Unicode string, except some codepoints below U+0020, U+FFFE and U+FFFF. Furthermore the characters '<' and '&', and in content the sequence ']]>' is not allowed. To include these characters in an XML document, you can use character references (charref) which can refer to an allowed Unicode character by its UCS codepoint. In addition there are predefined named entities (entityref): '<' for '<', '>' for '>', '&' for '&', ''' "for ' '', and '"' for '"'. XML is further complicated by the possibility to define named entities in a DTD. These entities can either stand for an arbitrary piece of content (*internal entity*) or as placeholder for some other data that is referenced by an URI

---

[59] The same name requirement that is one of the constraints that cannot be expressed in BNF.

[60] The uniqueness requirement of attribute names is another additional well-formedness constraint.

```
document  = prolog element misc*
misc      = comment | pi | s
s         = ( #x20 | #x9 | #xA | #xD )+
element   = starttag content endtag | emptytag
starttag  = "<" name (s attribute)* s? ">"
endtag    = "</" name s? "/>"
emptytag  = "<" name (s attribute)* s? "/>"
content   = text? ((element | reference | cdata | pi | comment) text?)*
text      = chars - (chars ("<" | "&" | "]]>") chars)
reference = charref | entityref
charref   = "&#" [0-9]+ ";" | "&#x" [0-9a-fA-F]+ ";"
entityref = "&" name ";"
value     = (text | reference)*
cdata     = "<![CDATA[" (chars - (chars "]]>" chars)) "]]>"
comment   = "<!--" (chars - (chars " " chars | chars "-") "-->"
pi        = "<?" pitarget s (chars - (chars "?>" chars)) "?>"
attribute = name s? "=" s? ( '"' (value - (value '"' value)) '"'
                           | "'" (value - (value "'" value ) "'" )
```

Figure 3.11.: Subset of the formal grammar of XML

(*external entity*).

Most entities are replaced by their content, when an XML document is read by an *XML processor* (a piece of software that parses the syntax of an XML document and provides access to its content and structure). However, some named entities can remain as unparsed artifacts because they are external or because the DTD is not taken into account by the processor. In practice the Simple API for XML (SAX) (Megginson 2004) is a common abstraction in XML processors, especially for the Java programming language. SAX is not a formal specification but it originates in an implementation of an XML parser that was first discussed in early 1998. The API of SAX provides a stream of parsing events that can be used to construct an XML document, if the stream of events follows the well-formedness constrain of XML (every XML document can be mapped to a stream of SAX events but not vice versa).

XML 1.0 defines two types of XML processors: validating and non-validating processors. Non-validating processors must only check whether a document is well-formed, but they do not need to process all aspects of a DTD.[61] Validating parsers must analyze the entire DTD, including other documents referenced from the DTD, and they must check whether the document matches the additional rules from its schema (see section 3.7.2). A processor may even change the content of an XML

---

[61] Some simple XML processors just ignore the DTD although this is against the specification. Removal of DTD is one of the most common request in discussions about a future "XML 2.0", as most XML documents have no DTD, and validating is mostly done by using other schema languages.

document by normalizing strings and by adding default values.

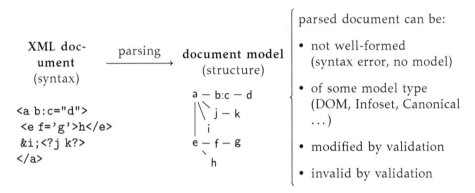

Figure 3.12.: XML document and XML document models

Parsing XML can best be understood as a process that converts XML syntax, given as sequence of characters, to another data structure (figure 3.12). In general the act of parsing an XML document is not reversible, because some aspects of XML syntax are considered as irrelevant (figure 3.13). The resulting data structure is a model not only of the parsed document, but of all other "logically equivalent" documents that result in the same model. Parsing XML can result in different structures. If the original data was not well-formed, there is no model, and the document is no XML by definition.[62] The specific type of model defines, which parts of syntax are translated to which parts of a model and which parts are omitted as irrelevant to the given model (figure 3.13). A processor may also modify the document to some degree or it may mark the document as invalid.

The most prominent models of XML are the *Document Object Model* (DOM) and *XML Infoset*. DOM evolved parallel to XML in the late 1990s. It was created to harmonize existing JavaScript-Interfaces that had been created by Web browser makers for manipulating HTML documents. The part of DOM that deals with XML documents is 'DOM Core'. Actually there are three variants: Level 1 is based on the tree structure of XML 1.0, Level 2 expresses the structure of XML with Namespaces, and Level 3 expresses a model compatible with XML Infoset (Cowan and Tobin 2004). Another model of XML is shared by XPath 1.0 and Canonical XML (Boyer and Marcy 2008), XPath 2.0 and XQuery define yet another model (Berglund et al. 2010). A given model may also be expressed in other languages but XML syntax. For instance *Fast Infoset* (International Organization for Standardization 2005) is a binary representation of Infoset based on ASN.1 and Tobin (2001) defines an RDF Schema to serialize XML document models as RDF instances.

Despite all minor differences, all document and processing models of XML share a basic structure, that can be described as ordered tree with nodes of different types.

---

[62] In practice you sometimes have to deal with not-well-formed documents that were intended to be XML. You can call this documents 'broken' XML if there is a chance to recover well-formedness.

- type of attribute delimiters ("/")

- type of character entities

- original character encoding

- CDATA sections

- standalone flag

- all entity references

- specified schemas

- whitespaces

- position of namespace declarations

- namespace prefixes

- attribute types (e.g. ID, IDREF...)

- explicit default attributes

- original form of normalized attributes

- original form of normalized Unicode

- comments

- processing instructions

Figure 3.13.: Some properties of XML considered as irrelevant by some processors

Basically, there are element nodes with exactly one element as root, attribute nodes, and text nodes. Other node types (processing-instructions, comments, external entity references etc.) are much less used to hold relevant information, and they more depend on the particular document model.

Each element node has a (possibly empty) set of unordered attribute nodes with unique attribute names, and an ordered (possibly empty) list of text and/or element nodes as child nodes. Attribute nodes cannot hold nested structures but only one text node each, and text nodes are Unicode strings with some code points excluded.

Each attribute and each element node has a name. The exact definition of a name from figure 3.11 depends on the specific XML model: in XML 1.0 a name is just a Unicode string that not contains some disallowed characters. The dependence on a particular version of Unicode was lifted with the fifth edition (Bray, J. P. Paoli, Sperberg-McQueen, et al. 2008). The most important (and often confusing) extension to XML 1.0 is XML Namespaces (Bray, Hollander, et al. 2009): namespaces allow names of elements and attributes to be qualified by an URI. This way names can be grouped together in vocabularies and elements from different vocabularies can be mixed in one document. In the model of XML with namespaces (and in other techniques that build upon namespaces, such as DOM Level 2 and 3, Infoset etc.) a name is triple consisting of the namespace URI, a local name, and a namespace prefix. In XML syntax namespaces are declared by special attributes that start with **xmlns** (in example 15 the namespace is declared at the root element so it applies to the whole document). Example 14 shows three XML elements that make use of a namespace declaration. In most cases only the namespace URI and the local name matter, so the first two examples should be treated as equivalent. The prefix is also included in most models, and some applications rely on it.[63] The third example

---

[63] See http://www.w3.org/TR/xml-c14n#NoNSPrefixRewriting for details.

14 is always different from the two above: in contrast to RDF Turtle syntax (see section 3.5.6), namespaces and local names cannot be used to construct a canonical name, but they must be used together to identify the full name of an XML element or attribute.[64]

element in XML syntax	namespace, local name, prefix
`<x:zz xmlns:x="http://example.org/"/>`	(http://example.org/, zz, x)
`<y:zz xmlns:y="http://example.org/"/>`	(http://example.org/, zz, y)
`<xz:z xmlns:xz="http://example.org/z"/>`	(http://example.org/z, z, xz)

Example 14: Namespaces in XML

To allow more complex graph structures, there are several techniques to extend the basic tree model of XML with links: attributes can be defined to only hold unique ID values or references to other identifiers (`IDREF` in DTD or keyref constraints in XML Schema). XLink (DeRose, Maler, et al. 2010) and XPointer (Grosso et al. 2003) describe other extensions to XML to create links to portions of XML documents. However, like other extensions to XML 1.0, this adds another layer of complexity and another model that first must be agreed on to achieve interoperability. To reduce complexity within the family of XML specification, simplified subsets have been proposed by Bray (2002), Clark (2010) and others, but none of them has widely been adopted yet. Nevertheless, XML is successfully being used to encode and exchange data on the Web and in other areas from markup languages such as TEI to structured metadata formats such as METS, MODS, and EAD. Furthermore several serialization forms of other formats in XML exist, for instance RDF/XML for RDF and MARCXML for MARC. As described by Wilde and Glushko (2008), many problems with XML arose from overbroad claims for XML, which in the end is just a format. It still suits best for marked-up textual data and other records that can be modeled well as ordered tree, but less for data with arbitrary order and links.

3.5.6. RDF

The *Resource Description Framework* (RDF) dates back to the Meta Content Framework (MFC) which Ramanathan Guha had created in the 1990s at Apple (Andreessen 1999; R. V. Guha 1996). R. Guha and Bray (1997) submitted the idea of MFC to the W3C, where it evolved to a general graph-based metadata framework, first released as RDF specified by Ora Lassila and Swick (1999). Merged with ideas of Tim Berners-Lee (1997), the focus had widened to metadata about any objects for creating a "Semantic Web", that can express knowledge about the world itself (T. Berners-Lee, J. Hendler, and O. Lassila 2001). The ambitious aim of RDF can be traced back further to the artificial intelligence project Cyc, which Guha was co-leader of in 1987–1994, and to

---

[64] Some vocabularies may specify *additional* identifiers for XML elements, for example in XML Schema each element has an URI that happens to be constructable by appending local name to namespace URI. However there is no general rule to do so in other vocabularies.

```xml
<?xml version="1.0" encoding="UTF-8"?>
<mods xmlns="http://www.loc.gov/mods/v3" version="3.4">
  <titleInfo>
    <nonSort>The </nonSort>
    <title>C programming language</title>
  </titleInfo>
  <name type="personal">
    <namePart>Kernighan, Brian W.</namePart>
  </name>
  <name type="personal">
    <namePart>Ritchie, Dennis M.</namePart>
  </name>
  <originInfo>
    <place>
      <placeTerm typo="toxt">Englewood Cliffs, NJ</placeTerm>
    </place>
    <publisher>Prentice-Hall</publisher>
    <dateIssued>1978</dateIssued>
  </originInfo>
</mods>
```

Example 15: MODS record in XML

the original proposal of the WWW (Tim Berners-Lee 1989). We will first describe the basic components of RDF, show how its structure can be described and extended, and list several serialization forms. Afterwards we will discuss how semantics is brought to RDF via an algebra over RDF graphs.

I. RDF components

In its most basic form — that is without additional techniques such as RDFS, OWL, SKOS, etc. — RDF is just a, graph-based data structuring language. The RDF data model is defined as abstract syntax by Klyne and Carroll (2004) as follows: an *RDF graph* is a set of *RDF triples* (also known as *statement*s) each consisting of a *subject*, a *predicate* (also known as *property*), and an *object*. The nodes of an RDF graph are its subjects and objects, and the edges are labeled by its predicates. Because RDF graphs are defined on mathematical sets, each particular combination of subject, predicate, and object is only counted once in a graph. In summary, an RDF graph can be described as multigraph with labeled edges, possible loops (triples where subject and object coincide), and partly labeled nodes. This multigraph may contain two kinds of graph labels: First an *URI reference* (or *URIref*) is an absolute, percent-encoded URI or IRI. Two URIrefs are equal if and only if they compare as equal as encoded strings.[65] URIrefs are treated as identifiers for *RDF resources*, which beside triples are the central part of the Resource Description Framework. No assumptions are made about the nature of resources, but the same URIref always refers to the same resource (P. Hayes and McBride 2004, section 1.2). RDF allows different URIrefs to refer to the same resource (synonyms), but unlike natural languages it is assumed to have no homonym URIrefs just by definition.[66] It should be noted that RDF graphs cannot contain resources which are not linked to other resources: you state that some resource plays a specific role in at least one RDF triple, but you cannot state that a selected resource only 'exists'.

The second type of graph labels are *RDF literals*. A literal is a Unicode string, which should be in Normalization Form C. Optionally it is combined with either a lowercase *language tag* as defined by Phillips and Davis (2006), or with a *datatype URI* being an URIref. Literals with datatype are called *typed literals* in contrast to *plain literals*. Two literals are equal if they hold the same Unicode string (also called its *lexical form*), and (if given) the same language tag datatype URI. Datatypes may enforce restrictions and normalization rules on lexical forms, but the details of this rules are out of the scope of basic RDF.[67]

In addition to labeled nodes, at least subjects and objects can be unlabeled *blank nodes*. Blank nodes are treated as variables for unknown URI references in one particular RDF graph. You can state that two blank nodes in one graph refer to the same resource, but blank nodes from different graphs are disjoint, unless you replace them with URIrefs. In practice, blank nodes are identfied by arbitrary identifiers, that are not shared among different graphs. As laid out by Carroll (2003), blank nodes can make it hard to check, whether two graphs are equal, to calculate a canonical representation of an RDF graph, and to remove all infereable tuples from a graph.[68]

Figure 3.14 shows a simple RDF graph consisting of six triples. URIrefs are depicted as rectangles, blank nodes as circles, and predicates are labeled arcs. Literals are shown in quotation marks, optionally followed by "@" and a language tag, or by "^^" and a datatype URI. The same graph in Turtle syntax is shown in figure 3.15.

---

[65] This definition of equality is not based on normalized IRIs, but on Unicode character string comparision (Klyne and Carroll 2004, p. 6.4). This makes `http://example.com/%41` and `http://example.com/A` two distinct URIrefs, although in most applications, after normalization of percent-encoding, the former results in the latter. The ambiguity cannot be solved in general, because there is no general canonicalization algorithm for all types of IRIs. It is possible but strongly discouraged to have two different URIrefs that percent-encode the same IRI.

[66] By this, RDF can be seen as one of many attempts to create a 'perfect language', in which same words always refer to same objects. The history of other attempts and their failures have been illustrated vivid by Eco (1995).

[67] To give an example, the XML Schema specification (Biron and Malhotra 2004) defines the datatype `xs:boolean` with four allowed lexical values ("`true`", "`1`", "`false`", "`0`") that map to the canonical literal values "`true`" and "`false`".

[68] It is assumed that the underlying graph isomorphism problem (GI) is strictly harder than polynomial time (P), and strictly easier than nondeterministic non-deterministic polynomial time (NP) (Köbler 2006).

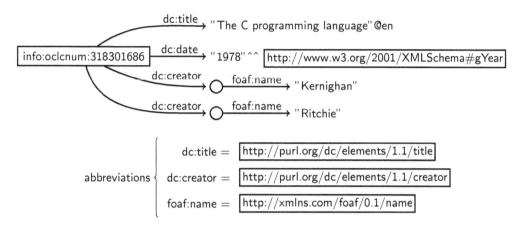

Figure 3.14.: Example of a simple RDF graph

RDF extension	subject	predicate	object	datatype	lang.	graph
standard	$U \cup B$	U	$U \cup B \cup L$	U	T	–
symmetric	$U \cup B \cup L$	U	$U \cup B \cup L$			
generalized	$U \cup B \cup L$	$U \cup B \cup L$	$U \cup B \cup L$			
full blanks		$U \cup B$		$U \cup B$		$U \cup B$
named graphs						U
language URIs					$U[\cup B]$	

U: URIref, B: blank node, L: Literal, S: Unicode string, T: language tag
$L = S \cup (S \times U) \cup (S \cup T)$ and U, B, L, S, T are pairwise disjoint.
The set of blank nodes B is partitioned into disjoint sets for different RDF graphs.

Table 3.11.: Definitions of the RDF data model and its extensions

II. The model and its extensions

An RDF graph can formally be defined as subset of the set $(U \cup B) \times U \times (U \cup B \cup L)$ of all triples, as laid out in table 3.11. You can think of several useful extensions of the standard RDF data model. First literals can also be allowed as subject of a triple. This extension to 'symmetric' RDF allows reversing the direction of any triple by switching subject and object. In standard RDF you cannot state, that a given literal is the 'name of' a given resource, but only that a resource is 'named as' a literal. Symmetric RDF is allowed at least internally in many RDF applications, for instance in SPARQL (Prud'hommeaux and Seaborne 2008, sec. 12.1.4.). Second you could allow literals and blank nodes at any part of a triple. This extension to *generalized RDF* is allowed for instance in OWL2 (Schneider 2009, sec. 2.1). An ORM model of generalized RDF is given in figure 3.17. Third you could allow blank nodes at every place where URIrefs are allowed, that means also as predicates and/or data types.

A different popular extension allows labeling whole RDF graphs by URIrefs. This extension was introduced as *named graphs* by Carroll, Christian Bizer, et al. (2005). It has been adopted for instance in triple stores (in this case also known as quadstores) that deal with multiple RDF graphs. Finally the replacement of language tags by URIrefs or blank nodes would repair another design failure of standard RDF.[69]

III. Serializations

The RDF data model is not bound to a specific syntax, but there a several serialization formats. The most common format is RDF/XML which uses XML (Dave Beckett 2004). Suprisingly, some allowed RDF graphs cannot be expressed in RDF/XML because they contain literals or predicate URIs with Unicode codepoints forbidden in XML 1.0. There are also numerous alternative ways to describe the same RDF graph in RDF/XML, which makes it hard to use generic XML tools to process general RDF data. *TriX* (RDF Triples in XML) is an alternative XML based syntax for RDF, that additionally provides for serializing several (named) graphs in a single document (Carroll and Stickler 2004). RDF/JSON and JSON-LD are serializations of RDF in JavaScript Object Notation (JSON), which is popular in several scripting languages (K. Alexander 2008; Sporny, Kellogg, and Lanthaler 2012). *N-Triples* is a simple, plain text serialization that was created for test cases (Grant and Dave Beckett 2004). RDF graphs in N-Triples are written one triple per line and the character set is 7-bit US-ASCII, but still the format is capable of encoding all RDF. *Turtle* (Terse RDF Triple Language) was created by David Beckett as more flexible and readable syntax extension of N-Triples (D. Beckett 2007). Turtle is probably the most popular RDF serialization format next to RDF/XML; an example is shown in figure 3.15. *TriG* syntax (Chris Bizer and Cyganiak 2007; Carroll, Christian Bizer, et al. 2005) extends Turtle by using curly brackets to group triples into multiple graphs, and to precede each graph by an URIref as its name. Apart from minor syntax variants, that can be added automatically (an equal sign before and a dot after each graph), TriG is also compatible with the syntax of *Notation3* (N3),[70] which is another superset of Turtle. N3 extends Turtle with features such as variables, formulae, logical implications, and functional predicates, that can be used to abbreviate common URIrefs and patterns of RDF statements (Tim Berners-Lee and Connolly 2008). A summary of syntax elements of Turtle and Notation3 is given in table 3.12.

IV. Vocabularies

A common technique used in all syntaxes (except N-Triples) is the abbreviation of URIrefs with namespace prefixes. In practice it is often assumed, that all resources, under one namespace prefix share same properties and that they belong to one

---

[69] In standard RDF you cannot refer to language tags in statements because language tags are disjoint with URIrefs and blank nodes.

[70] However both use different models of RDF: Trig is based on named graphs and N3 on standard RDF with a custom `rei:` reification vocabulary.

```
@prefix xs: <http://www.w3.org/2001/XMLSchema#> .
@prefix dc: <http://purl.org/dc/elements/1.1/> .
@prefix foaf: <http://xmlns.com/foaf/0.1/> .

<info:oclcnum:318301686>
  dc:title "The C programming language"@en ;
  dc:date "1978"^^xs:gYear ;
  dc:creator [ foaf:name "Kernighan" ] ,
           [ foaf:name "Ritchie" ] .
```

Figure 3.15.: Simple RDF graph in Turtle syntax

Syntax element(s)	purpose
@prefix	defines a namespace shortcut to abbreviate URIrefs
@base	defines a standard prefix for URIrefs
<X>	URIref with URI X
"...","""...""""	literals
"..."@X	literal with language tag X
"..."^^<X>	literal with datatype URIref X
.	marks the end of a statement
;	following statement(s) have same subject
,	following statement(s) have same subject and predicate
a	shortcut for rdf:type
_:X, [ ]	blank node with local id X or without specific id
numeric literals	xs:integer and xs:float as datatype
( )	rdf:List, rdf:first, rdf:rest, and rdf:nil.
#...	comment
=	owl:sameAs
!, ^, @forSome	statements with blank nodes
=>, <=	log:implies
{ }	statements with rei:reification and formulae
@forAll	rei:universals
?x, :y	variables in formulae

rdf: is a shortcut for http://www.w3.org/1999/02/22-rdf-syntax-ns#
owl: is a shortcut for http://www.w3.org/2002/07/owl#
xs: is a shortcut for http://www.w3.org/2001/XMLSchema#
log: is a shortcut for http://www.w3.org/2000/10/swap/log#
rei: is a shortcut for http://www.w3.org/2004/06/rei#

Table 3.12.: Syntax elements of Turtle (above) and Notation3 (additionally below)

common *RDF vocabulary*. An RDF vocabulary is a set of URIrefs and statements, that are created, described, and maintained for a specific use-case. If the vocabulary makes use of an RDF schema language like RDFS or OWL (see section 3.7.3), or if it implies other logical inference rules, the vocabulary can also be called an ontology.

The basic RDF data model as described by Klyne and Carroll (2004) includes only the predefined datatype URIref `rdf:XMLLiteral` for embedding XML in RDF literals. The standard further recommends to use datatypes from the XML Schema vocabulary (see section 3.7.2). Other parts of the RDF specification (Brickley and R. V. Guha 2004; P. Hayes and McBride 2004; Manola and Miller 2004) provide a basic RDF vocabulary to collect resources in classes (`rdf:type`), and resources that are used as properties (`rdf:Property`). In addition the RDF vocabulary contains resources to express containers (`rdf:Seq, rdf:Bag, rdf:Alt, rdf:_1, rdf:_2 ...`), collections (`rdf:List, rdf:first, rdf:rest, rdf:nil`), primary values (`rdf:value`), and *reification* (`rdf:Statement, rdf:subject, rdf:predicate, rdf:object`). Reification is the description of RDF triples using other RDF triples. This technique can be used for instance to express provenance and *n*-ary relationships, but it increases complexity and there are several competing reification ontologies.[71]

V. Semantics

A common misconception of RDF is, that RDF data automatically adheres to some semantics. The RDF data model imposes no conditions on the use of RDF vocabularies to only create 'meaningful' or 'well-formed' RDF graphs. On the contrary, an important principle of RDF is that "anyone can say anything about anything".[72] This means "RDF does not prevent anyone from making assertions that are nonsensical or inconsistent with other statements, or the world as people see it" and "it is not assumed that complete information about any resource is available." (Klyne and Carroll 2004). The latter important principle is also known as *Open World Assumption* (OWA): the absence of a particular statement from an RDF graph does not mean that the statement is false. We illustrate this by the first triple of the graph in figure 3.14 and figure 3.15. The triple can be read as "`info:oclcnum:318301686` is titled 'The C programming language' in English". More precisely, it says "the resource identified by URIref `info:oclcnum:318301686` has the English title 'The C programming language', assuming the concept of having-a-title as identified by URIref `http://purl.org/dc/elements/1.1/`." However this statement does not imply the absence of parallel titles. The resource may also have more than the two authors from the example — we just only know that there are two authors named at least "Kernighan" and "Ritchie" respectively. Once we start inferencing, it could also turn out to be one author with two names as shown in figure 3.16.

The semantics that is usually associated with RDF, does not origin from the RDF

---

[71] See `http://www.w3.org/TR/rdf-mt/#Reif`, `http://www.w3.org/DesignIssues/Reify.html`, and `http://purl.org/ontology/prv/core#` for other reification ontologies.

[72] This wording from the first RDF concepts document draft (Klyne and Carroll 2004) was later modified to "Anyone Can Make Statements About Any Resource" without changing the general declaration.

```
@base <http://viaf.org/viaf/>.
```

```
<info:oclcnum:318301686> dc:title         <info:oclcnum:318301686> dc:title
  "The C programming language"@en;          "The C programming language"@en;
  dc:date "1978"^^xs:gYear;                  dc:date "1978"^^xs:gYear;
  dc:creator <108136058>, <616522>.          dc:creator _:b1.
```

```
<108136058> foaf:name "Kernighan".        _:b1 foaf:name
<616522> foaf:name "Ritchie".                "Kernighan", "Ritchie".
```

blank nodes replaced by URIrefs   two blank nodes merged to one

Figure 3.16.: Two examples of RDF graph instances

data model, but from an algebra, that can be defined on RDF graphs.[73] The algebra allows you to freely merge and intersect RDF data based on simple set algebra. This is not possible in most other data structuring languages, for instance tree-based languages, which must have exactly one root element.[74] As blank nodes are always disjoint for different graphs, the simple set intersection of RDF graphs cannot contain blank nodes. The same applies to two RDF graphs A and B with $A \equiv B$. The RDF specification uses the word 'equivalent' in a different way, so we better call A and B 'set-equivalent' or 'identical' if $A \equiv B$.

The RDF specification defines another kind of equivalence and two additional relationships between RDF graphs: *graph equivalence*, *graph instance*, and *graph entailment*. Basically, two RDF graphs A and B are *equivalent*, written as $A \cong B$, if there is a bijection M that maps literals to equivalent literals, URIrefs to equivalent URIrefs, blank nodes to blank nodes. In addition the triple (s, p, o) is in A if and only if $(M(s), M(p), M(o))$ is in B (Klyne and Carroll 2004, sec. 6.3). It is recommended, but not required to apply Unicode Normalization before comparing graphs for equivalence.

An RDF graph H is called *instance of* an RDF graph G, if H can be obtained from G by replacing zero or more of its blank nodes by literals, URIrefs, or other blank nodes.[75] H is a *proper instance* of G, if at least one of its blank nodes has been replaced by a non-blank node, or if at least two blank nodes have been mapped to one. Two graphs A and B are equivalent if and only if both are instances of each other but neither a proper instance. Figure 3.16 shows two possible non-equivalent instances of the graph from figure 3.15.

---

[73] Some may argue, that the algebra is an inherent part of RDF. But this would neglect all RDF applications, which do not fully implement all aspects of the RDF algebra.

[74] You could define union, intersection, and relative complement also for INI files and some other record based data formats, but as described in section 3.5.2, these formats lack a precise definition.

[75] The term 'instance' is used also in RDFS and OWL for the rdf:type URIref.

Entailment is a relationship between two RDF graphs *A* and *B*, that holds, if a graph equivalent to *B* can be created from *A* by adding triples, based on specific inference rules. There is not only one kind of entailment but a variety of *entailment regimes* with different sets of inference rules.[76] A specific entailment regime can be defined by an ontology, by a set of inference rules, or by some application, that creates entailments. If the application can handle arbitrary inference rules in some rule language, it is also called a *reasoner*. To distinguish different entailment regimes, we say that *A* *x-entails* *B*, if *B* is an entailment of *A* in regime *x*. If some graph *G* is not *x*-entailed by any other graph, then *G* can be called *x-lean*.[77]

The RDF specification describes rules for simple-entailment, rdf-entailment, and rdfs-entailment (P. Hayes and McBride 2004, sec. 7). Simple entailment adds copies of existing triples by replacing URIrefs of subject and/or object with blank nodes.[78] You can understand simple-entailment as generalization: an RDF graph is always simple-entailment by all of its instances. *rdf-entailment* extends this rule to literals. The regime furthermore adds a rule that connect all URIrefs to `rdf:Property`, if they are used as property in some triple.[79]

Entailment is an important aspect of RDF, but it is not a feature of RDF data. The RDF specification only says how to apply entailment, but not whether and when to apply it. In many cases inference is expensive to calculate and would lead to a massive expansion of graphs. Some regimes have infinite entailments also for simple graphs. Even the general problem of determining simple-entailment between arbitrary RDF graphs is NP-complete (P. Hayes and McBride 2004), so most applications do not fully implement entailment unless it is explicitly required. Testing graphs for equivalence and instantiation is more common, but it also depends on entailment. Entailment is also used to detect inconsistencies in RDF data with respect to some regime. For instance in OWL, the triple { `?x owl:differentFrom ?x` } is a contradiction, that entails any possible triple, if description logic is applied. Reasoners for these entailment regimes usually detect such inconsistencies instead of infinitely adding triples.

The vision of the Semantic Web includes the idea of "intelligent agents" that can aggregate information from distributed sources and that can draw conclusions based on inferencing (T. Berners-Lee, J. Hendler, and O. Lassila 2001). This idea requires decisions about which sets of RDF data to combine, which entailment regimes to apply, and which URIrefs to rely on as non-ambiguous identifiers. All these agreements are out of the scope of RDF, which alone is just another method of structuring data.

---

[76] See `http://www.w3.org/ns/entailment/` for a non-exclusive list of common entailment regimes.

[77] The RDF specification only defines 'lean' for simple entailment, but it can also be defined for other entailment regimes. Finding lean graphs for a given regime is an area of ongoing research (Pichler et al. 2010).

[78] In Notation3: { `?s ?p ?o` } => { `?s ?p [ ] . [ ] ?p ?o` }.

[79] In Notation3: { `?s ?p ?o` } => { `?s rdf:type rdf:Property` }.

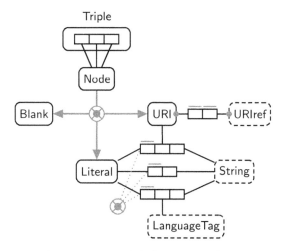

Figure 3.17.: Model of generalized RDF

3.6. Markup languages

A *markup language* is a formal language that is used to structure and annotate text. A good introduction into theory and history of markup languages until the late 1980s is given by Coombs, A. H. Renear, and DeRose (1987). The origin of markup languages is attributed to William Tunnicliffe who in 1967 made a presentation about the "Separation of Information Content of Documents from their Format" and to Stanley Rice (C. Goldfarb 1996). Tunnicliffe proposed to use descriptive tags (called *generic coding*) to mark up structural elements of publications instead of procedural formatting codes. Their ideas later evolved into the Generalized Markup Language (GML) that led to the Standard Generalized Markup Language (SGML) (C. F. Goldfarb and Rubinsky 1990). Both languages could be adopted to different kinds of documents by using a DTD (see 3.7.2). This shifted markup languages to data structuring languages, such as SGML's successor XML (see sec. 3.5.5). Eventually a *general* markup language is nothing but a kind of a readable data structuring language with strong support of character strings and other ordered lists, but little support of data types and additional relationships,beside simple hierarchy. The document structure imposed by markup languages is usually described as an ordered hierarchy of content objects (OHCO) (DeRose, D. G. Durand, et al. 1997; A. Renear, Mylonas, and D. Durand 1996), although there are attempts to extend markup languages with better support of multi-hierarchical structures (Pondorf and Witt 2010).

3.6.1. General markup types

The possibility to separate content and presentation has always been a strong argument for markup languages. With *descriptive markup* in contrast to *presentational markup* authors can focus on the structure of documents and mark what a text element *is* instead of how it should look like (Coombs, A. H. Renear, and DeRose 1987). Elements of a descriptive markup language are declared on the basis of their meaning — the markup is also called *semantic*.[80] However the distinction between layout and significance is less clear than it seems. Attributes like font size, color, and style may both serve readability and imply a special meaning. The meaning combined with a set of attributes can differ between texts or even within one text. And markup does not have to be descriptive per se. Sometimes bold text is just bold. Existing markup languages like HTML therefore often mix descriptive and presentational elements.[81]

In most applications markup is not presented directly to the user but only visible by means of its effects. A heading may be marked up as such but the reader can only differentiate based on layout properties (font size and style, section numbers etc.). With WYSIWYG editors, that provide direct visual feedback while editing, the descriptive markup is even hidden to the author. Although word processors support some separation of structure and layout via so called styles or templates, a 'What You See Is What You Mean' paradigm is difficult to achieve. Unless descriptive markup has some useful impact that is directly visible to the author (for instance automatic table of contents based on heading markup), one can unlikely motivate its usage. The concrete meaning of markup not only depends on the concrete markup language but also on its actual use and implications, and authors easily misuse markup elements for something other than their intended purpose. Eventually the markup's meaning is *only* its actual usage if we follow Wittgenstein. For a computer program, on the other hand, markup can only have an effect in form of *procedural markup* that indicates what to do with a given piece of text. Although procedural markup is mostly hidden to the user (descriptive and presentational markup is mapped to it internally), it affects the usage of markup as well. An author of an HTML document may use specific tags not (only) to indicate the meaning of some text or to shape its layout, but also to accomplish some behaviour in search engines, browsers and other programs that process the document.

Beside this three types of document markup there is a fourth class that gained importance with SGML and document types: a *prescriptive markup language* imposes a set of rules, which all matching documents must follow. A descriptive markup language in contrast describes document structures *a posteriori* rather than prescribing rules over them (Quin 1996; A. H. Renear 2000). The difference between the two lies in the purpose of validation, and applies not to single pieces of markup but to markup languages as a whole (Piez 2001). Prescriptive markup implies a strict validation that checks whether a document instance fits to a given document or not. Descriptive markup, in contrast, only provides loose validation but many degrees of freedom to describe documents of possibly unknown structure.

---

[80] This term is brought up with every new data structuring language: SGML, XML, RDF...

[81] HTML has descriptive elements like `<title>`, `<h1>`, `<em>`, and `<code>` but also purely presentational elements like `<i>` and `<tt>`. With HTML5 the standard is shifted more to descriptive markup with presentational capabilities separated in CSS (Hickson and Hyatt 2009).

3.6.2. Text markup languages

We will now look at some popular concrete markup languages for textual documents:

HTML, TEI, and DocBook are the major text markup languages. All were based on SGML and migrated to XML around the turn of the millennium. Each language covers a specific document type and mixes descriptive markup with some presentational markup (Burnard and Bauman 2007; Hickson and Hyatt 2009; Walsh 2010).

T$_E$X is a powerfull programming language for typesetting, created by Donald Knuth in 1978 (Knuth 1984). It is popular especially in mathematics and related disciplines because of its strong support of formulae. Its popular extension L^{A}T$_E$X defines a rich variety of macros; however there is no clear separation between descriptive markup, presentational typesetting, and programming (Lamport 1994).

troff is a presentational markup language that evolved from the very first text formatting program RUNOFF (1964). Several macro packages add descriptive markup for different document types (Dougherty and O'Reilly 1987). Troff has mainly been replaced by L^{A}T$_E$X and DocBook.

OpenDocument Format (ODF) is an XML based file format for several kinds of office documents. It includes detailed capabilities to encode text formatting, partly based on CSS and XSL-FO (OASIS 2012). Its extent and complexity limits the use a markup language to a subset of ODF, but to lesser degree than the rival "Office Open XML" file format by Microsoft.

Lightweight markup languages have a simple syntax, designed to be easy for a human to read and to enter with a plain text editor. Popular lightweight markup languages include reStructuredText, Markdown, Textile, POD, and several Wiki syntaxes. Examples of lightweight markup languages are shown in table 3.13, different markup languages cover same or overlapping document models by different syntax.

Rich Text Format (RTF) is a file format developed by Microsoft in 1987 to exchange text documents. It is not meant to directly be created by people but has a readable syntax and some concepts similar to T$_E$X (Burke 2003).

Extensible Stylesheet Language – Formatting Objects (XSL-FO) is an XML based markup language, that is used to describe the layout of documents, based on an area model (Berglund 2006, par. 6 and 4). The area model defines pages, blocks, and lines, partly derived from the CSS formatting model.[82]

---

[82] The XSL family of standards and its relation to CSS and XML is somehow confusing. In short the *Extensible Stylesheet Language* (XSL) consists of *i*) a query language for addressing parts of an XML document (XPath), *ii*) a programming language for transforming XML documents (XSLT) that uses

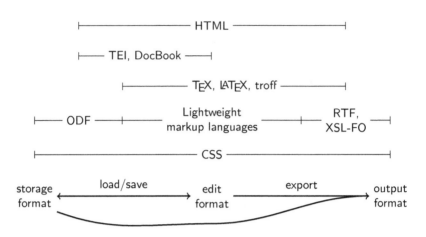

Figure 3.18.: Main applications of some markup languages

Cascading Style Sheets (CSS) is a stylesheet language to describe the presentation of elements in document markup languages (Bos et al. 2009). Introduced first by Håkon Wium Lie in 1994 for HTML, it has since been adopted for several other document types. In contrast to the other languages listed above, CSS does not markup text but describe the layout properties of elements in marked up documents.

Each language implies or defines a *document model* with entities such as pages, paragraphs, tables, lists, lines characters etc. Character encodings as described in section 3.1 provide the fundament of such models. Markup languages and document models are shaped by the focus of their application. We can divide *i*) storage formats, which are mainly used to store and exchange documents, *ii*) output formats, which procedurally or descriptively trigger a display device, and *iii*) edit formats, which are used to create, analyze, and modify documents (figure 3.18). Edit formats require the markup language to be expressed in a specific syntax; basically most markup languages are foremost defined by a markup syntax and 'markup' is often used as a synonym for a markup language's syntax. Syntax, however, should not be confused with the document model. Table 3.13 list four common concepts and their expression in syntax of different markup languages. As shown in table 3.14, the same document (here it is just a title) can be expressed differently in different form. Following the radical position of A. H. Renear and Wickett (2009), either the forms do not represent the same document or the document does not change if we transform one form to the other. But what is the document, if we only have markup language in form of syntax?

XPath, *iii*) an area model that defines layout properties, and *iv*) an XML syntax to specify documents based in the are model (XSL-FO). XSL builds on concepts of CSS and the *Document Style Semantics and Specification Language* (DSSSL) but not as its subset or superset.

language	bold face	italic face	monospace	sub-/superscript
DocBook	`<emphasis role='strong'>`	`<emphasis>`, `<firstterm>`	`<code>`. `<varname>`	`<subscript>`, `<superscript>`
HTML	`<b>`	`<i>`	`<tt>`, `<code>`	`<sub>`, `<sup>`
TEI	`<hi rend="bold">`	`rend="italics"`	`rend="typewriter"`	`rend="subscript"`, `rend="superscript"`
TeX	`\textbf {text}`	`\textit {text}`, `\emph {text}`	`\texttt {text}`, `\verb #text#`	`^{text}, _{text}`
RTF	`{\b text}`	`{\i text}`	`{\fmodern text}`	`{\sub text}`, `{\sup text}`
MediaWiki	`'''text'''`	`''text''`	`<tt>`, `<code>`	`<sub>`, `<sup>`
Markdown	`**text**`, `__text__`	`*text*`, `_text_`	`` `text` ``	`<sub>`, `<sup>`
Textile	`*text*`	`_text_`	`@text@`	`~text~`, `^text^`
reStructuredText	`**text**`	`*text*`	`` ``text`` ``	`:sub:'text'`, `:sup:'text'`
POD	`B<text>`	`I<text>`	`C<text>`	–
GNU troff (man)	`.fam B text .fam,` `\fBtext \fP`	`.fam I text .fam,` `\fItext \fP`	`.fam C text .fam,` `\fCtext \fP`	`~text~`, `~text~`

Table 3.13.: Comparison of markup languages

HTML	`Radiative &beta;-decay in <sup>141</sup>Ce`
LATEX	`Radiative \textbeta-decay in ^{141}Ce`
Textile	`Radiative &beta;-decay in [^141^]Ce`
non-standard markup	`Radiative β-decay in ^1^4^1Ce`
plain Unicode[a]	`Radiative β-decay in 141Ce` (superscript 141)
simplified transcription	`Radiative beta-decay in 141Ce`

Table 3.14.: An article title marked up in syntax of several markup languages

[a] This special title can be expressed in plain Unicode because the subscript digits 1 and 4 happen to be defined as codepoint U+00B9 and U+2074 and the upright beta is defined as codepoint U+03B2.

`<b><i>A</i></b>`	$\cong$	`<i><b>A</b></i>`	'A'
`<i><i>A</i></i>`	$\cong$	`<i>A</i>`	'A'
`<i>A</i><i>B</i>`	$\cong$	`<i>AB</i>`	'AB'
`<sup>a</sup><sup>b</sup>`	$\cong$	`<sup>ab</sup>`	ab
`a<sub>b<sup>c</sup></sub>`	$\ncong$	`a<sup>b<sub>c</sub></sup>`	$a_b^c \neq a_b{}^c$
`a<sup><sup>b</sup></sup>`	$\ncong$	`a<sup>b</sup>`	$a^b \neq a^b$

Figure 3.19.: Ambiguities and structural element differences in markup syntax

Defining a markup language by its syntax introduces some problems with escaping, concatenating, nesting, and alternatives. First, characters acting as syntax elements cannot directly be used in text but must be escaped or forbidden. For instance in HTML the less-than sign '<' (U+3C) must be escaped as '<', '<', or '<'. Second, syntax elements often cannot arbitrarily be nested and/or concatenated. For instance in Textile '**__B__**' encodes a bold, italic letter 'B' but if it is surrounded by other letters, it must be put in square brackets as 'A[**__B__**]C'. Alternatives occur especially if there is no isomorphism between syntax and document model (3.19). As each markup element has a special meaning you can rarely derive general rules for all parts of the syntax.

In most markup languages it is not even obvious which parts of a markup syntax are nested (tree model) and which are concatenated (sequence/event model). The interpretation of an element can depend on its position in a tree of elements, on its position in a sequence of elements, and/or on its position relative to other elements (see table 3.15, elements are shown underlined for better readability). In practise all markup language syntaxes have some tree-based parts and some event-based parts.

A widespread example of markup for metadata exists in citation styles and forms of heading, such as ISBD. Character strings that result from library cataloging rules, have mainly used for printing catalog cards and to support other forms of retrieval. Although often described as record, they can better be viewed as a special kind of document. As shown by Thomale (2010) for MARC, the origin as markup has also

syntax	model	document instance					
MediaWiki	events	`'''` bold	`''` bold-italic	`'''`		italic	`''`
invalid HTML	events	`<b>` bold	`<i>` bold-italic	`</b>`		italic	`</i>`
HTML	tree	`<b>` bold	`<i>` bold-italic	`</i></b><i>`italic			`</i>`

Table 3.15.: Event model vs. tree model in markup languages

influenced bibliographic data formats.[83]

Despite different applications and syntaxes, among markup languages you can find sets of shared concepts. Especially lightweight markup languages build on a common document model and differ mainly in details of syntax. Table 3.13 compares selected inline markup (bold, italics, monospace, subscript and superscript) in 11 different markup languages. Without loss of generality, we can limit analysis to inline formatting because that may more often occurr in other fields of metadata (see table 3.14). An integration of common parts will lead to a document model like the area model of XSL-FO or the formatting model of CSS. Much work of such integration has been done in the *pandoc* document converter software written by John MacFarlane.[84] Pandoc implements a set of parsers and a set of writers for various textual markup languages. They connect through a representation of parsed documents in a common document model, implemented as data structure in Haskell.

Example 16: The CSL text markup model

The *Citation Style Language* (CSL) is an XML based formal language for describing the formatting of in-text citations, notes and bibliographies (Zelle 2012). CSL does not require fixed input and output formats. Citations and bibliographic records must only conform to a common model and formatted bibliographies can be produced in different markup languages such as HTML/CSS, RTF, and TEX. Parts of the input may be formatted by additional markup as shown in table 3.14. CSL processors must be aware of this markup and transform it into a common text markup model. The markup includes italics, bold, and small caps as flags; nestable subscript and superscript; and quotations in up to two levels (pairwise quotation marks are treated as markup that can be modified by specific CSL styles). The implied text markup model is shown in figure 3.20. The model abstracts from alternatives as listed in figure 3.19.

---

[83] The treatment of existing markup in cataloging, which would result in markup in markup, has not been analyzed deeply yet. Most cataloging rules do not preserve font styles, emphasis, or even non-latin characters but make use of transcriptions and comments.

[84] http://johnmacfarlane.net/pandoc/

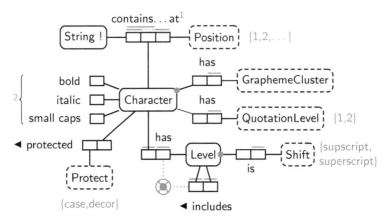

^{1} character positions of a string must have consecutive positions.

^{2} only if supported by the character's grapheme cluster.

Figure 3.20.: Text markup model of CSL

3.7. Schema languages

Und er kommt zu dem Ergebnis: / Nur ein Traum war das Erlebnis.
Weil, so schließt er messerscharf, / Nicht sein *kann,* was nicht sein *darf.*
— Christian Morgenstern: *Die unmögliche Tatsache* (1910)

Schema languages, data definition languages (DDL), or *data description languages* are primarily used to further restrict existing data structuring systems, such as database models, data structuring languages, or markup languages. The process of declaring a schema is often called *data definition* and the result is a data format or (logical) data schema. In data modeling, these schemas are located at the data realm (figure 2.6 at page 33), although some schemas (e.g. RDF schemas) also span to conceptual realm if used as conceptual modeling languages (see section 3.8).

The purpose of a schema can be both prescriptive specification of documents to be created and validation of existing documents. The expression of schemas in dedicated schema language better allows for sharing and analysis of schemas, independent of particular applications. Different schemas expressed in the same schema language can be used by a *validator* or parser (figure 3.21). Validators ensure common data structures based on shared schemas. Without such schema, data from one application may be rejected or lead to unexpected results in the other. The validator acts as interpreter that processes a schema in its schema language as program to transform documents as input to document analysis as output.

Each schema language has an inherent model of the data that schemas further restrict. In the case of regular expressions and Backus-Naur Form (part 3.7.1) this model is a simple sequence of characters. XML schema languages restrict

XML documents (part IV), RDF schema languages restrict RDF graphs (part 3.7.3), and SQL schemas restrict databases. Other methods used as schema languages (programming languages, forms, and the data format description language) are summarized briefly at the end of this section (part 3.7.5).

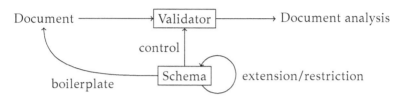

Figure 3.21.: Schema languages allow to express schemas for multiple applications

3.7.1. Regular Expressions and Backus-Naur Form

Regular expressions (RE) and Backus-Naur Form (BNF) are popular schema languages for sequences of symbols. Various similar notations for RE and BNF exist (Goyvaerts 2011) and elements of both are used within other schema languages. RE and BNF both originate from the mathematical definition of regular languages (REG) and context-free languages (CFL), which can be expressed as formal grammars by RE and BNF, respectively (see section 2.2.1). Other formal languages, such as visibly pushdown languages or boolean grammars, rarely have their own schema languages. Instead, they can be used as restricted or extended variants of REG and BNF.

Regular expressions are commonly used to define search patterns that match a set of character strings. In the mid-1960s Ken Thompson introduced RE by inventing a clever implementation for the text editor QED for the CTSS operating system. RE were then popularized by the command line tool 'grep' that became a standard feature of Unix. Descriptions and references of regular expressions for practical applications are given by Friedl (2006), the underlying theory and implementations are described by Cox (2007). In short, a regular expression is a sequence of character symbols that expresses a regular (Chomsky Type 3) language. When applied as search pattern, simple character sequences match themselves, except special metacharacters ($|$, $*$, $?$, $+$, $($, $)$,...). Metacharacters hierarchically group expressions into optional, repeatable, and alternative parts. The vertical bar denotes alternatives, a question mark denotes an option, star and plus denote zero or more respectively one or more repetitions, and parentheses group expressions. To match a metacharacter, it must be escaped with a backslash, which also acts as metacharacter. Several extensions of the traditional RE notation have added more metacharacters as abbreviation, for instance the dot to match any character or '\d' to match any digit. Another common extension, that goes beyond regular languages, are back-references: for instance '(a+)(b+)\1\2' matches the language of words with $i > 0$ occurrences of a, followed by $j > 0$ occurrences of b, followed by the same sequence of as and bs again (Carle and Narendran 2009). The most popular notation for regular expressions is Perl

Compatible Regular Expressions (PCRE). Some extensions of PCRE allow to express context-free grammars and more complex types of formal languages.

Backus-Naur Form (BNF) was introduced by John Backus and extended by Pete Naur to define the syntax of the Algol 60 programming language. The name was proposed by Donald Knuth in a letter to the Communications of the ACM (Knuth 1964). BNF since has widely been adopted to specify context-free languages. A schema (called grammar) consists of a set of named *rules* that map *non-terminal symbols* to one or more alternative sequences of symbols, that can be non-terminal symbols or *terminal symbol*s. A language in BNF is defined over all sequences of terminal symbols (usually all character strings) as the set of all sequences that can be constructed by the grammar's rewriting system (see page 27). There are many notations how to write down BNF grammars, for instance Wirth syntax (Wirth 1977), *Extended Backus-Naur Form* (International Organization for Standardization 1996), *Augmented Backus-Naur Form* (ABNF) (Crocker and Overell 2008), and W3C-BNF (Bray, J. P. Paoli, and Sperberg-McQueen 1998, sec. 6). Some variants introduce new grammar elements like grouping, options, repetitions, numeric factors, exceptions, etc. However, all variants can express the same set of formal grammars (Type-2 in the Chomsky hierarchy) and grammars in one variant can be converted to any other notation. Additional extensions to specific formal languages are often added by textual comments that explain language constraints, such as the uniqueness requirement of attribute names in XML. A summary of the syntax variant that is used throughout this thesis is given in table 3.16, some other syntax variants are shown in figure 3.22. Its non-BNF extensions difference and conjunction also allow for boolean grammars.[85] There are also graphical notations for BNF, known as *syntax diagram* or *railroad diagram*. A typical variant is depicted in figure 3.22.[86] A popular example of the use of syntax diagrams is the specification of JSON (Crockford 2002). The visual form of its publication, that can easily be followed by readers, was one reason for the quick success of JSON.

A general problem of Regular Expressions and Backus-Naur Form in practice is the conflict between ease of understanding and performance of implementation. In many cases, one formal language can be defined by multiple formal grammars of different structure. If the primary purpose of a schema is a specification that can automatically be used to implement an efficient parser, the grammar may be less readable for humans. To give a tiny example, a comment in XML must not contain the sequence '--'. The specification (Bray, J. P. Paoli, and Sperberg-McQueen 1998; Bray, J. P. Paoli, Sperberg-McQueen, et al. 2008) defines the syntax of a comment without explicitly using this sequence as:

```
comment = "<!--" ((char - "-") | "-" (char - "-")))* "-->"
```

This makes an efficient parser, but is more difficult to grasp than the following rule in natural language: a comment starts with '<!--', ends with '-->', and may contain

---

[85] General context free languages are not closed under difference, but the difference between a language in CFL and a language in REG is also in CFL, so one can use regular expressions as subtrahend in BNF.

[86] Repeating groups and boolean extensions are more difficult to picture.

non-terminal symbols		terminal symbols	
s =	defines a rule for symbol s	"..."	sequence of characters
a b	sequence of symbols	#xX	character with Unicode codepoint X
a | b	alternative symbols	[...]	regular expression character class
a?	optional symbol		
a+	repeatable symbol		
a*	optional repeatable symbol		
a:n	repeat n times	extended non-terminal symbols	
a:n-m	repeat n to m times	a - b	difference
a:n-	repeat at least n times	a & b	conjunction

Table 3.16.: Summary of BNF syntax with extensions

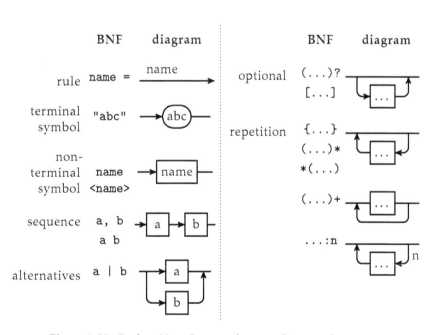

Figure 3.22.: Backus-Naur Form and syntax diagram elements

any (possibly empty) sequence of **char**, that does not contain '--' and does not end with '-'. One can translate this to BNF, equivalent to the specification, for instance as:

```
chars    = char+
comment  = "<!--" (chars? - (chars? "--" chars? | chars? "-") "-->"
```

3.7.2. XML schema languages

Since its first publication, XML (section 3.5.5) contains Document Type Definition (DTD) as native schema languag (Bray, J. P. Paoli, and Sperberg-McQueen 1998). DTD origins in SGML and uses a specific syntax, similar to Backus-Naur Form, so all XML parsers must implement one parser for DTD and one parser for XML element structure. DTD is criticized for its syntax and because of limited expressibility. For instance it does not support specification of XML namespaces without hard-coding the namespace prefix (Bray, Hollander, et al. 2009). For this reason several additional schema languages for XML were created with XML Schema and RELAX NG as most popular instances. Formal comparison of these languages, which are all based on formal grammars, are provided by Murata et al. (2005) and by Stührenberg and Wurm (2010). Schematron is another schema language that more differs from DTD, XSD, and RELAX NG. To some degree, query languages such as XPath and XML Query can also be used as (part of) XML schemas. As described by Nečaský (2006, 2008), by Sengupta and Wilde (2006), and by H. Chen and Liao (2010), XML schema languages only cover the logical level of data modeling, but conceptual modeling languages for XML are needed to better describe semantics of XML documents. In practice, however, conceptual modeling for XML is rarely applied (Mohan and Sengupta 2009) or no explicit schema is used at all (Wilde and Glushko 2008). The following section covers DTD, RELAX NG, Schematron, and XML Schema, in this order.

I. Document Type Definitions

Element content in DTD is specified in a special BNF variant with XML element names as non-terminal symbols. Element declarations can directly be mapped to BNF grammar rules as shown in example 17.

In addition, the special symbol EMPTY is used for elements without child elements (emptytag in the XML grammar, figure 3.11), the symbol ANY can be replaced by any element name, and the symbol #PCDATA is used for arbitrary character content. If XML elements should be allowed next to character content, one must define both in form of so called *mixed content*, that is a rule of the form (#PCDATA | e_1 | ... | e_n)* with $1 \leq i \leq n, n \geq 1$ where e_i is an element name. Processing instructions and comments are not treated as part of the document. DTD is the only XML schema language that supports declaration of XML entities (with the keyword ENTITY). The other languages treat a document as parsed model of a document where

```
<!ELEMENT  bib  ((author+|editor+),  year?,  title,  keyword*)>
<!ATTLIST  author  given    CDATA  #IMPLIED
                   surname  CDATA  #REQUIRED>
<!ATTLIST  editor  given    CDATA  #IMPLIED
                   surname  CDATA  #REQUIRED>
```

A bib element contains at least one author or at least one editor element, followed by an optional year, a title element, and an an optional list of one or more keyword elements. Both author and editor must have a surname attribute and may have a given attribute (the distinction between elements and attributes is not expressible in pure BNF).

```
bib    = ( editor+ | author+ ) year?  title  keyword*
author = ( given? surname )
editor = ( given? surname )
```

Example 17: DTD element declaration mapped to BNF rules

entity references and CDATA sections have been replaced by equivalent content (see figure 3.12 and page 3.5.5). DTD syntax for attribute declaration is different to element declaration, as attributes have no order and cannot be repeated at one element. Attributes can be marked as optional (keyword #IMPLIED) or mandatory (keyword #REQUIRED) and there are some limited capabilities to restrict possible attribute values, for instance to one value from a predefined list. Character content of XML element can not be restricted. One can specify default values for attributes and disallow changing attribute values (keyword #FIXED. Simple integrity condition are possible, by declaring some attribute values as unique identifiers (keyword ID) and some attribute values as pointers to these identifiers (keywords IDREF and IDREFS). A proposed ISO standard to further extend DTD has received little attention (International Organization for Standardization 2008c).

II. RELAX NG

The REgular LAnguage for XML Next Generation (RELAX NG) was developed as merger of Tree Regular Expressions (TREX) and Regular Language description for XML (RELAX), both experimental XML schema languages, created in 2000/2001 (Vlist 2003). RELAX NG was standardized at OASIS and published at ISO in 2003 and 2008 (International Organization for Standardization 2008b). A RELAX NG schema can be written in an XML syntax and in a more readable compact syntax, which is similar to Backus-Naur Form. Both forms can be translated to its counterparts without loss of information. The grammar from example 17 could be written in RELAX NG Compact as shown in example 18 (the datatype xs:gYear is added to the year element):

```
element bib {
  ( element editor { person }+ | element author { person }+ ),
  element year { xs:gYear }?,
  title,
  keyword*
}
person = {
  attribute given { text }?
  attribute surname { text }
}
```

Example 18: Grammar rules in RELAX NG Compact syntax

RELAX NG unifies syntax for element and attribute declaration and it provides functionality that goes beyond DTD. In particular, it better supports grouping, combining, and annotating grammar rules. It further adds context-sensitive content models, namespaces, unordered content, and datatypes for character content. Datatypes are not defined in RELAX NG but only referenced fro other specifications. The most common datatypes are those from XML Schema, for instance xs:integer for character sequences that represent integer values. Identifier attributes (ID, IDREF, IDREFS) and default attribute values are not supported but an official extension exists to add these features (Clark and Murata 2001). Additional rules can be embedded in RELAX NG schema by using other schema languages, especially Schematron.

III. Schematron

Schematron is a rule-based XML schema language, expressed in XML (Vlist 2007). It was first proposed in 1999 by Rick Jelliffe and later standardized as Schematron 1.3 (2000), Schematron 1.5 (2001) and Schematron 1.6 (2002). Schematron was published as ISO 19757-3 (2006) and an extended version is being published in 2011. The publication at ISO may be one reason why Schematron is less known and less used than other schema languages described in this section. In contrast to grammar-based languages, a Schematron schema does not specify the whole tree structure of an XML document, but it defines a set of additional constraints. Schematron constraints are expressed by two XPath expressions: the context defines which part of a document to check and the test specifies a condition that must be true for each context element. A condition can trigger a message if it is met (with report) or if it is not met (with assert). One or more conditions with same context are grouped in a rule and one or more rules are grouped in a pattern, which may further be associated to phases. Schematron also supports variables and abstract patterns as pattern templates, as shown in example 19: this Schematron schema can be used to restrict author and editor names from the previous schemas (example 17 and

18) by checking that given names are not empty strings and surnames do not end with a dot, unless there is a given name. Such interdependencies are difficult or not possible to express in other schema languages.

```
<schema xmlns="http://www.ascc.net/xml/schematron">
  <title>Person name checks</title>
  <pattern abstract="true" id="person">
    <rule context="$p[@given]">
      <report test="0 < string-length(normalize-space(@given))"
      >person with valid given name</report>
    </rule>
    <rule context="$p[@surname and not(@given)]">
      <let name="s" value="normalize-space(@surname)"/>
      <let name="l" value="string-length($s)"/>
      <assert test="0 < $l and substring($s,$l) != '.'"
      >Surname without given name must not be abbreviated</assert>
    </rule>
  </pattern>
  <pattern is-a="person">
    <param name="p" value="author"/>
  </pattern>
  <pattern is-a="person">
    <param name="p" value="editor"/>
  </pattern>
</schema>
```

Example 19: Simple Schematron schema, restricting person names

Schematron conditions can also be documented with icons, diagnostic messages, and other hints. In contrast to other XML schema languages, Schematron is primarily targeted to human users, as its core output of validation are messages. This makes schematron together with its structured output format Schematron Validation Report Language (SVRL) more a reporting language for business rules. Schematron can report (violations of) several rules as independent properties of an XML document. By this, it can be applied more flexible and less strict than a global schema, which eventually has a boolean output as either valid or not valid.

IV. XML Schema

XML Schema (XSD) is the most comprehensive and most used schema language for XML documents. It started as an extension of DTD in XML syntax, influenced by several other schema languages that were discussed as candidates for an official W3C recommendation during 1998 and 2000.[87] XSD 1.0 became W3C recommendation in 2001 with a second edition in 2004. XSD 1.1 is being published as extended successor in 2011. The recommendation consists of one part on structure (Thompson et al. 2004) and one part on datatypes (Biron and Malhotra 2004), the second of which also referred to in other schema languages such as OWL (page 132).

An XML Schema mainly consists of element declarations, attribute declarations, and type definitions. Declarations define which XML elements and attributes may or must exist in an XML document, while type definitions are referenced by element and attribute declarations. There are also methods for grouping and reusing parts of a schema, annotations as human- and machine-targeted documentation, and uniqueness and reference constraints that go beyond the identifier attributes (ID, IDREF, IDREFS) in DTD. XSD 1.1 adds assertions and boolean conditions (as XPath expressions) that can be used for conditional constraints and type assignment, similar to rules in Schematron. Element and attribute declarations are similar to declarations in DTD, but element and attribute content is always defined with a type. There are simple types that define constraints on strings for attribute values and text-only content, and there are complex types that define constraints on attributes and child elements. XSD offers various syntax variants to express the same format, but all are very verbose and hard to read and write compared to DTD and RELAX NG Compact.[88] For this reason XSD is mostly created with specialized XSD editors and similar software tools that provide graphical user interfaces or automatic generation of schemas. Example 20 shows a schema in XSD that combines the rules from example 17 to 19. Repeatability and optionality can be specified with a minimal (minOccurs) and maximal number (maxOccurs) for elements or with use="required" for attributes. Element content is defined with xs:complexType as ordered sequence (xs:sequence), or as choice (xs:choice) of other components. One can group elements with xs:any, if the elements of a set can occur in any order, but with at most one occurrence of each element — this allows specification of unordered content to a more limited degree than RELAX NG. Wildcards, similar but more customizable then the ANY keyword in DTD, are also supported.

Derived types can be defined based on existing types by constraints (xs:restriction) or by allowing additional content (xs:extension). Simple types can also be combined to union types (xs:union) and list types (xs:list). A predefined set of (mainly simple) types is provided in the second part of XSD specification (Biron and Malhotra 2004). The practical relevance of these XSD datatypes, also beyond pure applications of XML, demands a more detailed description. As noted in the recommendation, XSD datatypes were influenced by data types in programming and database languages and by ISO 11404 (International Organization for Standardization (2007a)).

---

[87] In detail, XSD was influenced at least by the Document Definition Markup Language (DDML) and Schema for Object-Oriented XML (SOX), both proposed as W3C note in 1999; Document Content Description (DCD) a W3C submission from 1998; and XML Data Reduced (XDR), proposed by Microsoft in 1998-2001.

[88] You could use a compact syntax for XML, but proposals such as Wilde (2003) have not received much adoption.

```
<xs:schema xmlns:xs="http://www.w3.org/2001/XMLSchema">
  <xs:element name="bib">
    <xs:complexType>
      <xs:sequence>
        <xs:choice>
          <xs:element name="author" type="person"
                      maxOccurs="unbounded"/>
          <xs:element name="editor" type="person"
                      maxOccurs="unbounded"/>
        </xs:choice>
        <xs:element name="year" type="xs:gYear" minOccurs="0"/>
        <xs:element name="title" type="xs:string"/>
        <xs:element name="keyword" type="xs:string"
                    minOccurs="0" maxOccurs="unbounded"/>
      </xs:sequence>
    </xs:complexType>
  </xs:element>
  <xs:complexType name="person">
    <xs:attribute name="given" type="myString"/>
    <xs:attribute name="surname" type="myString" use="required">
      <xs:alternative test="not(../@given)">
        <xs:simpleType name="noAbbrev">
          <xs:restriction base="myString">
            <xs:pattern value=".*[^\.]"/>
          </xs:restriction>
        </xs:simpleType>
      </xs:alternative>
    </xs:attribute>
  </xs:complexType>
  <xs:simpleType name="myString">
    <xs:restriction base="xs:string">
      <xs:minLength value="1"/>
      <xs:whiteSpace value="collapse"/>
    </xs:restriction>
  </xs:simpleType>
</xs:schema>
```

Example 20: XML Schema, including features of XSD 1.1

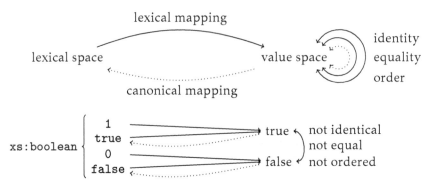

Figure 3.23.: Lexical space and value space of XSD datatypes with boolean as example

A datatype consists of a *value space*, which is a set of abstract values; a *lexical space*, which is set of Unicode strings used to denote the values; a surjective *lexical mapping* function that maps from the lexical space to the value space; and an equality relation for the value space (figure 3.23). Furthermore datatypes may have an order relation for the value space, a *canonical mapping* that maps each value from the value space to its preferred representation in the lexical space. In addition, there is an identity relation that in most cases is the same as the equality relation.[89] There are 50 build-in datatypes, each referencable by an URI. Grouped by purpose one can identify:

- a type for Unicode strings, limited to the characters allowed in XML (xs:string), and two types for strings with normalized whitespace (xs:normalizedString and xs:token),

- various numeric types (see table 3.17),

- a boolean type (xs:boolean, as shown in figure 3.23),

- twelve different types for dates, times, and their parts or combinations,

- two binary types for encoded byte sequences (xs:base64Binary, xs:hexBinary),

- a type for URIs (xs:anyURI) and for tuples of namespace URI and local name to represent XML element names with namespaces (see example 14),

- a type defined equivalent to xs:QName but for XML Notations (xs:NOTATION),

- six special types derived from xs:token to represent differnt kinds of identifiers (xs:language, xs:Name, xs:NCName, xs:ID, xs:IDREF, xs:NMToken),

---

[89] The distinction between equality and identity was introduced in XSD 1.1. For instance the lexical values −0 and 0 were both mapped to value zero for the datatype xs:float, but now they are mapped to non-identical but equal values, to better mirror floating point number encoding (see page 58). Another example from xs:float is the value of NaN (not a number), which is identical but not equal to itself.

datatype	value space
xs:anyType	all types (simple and complex)
–xs:anySimpleType	all simple types
– –xs:anyAtomicType	all simple types that are not lists or unions
– – –xs:decimal	$\{x/10^y \mid x \in \mathbb{Z}, y \in \mathbb{Z}_{\geq 0}\} \subset \mathbb{R}$
– – – –xs:integer	$\mathbb{Z} = \mathsf{Int}$
– – – – –xs:long	Int_{64}
– – – – – –xs:int	Int_{32}
– – – – – – –xs:short	Int_{16}
– – – – – – – –xs:byte	Int_8
– – – – –xs:nonNegativeInteger	$\mathbb{Z}_{\geq 0} = \mathsf{UInt}$
– – – – – –xs:positiveInteger	$\mathbb{Z}_{>0}$
– – – – – –xs:unsignedLong	UInt_{64}
– – – – – – –xs:unsignedInt	UInt_{32}
– – – – – – – –xs:unsignedShort	UInt_{16}
– – – – – – – – –xs:unsignedByte	UInt_8
– – – –xs:nonPositiveInteger	$\mathbb{Z}_{\leq 0}$
– – – – – –xs:negativeInteger	$\mathbb{Z}_{<0}$
– – –xs:float	32 bit IEEE 754 floating point (except sNaN)
– – –xs:double	64 bit IEEE 754 floating point (except sNaN)

Table 3.17.: Predefined numeric datatypes in XML Schema

- derived list types for three token types (xs:ENTITIES, xs:IDREFS, xs:NMTOKENS),

- the special types xs:anyType, xs:anySimpleType, and xs:anyAtomicType as base types of all other predefined types.

The recommendation groups its datatypes into primitive types and derived types. Each derived type must have exactly one base type with xs:anyType as base type of all other simple types. A subset of the derivation tree is shown in table 3.17. A derived type can specify restrictions in predefined constraining facets that serve to normalize or constrain its lexical space and/or its value space. Possible facets include length of the lexical representation, a regular expression pattern that all lexical values must match, and lower/upper bounds on its value space for ordered values. Beside derivation one can define new types as lists or as unions of existing types. It should be noted, that the lexical mapping of an union type may be no function, because the same lexical value can represent multiple values for different types (for instance the string "2" and the number 2).

The XSD type system includes some more caveats: for instance primitive datatypes are disjoint (the number 2 as xs:float is incomparable to the number 2 as xs:double and as xs:decimal). xs:float and xs:double have no common base type although they both decode subsets of $\mathbb{R}$ and there are unrelated types with the same value space (xs:base64Binary and xs:hexBinary, which both map to the set of finite-length sequences of binary bytes). Another problem may arise from the fact that validation with a XSD instances may modify a document by adding default values and type information. The set of XSD datatypes has also been criticized for being an arbitrary selection (Ogbuji 2002). For instance there are various types for dates and times but no types for other dimensions such as length and geographic location. Facets like length of the lexical value neither consider Unicode normalization forms which can be relevant to textual content. Alternatives and extensions to XSD data types such as "Extensible Datatypes" and the Character Repertoire Description Language (CREPDL), both published as part of ISO 19757 (2008), are mostly ignored in the XSD community, possibly because of the "Not Invented Here syndrome": unlike RELAX NG and Schematron, XSD is not designed by a small team, but by a large working group that incorporates interests of database vendors and other companies. As a result, the specification is large, complex, and difficult to implement with all features. XSD is also criticized for being difficult to read and write without additional tools, it does not allow *ambiguous rules* that result in multiple term parse for the same XML document,[90] and for other reasons (Clark 2002). As pointed out by Ogbuji (2002), there is a cultural gap between use of XML technology with a background in markup languages (see section 3.6) and user with a background in relational databases and object-oriented development. XSD clearly origins from the second culture.

3.7.3. RDF schema languages

Schema languages for RDF (see section 3.5.6) are also known as ontology languages, with the Web Ontology Language (OWL) as their most popular instance. RDF schema languages are usually based on formal logic systems such as first-order predicate logic or description logic, and they originate in knowledge representation languages from artificial intelligence research. In its most general form, an RDF ontology can be described as any collection of RDF resources, at least if the resources are used (or proposed to be used) in RDF triples either as predicate, or as datatype, or as object if the predicate is `rdf:type`.[91] RDF resources from one ontology are usually summarized as RDF vocabulary under one common namespace. In addition, ontologies can include rules that restrict the use of their resources in RDF data, and that allow logical inference for entailment in a specific entailment regime (see page 111). Given this definition of an ontology, an RDF schema language is a defined method to specify and describe ontologies. Most current RDF schema languages are also RDF ontologies, that means these languages are expressed by RDF triples. An exception is the definition of RDF datatypes, that make use of XML Schema (see section 3.7.2). Example 21 shows some RDF data together with parts of the Friend of

---

[90] The concept of ambiguous and deterministic rules in XML is an extension of ambiguous and deterministic grammars for formal languages (section 2.2.1) to tree languages. A detailed analysis of computability classes for XML schema languages is given by Stührenberg and Wurm (2010), based on Murata et al. (2005).

[91] This automatically makes `rdf:type` part of an ontology, because it is used as predicate.

a Friend (FOAF) ontology and the DBPedia ontology. The example already shows that in practice one rarely deals with a schema language as a whole but with specific features of schema languages.

Although a general schema language for RDF graphs could be created as a rewriting system on graph patterns (see page 27), existing schema languages do not allow arbitrary graph patterns, but adhere to a object-oriented system with classes, properties, and individuals. In short, RDF schema languages provide resources to document parts of an ontology (`rdfs:isDefinedBy`, `rdfs:label`, `rdfs:comment`, `vs:term_status...`), to define (specific kinds of) classes and properties (`rdf:type`, `rdfs:Class`, `rdf:Property`, `owl:AnnotationProperty`, `owl:FunctionalProperty...`), and to define rules and relations between these entities (`rdfs:subClassOf`, `owl:disjointWith`, `rdfs:domain`, `rdfs:range...`).

The most basic schema language is the basic RDF vocabulary with the property `rdf:type`, the resource `rdf:Property`, the datatype `rdf:XMLLiteral`, and the rules of rdf-entailment (P. Hayes and McBride 2004, section 3). This minimal ontology language is extended by Brickley and R. V. Guha (2004) to the RDF Vocabulary Description Language, which is called *RDF Schema* (RDFS). RDFS is further extended by the OWL family of ontology languages. OWL was first published as working draft by Dean et al. (2002) and extended to OWL2 (Schneider 2009). OWL has since superseded other general ontology languages such as DAML+OIL. In addition, there are rule languages, such as the *Rule Interchange Format* (RIF) (Kifer and Boley 2010) and *SPARQL Inferencing Notation* (SPIN) (Knublauch, J. A. Hendler, and Idehen 2011). The usability of ontology languages can partly be improved by specific syntaxes, such as the Manchester Syntax for OWL (Horridge and Patel-Schneider 2009) and by using specialized ontology editors. One can also use other logic languages and even natural language. In fact many ontologies contain additional rules and descriptions that are only provided in natural language, because using a formal rule language would be too complex or too strict. For instance the restriction of `foaf:birthday` to strings of the form "`mm-dd`" in example 21 is only given as deontic comment, although it could also be expressed as formal constraint. Some rules can also be expressed in Notation3: its syntax supports statements in first-order predicate logic by using formulae with quantification and logical implication. The processing of this rules, however, is much less supported by applications then standard RDFS and OWL. To reduce complexity and to facilitate implementation and computation, OWL is split up in three different sublanguages (Dean et al. 2002) or three different profiles (OWL2). With limited expressibility there are the following dialects:

- OWL-Full contains all features of the original Web Ontology Language. It is now replaced by OWL2.

- OWL-Lite was intended as subset of OWL for easy implementation. As it turned out to be more complex then intended, OWL-Lite is now deprecated.

- OWL DL and OWL2 DL are similar subsets of OWL and OWL2 that can be mapped to an extension of description logic with useful computational prop-

```
# RDF vocabularies
@prefix rdf: <http://www.w3.org/1999/02/22-rdf-syntax-ns#> .
@prefix rdfs: <http://www.w3.org/2000/01/rdf-schema#> .
@prefix dc: <http://purl.org/dc/elements/1.1/> .
@prefix foaf: <http://xmlns.com/foaf/0.1/> .
@prefix dbp: <http://dbpedia.org/property/> .
@prefix owl: <http://www.w3.org/2002/07/owl#> .
@prefix vs: <http://www.w3.org/2003/06/sw-vocab-status/ns#> .

# RDF data that uses the RDF resources foaf:Person, foaf:name,
# foaf:birthday, dbp:dateOfBirth, and xs:date from ontologies.
<http://viaf.org/viaf/616522> rdf:type foaf:Person ;
  foaf:name "Dennis M. Ritchie" ;
  foaf:birthday "09-09" ;
  dbp:dateOfBirth "1941-09-09"^^xs:date .

# Parts of RDF ontologies, described by RDF schema languages:

## FOAF ontology
<http://xmlns.com/foaf/0.1/> rdf:type owl:Ontology ;
   dc:title "Friend of a Friend (FOAF) vocabulary" .

foaf:Person rdf:type rdfs:Class ;
   rdfs:isDefinedBy <http://xmlns.com/foaf/0.1/> ;
   rdfs:label "Person" ;
   rdfs:subClassOf foaf:Person ;
   owl:disjointWith foaf:Document, foaf:Organization, foaf:Project ;
   vs:term_status "stable" .

foaf:birthday rdf:type owl:AnnotationProperty, owl:FunctionalProperty;
   rdfs:comment """The birthday of this Agent, represented in
                  mm-dd string form, eg. '12-31'.""" ;
   rdfs:domain foaf:Agent ;
   rdfs:range rdfs:Literal ;

## DBPedia ontology
dbp:dateOfBirth rdf:type rdf:Property ;
   rdfs:label "DATE OF BIRTH"@en .
```

Example 21: RDF data and its ontology, described by RDF schema languages

erties. The underlying logic model of OWL2 DL is called $\mathcal{SROIQ}$ (Horrocks, Kutz, and Sattler 2006).

- OWL2 EL, OWL2 QL, and OWL2 RL are subsets of OWL2, each designed for efficient computability in different application scenarios: EL has polynomial time reasoning complexity, QL supports fast query answering, and RL can be implemented using rule-based reasoning systems.

OWL also adds two new numeric data types (`owl:real` and `owl:rational`). Although RDFS and OWL allow undecidable statement (RDFS is not on OWL DL) most schemas only use a limited set of features. Furthermore, most existing ontologies can easily be patched to belong to a less complex dialect (Martinez-Gil, Alba, and Aldana-Montes 2010; Wang, Parsia, and James Hendler 2006). A general property of RDF schema languages is their use of the Open World Assumption as default: An RDF ontology assumes that any unspecified statements may exist (unless declared otherwise, for instance with statements like `owl:oneOf`, `owl:disjointWith`, and `owl:complementOf`), while non-RDF schemas assume that unspecified data elements are not allowed (unless declared otherwise, for instance with wildcards, such as `ANY` in XML).

3.7.4. SQL schemas

The first data definition language that was used under this name, was used to define schemas of relational databases and later specified as subset of SQL. In addition to this SQL schema definition language, SQL-92 introduced a schema manipulation language and schema information tables, which provide views to database schemas in form of SQL tables (Date and Darwen 1997). Alternatives to the SQL schema language, such as Tutorial D by Date and Darwen (2006) have little practical relevance, so most SQL schemas should be written in one common schema language. The exact specification of this language, however, much depends on the particular RDBMS, because each database system implements its own subset of some version of the SQL standard with its own additions and modifications. In general, a schema consists of a set of `CREATE` statements. The most important statement is `CREATE TABLE` to define database tables. In addition one can define derived datatypes with `CREATE DOMAIN` or a similar command, and group table and datatype names in namespaces with `CREATE SCHEMA`. Derived datatypes can have their own default values and an optional `CHECK` clause, for instance to limit the possible values to a custom range, but this features are not fully supported by all RDBMS. A table definition consists of a non-empty sequence of column definitions, where the order of fields is irrelevant for most applications. Each column is identified by a name, unique per table, it is associated with a datatype (see below) and it can have an optional default value. The default value which may also be generated automatically with the `IDENTITY` statement (also known as auto-increment) and a selected numbering scheme). In addition, each column and the table as a whole can be shaped by the following constraints:

- UNIQUE marks column values to be unique per table, so each row can be identified by its value, unless the value is NULL.

- NOT NULL enforces a column to not contain NULL value.

- PRIMARY KEY marks up to one column per table. It implies UNIQUE and NOT NULL.

- FOREIGN KEY values must reference an existing PRIMARY KEY in a specific table. This constraint is important to connect multiple tables of one schema.

- CHECK can limit values based on boolean expressions over one or more columns. For instance one can check that the date of death is not before the date of birth for a table with two columns BIRTH and DEATH.

SQL-92 also introduced a CREATE ASSERTION statement for constraints that can span multiple tables, but this feature is not supported by most RDBMS. Triggers and other settings may also shape the actual database content, similar to a schema, but this highly depends on the specific database application. In addition to tables, there can be views, defined with CREATE VIEW. Views are virtual tables that map to normal tables via an SQL query. If there is a one-to-one relationship between rows in a view and rows in tables it refers to, among other limitations, the view may be counted as part of a schema. The list of SQL datatypes for column definitions has slightly changed with each version of the standard, and support of datatypes differs among RDBMS. In summary there are:

- numeric types, including integer types and decimal types with fixed or arbitrary precision, and floating-point types

- character string types with variable or fixed length, possibly padded by whitespaces

- temporal types for dates, times, and intervals

- binary data types for sequences of bits or sequences of bytes

- a boolean type (not exactly supported by most systems)

- an XML type to store XML documents and fragments

- an ARRAY type for one- or multi-dimensional sequences of same type and a (rarely supported) MULTISET type for unordered collections of same type value. Some systems also support non-standard nested tables and associative arrays.

- composite types to group one or more unconstrained columns to be used as datatype in another column

- types for specialized domains, such as monetary types and spatial types

Example 29 in section 4.2.1 includes a simple SQL schema for illustration.

3.7.5. Other schema languages

Given XML schema languages for XML data, RDF schema languages for RDF data and SQL schema language for SQL data one can think of many more schema languages for each particular data structuring method: there are several proposals for JSON and YAML (Kwalify, JSON Schema, Rx, Simple Declarative Language etc.) and several data binding languages come with their own data definition language (see part 3.5.1 and table 3.8). Terminology among schema languages differs — the same concept may be called 'schema', 'format', or 'message' in different languages — but in general schema languages share a set of common concepts, similar to type systems of programming languages: there is a set of predefined, possibly extensible data types and data elements can be named, grouped, and constraint as mandatory or optional. In addition one can often find methods to combine, extend and restrict schemas. To give an example, example 22 lists predefined data types and methods of constraining in the Rx schema language (Signes and Cappiello 2008). Table 3.9 (page 95) includes another example with data types from Protocol Buffers. Some schema languages make use of regular expressions and elements from context free grammar when defining hierarchical or sequential data. Methods to specific context-sensitive rules which correlate multiple data elements are less frequent, and they are often restricted to a set of rule types, such as referential constraints with keys and foreign keys. Less limited languages to defined and describe data structures will be covered as modeling languages in section 3.8. In the following, programming languages, forms, and the Data Format Description Language (DFDL) will be explained briefly.

Type	Content
nil	the lack of a value (undef, null, nil, etc)
def	any defined value; anything that is not nil
bool	a value that is either true or false
num	a number; may be parameterized by a range (fixed or inclusive or exclusive minimum and/or maximum value)
int	an integer; may be parameterized by a range
str	a string, even the empty string
one	any of bool, num, int, and str
arr	a list of values all of one type; may be parameterized by a range as length
seq	a list of values of different, given types
rec	a record of named entries, each with its own schema and a required/optional flag
map	a map of names to values, with all the values of one type
any	either anything at all, or any of a given list of types (union)
all	a combination of types (intersection)

Example 22: Predefined data types and elements of the Rx schema language

I. Programming languages

Many schemas are expressed in some programming language, either explicitly by the language's type system or implicitly by the behavioral logic of a specific program.

A schema, expressed in a particular schema language, can also be viewed as source code that is run by a validator (see image 3.21). One can create a program for validation of documents in any Turing-complete programming language. This implies programming languages can be used as schema languages for decidable data format. Such program makes the data format implicit because the program will contain many parts which are not directly related to the data format. With implicit schemas, hard-coded in programming languages, it is more difficult to share and compare schemas. These also applies partly for schemas that are automatically created by other tools, so the created schema is only a compiled artifact from an original schema in another program or language. In exchange validation may be more performant and provide better document analysis, for instance more helpful error messages. In practice many data formats have no explicit schema, so the programs that read and write data are the only reliable source to infer common data structures. Even programs that make use of explicit schemas may modify its rules, for instance by adding practical limits on length of values or other constraints which cannot be expressed in the particular schema language. Therefore one should always distinguish the explicit part of a schema, as expressed in a schema language, and the implicit part of a schema, as only implemented in applications. Especially the meaning of a data element can often better be determined by looking at its use in applications instead of relying on labels and descriptions in official schemas.

II. Forms and questionnaires

Standardized forms and questionnaires are ubiquitous methods to collect and edit data, predating all digital data management. The *Marcufli Formulae* from the late 7th century can be considered as first collection of forms (Zeumer 2001): it contained boilerplates for deeds, that were used in the Frankish Empire. Modern printed forms have been used from the 19th century on, also with legal pleadings and contracts as first applications. Their primary purpose is attestation: documentation of statements. In contrast to other documents, a form highlights the relevant statements to be documented by forcing them into predefined structures. By this, a form can be seen as kind of schema and as visible interface to a data format. The form gives a frame to actual data and it can influence what and how data is entered, for instance in form of good or bad usability. A deeper analysis of dedicated forms could explain some artifacts in the data that was edited through them, but this would go beyond the scope of this thesis. Most aspects of the history of forms still have to be written. For a starting point see Becker (2007) and Grosse and Mentrup (1980).

III. Data Format Description Language

The Data Format Description Language (DFDL) is an extension to a subset of XML Schema to describe binary and text formats for mapping them to XML (Beardsmore 2007; Powell, Beckerle, and Hanson 2011). Version 1.0 of DFDL has been published as proposed recommendation in 2011. A DFDL schema consists of an XSD schema that defines XML elements (XML attributes are not supported) and mappings from these elements to data elements in the non-XML format to be described. DFDL supports sequences, choices, grouping, optional, and repeatable elements, so one can use it like Backus-Naur Form to parse word in formal languages to syntax trees in XML. DFDL also supports unordered sequences, delimiters, length indicators and padded fields of fixed length, tags, terminators, default values, escape characters, regular expressions etc. that facilitate the description of binary and textual formats. A subset of XPath 2.0 can be used to express dependencies and calculations that even span local boundaries, similar to context and test expressions in Schematron.

3.8. Conceptual modeling languages

Essentially, all models are wrong, but some are useful.
— George Box (on statistical models)

Conceptual modeling languages (Frederiks, Hofstede, and Lippe 1997) or *semantic modeling languages* (Hull and King 1987; Peckham and Maryanski 1988) are used to formally capture an universe of discourse (see section 2.2.3 on data modeling). They often come in a graphical notation, known as data model diagram or data structure diagram. Originally, such diagrams were introduced by Bachman (1969) for logical schema design of network databases. They have since evolved to many notations from simple labeled graphs to detailed graphical rules (see section 3.9).

The by far most influential conceptual modeling language, both to academia (C. Chen, Song, and Zhu 2007) and to practitioners (Simsion 2007), is the *Entity-relationship model* (ERM), presented in part 3.8.1. ERM is rarely used in its original form but in form of various variants and extensions. An extensive evolution of modelling languages has been identified by (Patig 2006) and the plethora of modeling languages has even been named 'yama syndrome' (Yet Another Modeling Approach) Oei et al. (1992). The amount of academic work on conceptual modeling languages notwithstanding, modelers often ignore these languages and prefer to work directly in a data description language (see section 3.7), as pointed out by Simsion (2007, p. 345). At the same time, modelers try to express not only a logical model but a model of reality that only exist in our minds, The reality as 'territory' is easy to confuse with a conceptual model as 'map' and the conceptual model is easy to confuse with a logical model as 'map copy'.[92] In the following the term 'model' refers to a conceptual model, as symbolic abstraction between mind and logical schema (see figure 6.1 on page 223). Examples of conceptual models from the cultural domain include FRBR (IFLA Study Group on the Functional Requirements for Bibliographic Records 1998), CIDOC-CRM (Crofts et al. 2011), and CHARM (Gonzalez-Perez et al. 2012).

Beside ERM (part 3.8.1) this section presents fact-oriented Object Role Modeling (ORM) (part 3.8.2) and the Unified Modeling Language (UML) (part 3.8.3) as concrete examples of unique conceptual modeling languages. Their common conceptual properties as base of general modeling paradigms and patterns can further be identified by meta-modeling and a look at the motivation of domain specific modeling (part 3.8.4). Modeling languages for processes and dynamic systems, such as Petri Nets and Business Process Model and Notation (BPMN) are not included because of the focus on stable digital documents.

---

[92] The expression "the map is not the territory" is attributed to Korzybski (1933) and applied to data modeling by (W. Kent 1978).

3.8.1. Entity-relationship model

The *Entity-Relationship Model* (ERM) is known as the most influential conceptual modeling language. It was originally proposed by P. P. Chen (1976) to unify network databases and relational database views (see section 3.4). The basic components of an ERM model are *entity types*, *relationship types*, and *attributes*, together with rules how to connect them: relationship types must connect at least two entity types and attributes must be connected to entity types or relationship types. Strictly speaking, entities and relationships in ERM refer to concrete objects in the universe of discourse. For instance, you can think of different books and authors as entities and authorships as relations. Entities and relationships are then modeled with entity types such as 'book' and 'author', and relationship types such as 'authorship'. For simplicity the terms entity and relationship are often used for entity types and relationship types and concrete objects referred to as instances of entities or relationships. Entity-Relationship models are mainly expressed and explained by graphical notations. A graphically expressed model is called an Entity Relationship Diagram. Figure 23 shows an ERM diagram in Chen's notation. Elements of other ERM notation variants (IE and Barker Notation together with ORM and UML) are included in table 3.18.

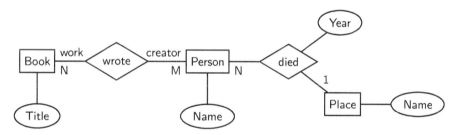

Example 23: ERM diagram in Chen's notation plus attributes

Since introduction of ERM, a large number of variants have evolved (Patig 2006). These variants often add new features and come with different graphical notations. The diversity of ERM variants and notations requires to check carefully which conventions and semantics apply in a given application. As shown by Hitchman (1995), many additional constructs like subtypes, n-ary relationships, and naming both ends of a relationship are rarely used and not well understood. In its original form, ERM is rarely used in data modeling practice (Simsion 2007, pp. 49, 345). Widely used variants and notations include information engineering notation (IE), also known as "crow's foot notation" (Finkelstein 1989; Martin and MacClure 1985) and Barker Notation (Barker 1990). Both add some additional constructs to ERM but also limit relationship types to binary associations only (T. Halpin and Morgan 2008, pp. 318ff.). The full variety of ERM dialects between 1975 and 2003, has been analyzed in a study on ERM evolution: Patig (2006, p. 72ff) identified 33 conceptual constructs in addition to labeled entity types, relationship types, attributes and the basic rules how to connect them. These constructs can be grouped in constructs of the basic model structure, integrity conditions on model instances, and constructs that are motivated by specific applications or by specific domains. The following list summarizes basic some conceptual constructs, derived from similar collections by Patig (2006) and W. Kent (1983a):

entity types group sets of entities to be modeled, for instance people in a Person entity type.

relationship types must be connected to at least two entity types.

attributes can be connected to entity types and to relationship types.

attribute values may explicitly be defined with data types or lists.

multivalued attributes can have multiple values For instance a person may have more than one name. In addition, multiple values may be ordered or unsorted.

attributes of attributes may be allowed, for instance the percentage of a value or the language of a name.

labels uniquely identify and describe entity types, relationship types, and attributes.

roles uniquely identify and describe connections. They are needed, in particular if there are multiple connections between two components (recursive or circular relations).

aggregations treat selected relationship types as entity types, so they can be connected to other relationship types. In ORM this is known as 'objectification'.

conditions limit the set of possible entity instance, relationship instances, or attribute values, based on arbitrary propositions. Frequent types of conditions are often expressed by additional modeling constructs, such as the following:

primary keys mark selected attributes relationship types to have unique values/instances among all entity instances.

inference rules can define that parts of a model instance (entity types, relationships, attribute values etc.) can be inferred from other parts. For instance the current age of a person could be inferred from its date of birth and the current date.

frequency constraints limit the total number of concrete entities or attributes of some type in a model instance.

cardinality constraints limit the minimum and/or maximum number of times that an entity can be connected to a relationship. In detail, you can distinguish between simple participation cardinality and look-across cardinality, which is only relevant to relationships with more than two entities. For instance a library user may only loan a maximum number of books (participation cardinality), but only another maximum number of books on each single day (look-across cardinality).

optionality and mandatory constraints define that specific connections are optional or required. These constraints are often confused with minimum cardinality constraints zero or one, but they can also be used independently. For instance a publication does not need to have a review (optionality), but if it is reviewed, it must have at least two reviews (cardinality).

exclusive constraints mark connections as mutually exclusive.

inheritance allows direct connections between a supertype entity and a subtype entity, which then shares all attributes and relationship connections with its supertype. For instance an Author can be a subtype of a Person (see example 25). Simple cases of subtyping can also be expressed by euler diagrams. Subtypes can have their own subtypes but all subtyping connections must form a directed acyclic graph.

identity relationships connect two or more entity types to state that their instances refer to the same objects in the universe of discourse. For instance an author entity could be identical with a translator entity.

specialized types group selected entity types, relationship types or attributes as being of a same kind. Specialized types can be domain-specific, for instance geographic entity types or causal relationship types, or more general. The most common specialized types are aggregation and composition relationships, both available in IE and in Barker Notation.

transactions describe possible changes of model instances.

temporal connections distinguish structure and constraints of the model at different times.

multidimensionality helps to highlight components of a schema as dimensions and facts for aggregation in data warehouses.

uncertainty can be introduced to mark selected parts of a model (entities, relationships, attributes and connections) not known exactly.

As found by Simsion (2007, p. 345) "the impact of the very substantial amount of work on modeling languages appears to be minimal, with modelers apparently preferring to work with the DBMS language." If ERM is used, it is mostly used in a limited variant. The most important modification is a limitation to binary relationship types, which are then drawn as simple lines instead of diamonds. N-ary relationship types can be modified to entity types with N mandatory connections, as shown in example 24. Together with roles, such simplification actually means removal of relationships from ERM as implemented in Object role modeling (see part 3.8.2). Attributes can also be replaced by entity types, as suggested by W. Kent (1983a, 1984) and also shown in example 24, but most applications keep attributes for simplicity and brevity. It should be noted that such transformations are often subject to interpretation because they may result in different models (see example 33 in section 4.2.4).

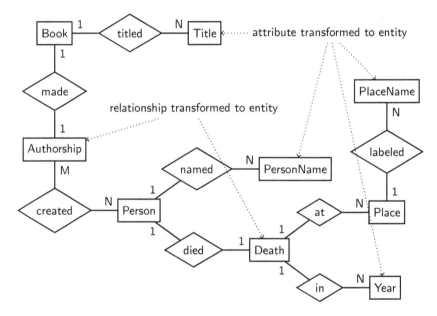

Example 24: ERM model transformed from example 23

Another limitation of most ERM variants is less obvious: all entity types are assumed to be disjoint, unless they are connected by inheritance or by identity relationships. For instance in example 23 and 24, an entity is *either* instance of Book, Person, or Place. This implicit rule can cause problems with entity types that are less easy to separate, such as Title, PersonName, and PlaceName in example 24: here the disjointness constraint becomes an artifact of the model, that is not present in the universe discourse — normally a book, a place, and a person can have the same name without being the same object. The disjointness assumption of ERM can also be found in other conceptual modeling languages and in most schema languages.[93]

---

[93] An exception are RDF schema languages (section 3.7.3), because of the Open World Assumption: An RDF entity ('resource' in RDF terminology) can be of multiple entity types ('classes'), unless an explicit disjointness constraint is enforced by a specific ontology.

3.8.2. Object Role Modeling

Object-Role Modeling (ORM) is a fact-oriented modeling language that evolved from the *Natural-language Information Analysis Method* (NIAM) by Gerardus M. Nijssen and Eckhard Falkenberg (Falkenberg 1976; Nijssen and T. Halpin 1989). The current version (ORM2) is mainly based on works of Terry Halpin and best described by T. Halpin and Morgan (2008). Unlike ERM and UML, ORM is build from a linguistic basis using structured sentences in natural language as a starting point. ORM does not make use of the notion of attributes but views the universe of discourse in terms of objects playing roles. Objects are classified in sets of *entity types* and *value types*. Entities can be any (possibly abstract) concepts and they are references by values. For instance a person (entity) may be referenced by its name (value). Modeling starts with factual examples that are split into *elementary facts* and translated into *predicates*. This process will be exemplified in the following.

The sentence 'Frankenstein was written by Shelley' is an elementary fact because it cannot be split into smaller statements collectively provide the same information. With background knowledge about its meaning can be translated into 'The book referred to by title 'Frankenstein' was written by the person referred to by name 'Mary Shelley''. You can then infer first the entity types Book and Person, second the value types BookTitle and PersonName, and third the predicate ...was written by.... General prredicates in ORM can be named in two directions (...was written by.../...wrote...) and connect any positive number of objects. For instance in the fact 'Mary Shelley is dead' the predicate ...is dead is unary and in the fact 'Mary Shelley died 1851 in London' the predicate ...died...in... is ternary. Each "..." slot of a predicate is called a *role*. Roles may be named and the number of roles is the predicates *arity* as in predicate logic.

ORM2 includes a detailed graphical notation to express models with objects types, roles, and constraints (see figure 2.7 for a very simple example). An object type is drawn as rectangle with rounded corners containing its name. Entity types use solid border lines and value types use dashed border lines. Predicates are drawn as sequence of concatenated role boxes that are linked to object types by lines. Role names can be shown in square brackets and blue color next to a role box. Figure 25 shows an ORM diagram of the model derived from example 23. Value types that uniquely identify instances of an entity type (in this example BookTitle, PersonName, and PlaceName) are shown as *reference mode* below the entity's name. In addition the model introduces the Author entity type which is a subtype of the Person entity type, so every author is a person. Subtype connections are indicated by bold arrows that show the inheritance. The diagram also contains some *constraints*, which are shown in magenta: a dot at the line connecting the Author with the creator role depicts a *mandatory role constraint*. This kind of constraint demands that every author must have written at least one book. The arrow between the first role of ...is dead and of ...died...in... shows an *external constraint*, in detail a *subset constraint*. It states that the set of people who died in a specific year and place must be a subset of the set of people who are dead. To create a precise conceptual model, you must carefully reveal such connections which may be obvious only to experts in the universe of discourse. The bar below the first role of the predicate ...died...in... is a *uniqueness constraint*. It can be read as "each person died at most once". On all predicates there is an implicit uniqueness constraints that spans all roles combined. For instance a person is only dead once: if "Mary Shelley died 1851 in London" is an elementary fact, it does not make sense to include it twice in the same model population. This is also due to the interpretation of ORM predicates as factual statements in predicate logic.

A *model population* (or *model instance*) is a set of objects and roles played by them, that fulfills all model's constraints. In terms of ontology languages, a model is a TBox and a model population is a ABox. ORM offers practical means of communicating via unambiguous, controlled natural language language and examples of data by *verbalization* (T. Halpin 2004). Given some basic language templates you can even provide verbalizations in multiple languages, as implemented by (Jarrar, M. Keet, and Dongilli 2006). This verbalization is similar to standardized verbalization forms of fact-oriented business rule such as those based on the Semantics of Business Vocabulary and Business Rules (SBVR).[94]

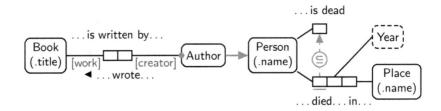

Example 25: ORM diagram expressing a conceptual model

Among the special ORM features not included in example 25, there are ring constraints, frequency and value constraints on entity types and roles, deontic rules, and objectification. Ring constraints can be applied to pairs of roles that may be populated by the same entities. The simplest case if a binary relationship with both roles played by the same entity type, but rings can also occur on longer predicates and indirectly because of subtypes. There are 10 ring constraints (reflexive, irreflexive, purely reflexive, symmetric, asymmetric, antisymmetric, transitive, intransitive, strongly Intransitive, acyclic) with 26 legal combinations. Example 26 a) shows a model in which a Person can be child of a Person. The predicate is constraint as acyclic (left), because no one can be its own child or ancestor. A frequency constraint ('≤ 2') is added to the parent role to state that a person is child of at most two people. An additional strongly intransitive ring constraint is given as deontic (right, in blue). This means, if one person is child of another, there should be no other chain of child-of-relationships between the two. By this deontic rule, incest is forbidden, but

---

[94] See http://www.rulespeak.com/ for an example. In brief, SBVR was influenced by fact-oriented modeling, but it lacks a graphical notation.

still possible, while circular ancestorship or more than two parents of one person are impossible.

A special feature of ORM that is rarely found in other conceptual modeling languages is *objectification* or 'nesting'. Objectification allows instances of relationships to be treated as entities in their own right (T. Halpin and Morgan 2008, ch. 10.5.). In contrast to transformations of relationships to entities in example 24, an objectified relationship may still be used as relationship. In example 26 b) the relationship wrote is objectified as Writing. In natural language objectification is related to the activity of nominalization. For instance the statement 'Shelley wrote Frankenstein' may be nominalized as 'Shelley's writing of Frankenstein'. The interpretation of objectified facts, bears some difficulties: relationships one the one hand represent possible propositions, which can either be true or false: Shelley either has written Frankenstein or not. Entities on the other hand are states of affairs. It makes no sense to say that Shelley's writing of Frankenstein is true or false, but you can make statements about this event, for instance it started in summer 1816 in Geneva, it was not known when the novel was first published anonymously in 1818, and it is described in other books. For this reason a relationship and its objectification should be seen as distinct objects connected by a 1:1 relationship. If you further analyze nominalization, different ontological types of objectification may be distinguished (Moltmann 2007), for instance to differentiate statements like 'I know that Shelley wrote Frankenstein' and 'I know the particular circumstances of Shelley's writing of Frankenstein'. General problems of mapping between relationships and entities will be dealt with in section 4.2.4.

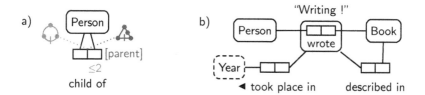

Example 26: Additional constraints and features in ORM

3.8.3. Unified Modeling language

The *Unified Modeling language* (UML) was developed in the 1990s as modeling language for object-oriented software systems. It was standardized by the Object Management Group (OMG), published as ISO specification in 2005, and since extended to UML 2.4.1 (OMG 2011). Similar to CORBA, ORM's other popular standard, UML at large is fairly complex and expressive.[95] UML provides graphical notations

---

[95] Complexity and standardization without reference implementation has been identified by Henning (2006) as reasons why CORBA's failed. UML in contrast is quite popular, but its broad coverage maked it difficult to know, to what in particular applications refer to with UML.

for several types of diagrams, that can also be combined. The major kinds of UML diagrams are structure diagrams and behavior diagrams. Behavior diagrams are not relevant to this thesis because of the static nature of digital documents. Structure diagrams show the static structure of a software system and its parts, so they can also be used to depict data structures. Relevant structure diagram types for modeling in UML are:

class diagrams describe the structure of a system in terms of object orientation: *classes* correspond to ERM entity types and *objects* correspond to entities. UML classes can have attributes, which may have datatypes, and cardinality constraints, among other properties. Classes may further be connected by inheritance, dependency, composition, aggregation, and general binary relationships (called associations). UML objects can either be simple class instances or so called (static) classifiers, which are shared among all class instances. An instance of a model, which is depicted by an UML class diagram, can have multiple instances per class but only one classifier.

object diagrams show (partial) model instances by depicting concrete objects with their class memberships and attribute values.

component diagrams and **package diagrams** group parts of an UML diagram, to better abstract from distinct parts and layers.

deployment diagrams show how parts of a software system are located on different computers and other resources, including storage.

profile diagrams can define extensions of UML in form of specialized classes or other constructs. These extensions are called stereotypes and they may introduce their own graphical notation. Most applications of UML stereotypes can also be replaced by inheritance between normal classes. To some degree profile diagrams allow metamodeling, because they specify the way that other models can be expressed.

composite structure diagrams show the internal structure of a class or another component. The internal structure may imply the existence of other classes and relationships, but the meaning of this diagram type is not well understood among engineers (Oliver and Luukala 2006).

With class diagrams, UML can be seen as a variant of ERM, enriched with other diagram types and metamodeling. As suggested by the attribute 'unified', UML in theory subsumes other modeling languages and provides a tool to exchange conceptual models. In practice, however, support and interpretation of UML's exchange format XML Metadata Interchange (XMI) varies among tools. In addition, the semantics of UML constructs differs among users, as described by Oliver and Luukala (2006) for composite structure diagrams. Typical misues and wrong expectations of UML have been collected by Bell (2004). A general problem is the primary use of

UML for describing logical and physical data models which can directly be transformed to software. Conceptual concepts in contrast, must rather match a specific
domain, independent from its technical implementation.

Example 27 shows an UML class diagram that depicts a conceptual model similar
to the ERM and UML models above. The ternary relationship between Person, Year,
and Place has been replaced by a DeathEvent entity. The model makes use of attributes
and data types (string and year). n-ary relationships and additional entities connected
to binary relationships are also supported by UML but not shown in example 27.

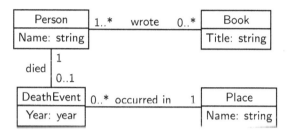

Example 27: UML diagram with a model similar to example 23 and 25

3.8.4. Domain specific modeling and metamodeling

In addition to generalized conceptual modeling languages, such as ERM, ORM, and
UML, the idea of *Domain Specific Modeling* (DSM) and *Domain Specific Languages*
(DSL) have recently gained popularity (Kelly and Tolvanen 2008). In short, a domain-
specific modeling language is a custom formalism for a specific domain, for instance
the domain of mobile applications or the automotive industry. Each language is
designed to model an universe of discourse within the specific domain. A DSL consist
of a set of language concepts and their rules, together with a graphical notation. For
instance a business modeling language could consist of customer types, contract
types and service types, instead of general entity types and relationship types. DSM
and DSL have been proven useful in software engineering especially to bridge the gap
between domain experts and software architects and to maintain changing models
(Cao, Ramesh, and Rossi 2009). In addition to conceptual modeling, specialized
modeling languages are also used for automatic generation of software systems. For
this reason the boundaries between domain specific modeling languages, domain
specific schema languages, and domain specific programming languages are fluid.
The lack of a clear separation increases the existing danger of confusing real world
models and software models (Génova, Valiente, and Nubiola 2005).

Domain specific modeling languages have a history in Computer-aided software
engineering (CASE) tools with the Problem Statement Language/Problem Statement
Analyzer (PSL/PSA) by Teichroew and Hershey (1977) as first instance. To some
degree you can also use generalized modeling languages that allow some customization, for for instance UML with its profile diagrams. Most DSL, however, are created

with specialized DSM tools such as MetaEdit+ (Kelly and Tolvanen 2008) and DSL tools of Microsoft Visual Studio (Cook et al. 2007). The former has its origin in a research project at University of Jyväskylä which laid the theoretical and practical foundation of *metamodeling*.

The term *metamodel* first refers to any specialized DSL which can be used to create concrete models in its domain. The task of creating specialized modeling languages, is then called metamodeling. Each DSM tool provides its own (graphical) language for metamodeling; this metamodeling language is based on a meta-metamodel which defines how metamodels can be expressed. Several meta-metamodels are compared by Kern, Hummel, and Kühne (2011), among them GOPRR from MetaEdit (Kelly and Tolvanen 2008), the metamodel from Microsoft DSL tools (Cook et al. 2007), and Ecore from Eclipse Modeling Framework (Steinberg et al. 2009). The list of metamodeling concepts from this comparison is similar to the list of conceptual ERM constructs in part 3.8.1. There are entity types (also refered to as object types) and relationship types (possibly limited to binary relationships), attributes, roles, and inheritance, which each can be subject to several constraints and extensions. Additional concept in meta-modeling include entity-sets and composition, port typess that further define how entities can be connected by relationships, grouping of metamodel elements, and model types to group and refer to models with common properties. An example of a modeling language specified by a metamodeling is ConML (Gonzalez-Perez 2012), which was specified using UML. ConML on its part supports creation of conceptual models such as CHARM for cultural heritage, including aspects such as subjectivity and temporality.

Several independent attempts have been made to unify conceptual modeling languages by mathematical descriptions, for instance with category theory (Frederiks, Hofstede, and Lippe 1997) and with description logics (C. M. Keet 2008a). The practical outcome of this (meta)-metamodeling, however, is questionable as it comes with more complexity and less readability. This contradicts the original purpose of conceptual modeling as translating between domain experts and programmers. Alternative uses of modeling languages for knowledge representation and schema design may better benefit from mathematical metamodels, but both veers away from the 'territory' of reality, which is not build from entities, relationships, attributes, and roles, but from experience and assumptions. A general limitation of conceptual data modeling is its foundation on crisp set theory, in contrast to the fuzzy nature of natural language. Even if conceptual language is based on language (like ORM), it only uses traditional logic statements with sets of disjoint objects. And even an exact metamodel with clearly defined semantics does not ensure that the meaning of a model is equal to all participants: As shown for both ERM Hitchman (1995) and UML (Oliver and Luukala 2006) the "semantics [of UML constructs] are often based on the engineer's expectations and *perceived meaning* rather than on the actual, intended semantics". Nevertheless conceptual modeling is practiced, either explicit with conceptual modeling languages or implicit by directly creating logical schemas. The analysis of important modeling languages and metamodeling principles in this section has revealed some common constructs which lead to more concrete patterns

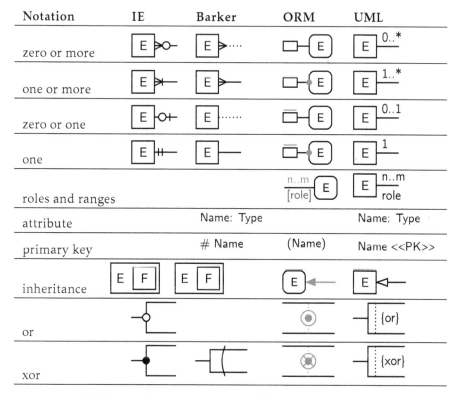

Notation	IE	Barker	ORM	UML
zero or more				
one or more				
zero or one				
one				
roles and ranges				
attribute		Name: Type		Name: Type
primary key		# Name	(Name)	Name <<PK>>
inheritance				
or				{or}
xor				{xor}

Table 3.18.: Some conceptual modeling notation variants

in chapter 5.

3.9. Conceptual diagrams

Thomson: I usually write down data structures before I write down code. I don't write algorithms — no flowcharts, or stuff like that. But stuff you have to refer to on almost every line of code — data structures.

Seibel: If you're writing a C program, does that mean C code that would define those data structures?

Thomson: No, little boxes with arrows and stuff.
— Ken Thomson interviewed by Seibel (2009, p. 459)

Drawings and graphical symbols predate written language. In contrast to character based writing systems, a diagram can convey meaning rather directly using elements and space as visual and spatial methaphors (Tversky 2001; Winn 1990). Beside spatial data in geographic maps, however, the use of diagrams to convey data is relatively new (Tufte 2001). Common diagram types such as bar chart, pie chart, and line graph were developed by William Playfair (1759-1823). The focus of this thesis is data as bits instead of data as measures and numbers. For this reason the majority of graphical methods for statistical data, as widely used in *data visualization* (Friendly 2009) are not relevant to this thesis. Diagrams as methods for data description and structuring can best be summarized as *conceptual diagrams*: an example of a conceptual diagram is an organizational chart which represents organizational parts and their relationships in a company.

Conceptual diagrams are popular methods especially to abstract from an universe of discourse in the act of data modeling. Pictoral and graphical representations even turned out to be the most mentioned theme in a survey among 104 data modeling practitioners, asked for a definition of data modeling (Simsion 2007, p. 192).

Conceptual diagrams can structure and describe data but they are also a form of data if they follow the visual notation of a diagrammatic writing system. To justify this view we can compare diagrams with written text – both can be based on defined symbols (see section 3.1). Once these symbols are identified in a visual notation, the diagram or text can be reproduced without any loss of information. A *visual notation* is formed by a set of *visual symbols* and a set of rules how to combine these symbols to valid diagrams (Costagliola, Deufemia, and Polese 2004; Moody 2009). The argument for treating conceptual diagrams as data is outlined in appendix B. The primary problem is a problem of digitization, similar to optical character recognition (OCR) for textual data.

The following section will first list existing types of conceptual diagrams (section 3.9.1) and second summarize their common properties and elements (section 3.9.2). Diagram types for processes, such as flow charts, business rules and visual programming languages are not included because of the focus of this thesis on static digital documents.

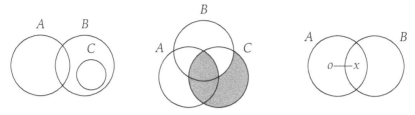

Figure 3.24.: Euler diagram, Venn diagram, and Peirce's extension to Venn

3.9.1. Diagram types

I. Conceptual modeling notations

An early and influental graphical notation for data was introduced by Bachman (1969) as *data-structure diagram*, also known as Bachman diagram . Bachman compared his diagrams with Critical Path Method (CPM) and Program Evaluation and Review Technique (PERT) diagrams that had been developed for project management in the late 1950s. A simple example of a data-structure diagram is included in figure 3.5. Based on Bachman, P. P. Chen (1976) introduced ERM (section 3.8.1) together with entity-relationship diagrams. Similar conceptual diagram types are associated with other conceptual modeling languages such as UML (section 3.8.3) and ORM (section 3.8.2). Elements of these diagram types, such as notations for entity types, attributes, roles, rules, and constraints (see figure 2.7) mirror elements and constructs of their modeling language, as listed and described at page 142 in section 3.8.1. An example of visual notation variants is given in table 3.18.

II. Diagrammatic logic systems

A second tradition of conceptual diagrams is more connected to formal logic. Intersection, union, and subset relationships between sets can be depicted by Euler diagrams and Venn diagrams. *Euler diagrams* (Euler 1768) consist of circles, ellipses, or similar closed curves that together divide the plane in zones. The whole plane depicts the universal set, zones build from overlapping curves depict set unions, and missing zones depict empty sets. A *Venn diagram* (Venn 1880) is an Euler diagram in which all possible set intersections are represented and shading can be used to depict empty zones. Figure 3.24 shows an Euler diagram (left) and a Venn diagram (center), both representing three non-empty sets A, B, and C with $A \cup B \neq \emptyset$, $A \cup C = \emptyset$, and $C \subsetneq B$.

Peirce (1933) extended Venn diagrams to also express existential statements and disjunction. He used the symbol o instead of shading to denote empty sets and the symbol x to represent the existence of an element in a set. These symbols can be connected by lines that represent disjunctive statements. Figure 3.24 (right) shows a graphical representing of the statement $A \setminus B = \emptyset \vee A \cup B \neq \emptyset$ for two sets A and B. Peirce's diagrams were further modified by Shin (1995) in two variants that both use

Figure 3.25.: Spider diagram and constraint diagram

Venn's shading instead of Peirce's symbol o. Several extensions and modification to these diagram types have since been proposed (Dau 2009b; Howse 2008) and it has been shown that diagrammatic logic systems can be as complete and as precise as other symbolic systems for logic sentences and proofs (E. Hammer 1994).

Two particular extensions to Peirce/Shin diagrams are spider diagrams and constraint diagrams, both shown in figure 3.25. *Spider diagrams* (Gil, Howse, and S. Kent 1999b)[96] extend Euler diagram by shading and so called 'spiders' to place lower and upper limits on the number of elements in a set. Spiders are similar to Peirce's connected x symbols: a spider represents an element, depicted as a tree with nodes (shown as dots instead of x) in different zones of the Euler diagram. Figure 3.25 (left) shows a spider diagram with two spiders. The first spider indicates that there is an element which is either in A or in B but not in their intersection. The shading of B indicates that this element is the only element in B. The second spider indicates that there is another element which is either in $A \setminus B$ or in $A \cup B$ (being the only element in this intersection) or neither in A nor B. The expressivity of spider diagrams is equivalent to monadic first order logic with equality. *Constraint diagrams* (Gil, Howse, and S. Kent 1999a, 2001) extend spider diagrams by binary relations between sets and by explicit universal quantification. Figure 3.25 (right) shows a constraint diagram with two sets A and B and two disjoint relations f and g ($\forall x \in A, \langle x, y_1 \rangle \in f, \langle x, y_2 \rangle \in g : y_1 \neq y_2$). Constraint diagrams have been proposed to replace the Object Constraint Language (OCL), a notation for first order predicate logic, that is part of the UML modeling language. While spider diagrams and constraint diagrams have a strong mathematical background, their actual usability in data modeling is an open question. Many constraints could also be formulated in a data modeling language such as ORM or in natural language with less rigour and more readability.

Another graphical notation for logical sentences, also created by Peirce (1933) are *existential graphs*. This diagram type is divided into three parts. The first ('Alpha') corresponds to propositional logic, the second ('Beta') corresponds to first-order predicate logic, and the third ('Gamma') adds elements of higher-order logic and modal logic, among others. The full system, however, was not finished and existential graphs received little attention until Sowa (1976) adopted them to its own *Conceptual graphs*. Introductions to conceptual graphs are given by (Sowa 1992a,

---

[96] In different context, the term 'spider diagram' is also used for other kinds of diagrams, among them mind maps.

2008) and Dau (2009a). A specification, including the Conceptual Graph Interchange Format (CGIF) was published as part of ISO/IEC 24707 (2007). An example of a conceptual graph from Sowa (2008) is shown in example 28 with its notation also translated to extended CGIF. The graph represents the statement "if a cat is on a mat, then it is a happy pet" – this interpretation, however, requires background knowledge in form of a mental model of the real world. According to Sowa (2008) the "Attr relation indicates that the cat, also called a pet, has an attribute, which is an instance of happiness" but what does "having an attribute, which is an instance of happines" mean? One the strict logical level of concetual graphs, there is no relation between this formal statement and the idea of "being happy" and no knowledge about whether "being happy" has a different ontological status than "being a pet".[97] With their grounding in sets and relationships, diagrammatic logic systems share strength and weaknesses of formal logic (section 2.1.1): they can be very precise but they poorly cover non-traditional logic that better fit to descriptions of reality.

A comparision of several diagrammatic logic system for use in artificial intelligence is given by Sowa (1992b). Diagrammatic logic systems are very similar to conceptual modeling notations based on entities and relationships.[90] Both types of diagrams can be formalized as multi-bipartite graphs or directed multi-hypergraphs from a graph-theoretic view.

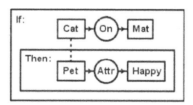

[If: [Cat *x] [Mat *y] (On ?x ?y)
[Then: [Pet ?x] [Happy *z] (Attr ?x ?z)]]

Example 28: A conceptual graph in graphical and CGIF notation

III. Knowledge structuring diagrams

The third tradition of conceptual diagrams can best be described as *knowledge structuring diagrams*. Popular instances include mind maps, concept maps, topic maps, and spatial hypertext. Eppler (2006) provides a comparision of mind maps, concept maps and two additional mapping methods. As shown by Sowa (2006), knowledge structuring diagrams have less precise semantics than logic diagrams and conceptual modeling notation. In data modeling (see figure 2.6 that itself is

---

[97] It is said that cats have no master, so 'pet' may be an attribution just like 'happy'.

[98] In the first publication on conceptual graphs, Sowa (1976) used them to represent the conceptual schemas for database systems. In later publications he applied them to a wider range of topics from artificial intelligence and cognitive science.

an example of a knowledge structuring diagram) they help to find and formulate mental models without constraints of precise formal logic.

Mind maps (T. Buzan and B. Buzan 1996) arrange topics as possibly colored bubbles or pictograms with labels in a hierarchical layout around a central topic. Mind maps are used as tools for brainstorming and note taking, but they can be hard to read without additional explanation. An example of a mind map is given in figure 3.26 to depict a classfication of spatial relationship types. In this example topics are drawn as gray bubbles (boxes) with labels inside and connected by lines. An simple pictogram is shown next to selected topics (spatial concatenation) for illustration.

Concept maps (Novak and Cañas 2006) arrange labeled boxes connected by arrows, also starting with a main topic. While mind maps basically have the graph structure of a labeled tree, concept maps are directed labeled graphs. In *spatial hypertext* (Marshall and III 1995) the basic elements represent documents. Links between documents are shown with lines and arrows, by inclusion and visual proximity. *Topic Maps* (Pepper 2010) are more formally defined, but they neither have precise semantics such as diagrammatic logic systems. Topic maps are based on connected topics, similar to concept maps. In addition to elements for topics, there are associations (*n*-ary relationships between topics with optional roles) and so called ocurrences. Ocurrences represent information resources (documents) relevant to particular topics and they may have a datatype. As in all conceptual diagrams, elements of topic maps can be labeled by names. It is possible to treat a topic map as single topic in another topic map (reification) but its not clear whether one topic map can refer to itself in a meaningful way. In contrast to other knowledge diagram types, there are defined methods to express topic maps in an XML based data format and other precise syntax, and topic maps are standardized in ISO/IEC 13250 (2000).

IV. Domain-specific visual notations

Many visual notations exist in specific domains, such as electrical circuit diagrams, musical notation, and written singn language (Sutton 2002). Most of them follow some standard that defines the meaning visual symbols and their aggregations. The common properties and elements of these domain-specific visual languages, however, have received little attention so far. Tversky (2001, 2011) suggests that visual languages convey meaning rather directly by properties of the page. Spatial patterns such as proximity, containment, size, and order etc. help to structure memory, communication, and reasoning.

3.9.2. Diagram properties

Frameworks to describe and evaluate visual diagram notations are given by Moody (2009) by Costagliola, Deufemia, and Polese (2004), and by Bertin (2011).[99] There are several approaches to describe diagram notations by formal grammars (see

---

[99] First published by Bertin (1967) in French.

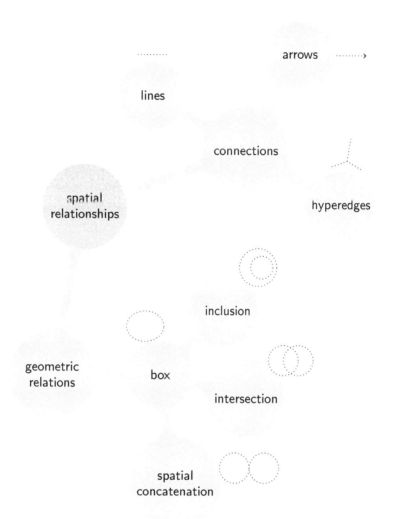

Figure 3.26.: Mindmap of spatial relationship types in conceptual diagrams

example 3 for a simple diagrammatic rewriting system). The visual symbols of these grammars are constructed by combinations of visual variables (shape, size, color...) and related to each other by spatial relationships. The basic relationship types as identified by Costagliola, Deufemia, and Polese (2004) are shown in figure 3.26. Spatial concatenation can further be divided by direction (above, below, left, right). A taxonomy of visual variables has been created by Bertin (2011): The basic dimensions are position, size, brightness value, texture, color, orientation, and shape. Bertin classified these dimensions according to their suitability to depict quantity, order (ordinal values), selection (nominal values), and associativity (nominal values with similarity). As described by Moody (2009) these dimensions can be used as degrees of freedom to encode information, in addition to textual labels as "non-visual" elements. All visual elements and dimensions are based on likenesses and on proximity, at nominal, ordinal, and interval levels (Tversky 2001). They help to structure memory, communication and reasoning just like other kinds of patterns. Although the treatment of diagrams as data requires a first encoding (see appendix B) and although the domain of non-visual digital data is much more restricted, it is likely that some visual patterns have counterparts in the domain of non-visual data.

3.10. Query languages and APIs

For the main part, query languages and Application programming interfaces (APIs) are not used to structure and describe data but for access and modification. Such dynamic applications are out of the scope of static digital documents, as collected in chapter 3. Nevertheless query languages and APIs take a relevant part in structuring and description as briefly described below.

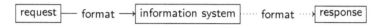

Figure 3.27.: Interaction with an information system

To limit the analysis to parts relevant to this thesis, one first needs to look at the general interaction with an information system via APIs and query languages (figure 3.27): an information system is accessed by sending a request which may result in a response. For instance a digital library is an information system that can be accessed by requests to add, modify, delete, and select stored documents. Both request and response are digital documents in a defined format, specific to the information system. To exclude dynamic properties of information systems, we limit the analysis to requests that do not modify the visible behaviour of the system. In particular, all these requests must be stateless and cacheable in terms of the Representational State Transfer (REST) model (R. T. Fielding 2000): "each request [...] must contain all of the information necessary to understand the request" and "requests that are equivalent [...] result in a response identical to that in the cache". Requests of this type are mostly known as information retrieval requests. Examples of query languages, formats, protocols, and APIs for document retrieval include Z39.50, SRU, CQL, and OpenSearch. Beyond information retrieval queries there are further other kinds of queries. A classification of queries types for information systems has been undertaken by Reiner (1988, p. 33) by distinguishing queries that ask for one of:

- documents (which),

- facts (where, when, who, what, ...),

- decisions (yes or no),

- explanations (how, why).

For all kinds of these queries, a universal query language called Intermediary Query Language (IQL) has been built up based on predicate logic (Reiner 1988, 1991). With a clearly defined syntax and well-founded semantics this language can be expressed in semantically equivalent formal languages.[100] A query can be asked

---

[100] Reiner (1988, 1991) in her thesis implements the Untrained User Query Language (UUQL) and the Trained User Query Language (TUQL).

to an information system in any of these languages, given a defined request format of the query language. The response of the information system is a set of documents, facts, or explanations, also expressed in a defined format.

The concept of query language and request formats corresponds to the use of an identifier, as described in section 3.2: given an information system, a request is a piece of data that refers to a response document, which is another piece of data. The information system fulfills the role of an identifier system (section 3.2.3) which defines how request and response must be structured and which request maps to which response. In contrast to identifiers, there is no general uniqueness requirement: multiple requests (queries formulated in different query languages or different forms to express the same query in one language) may result in the same response. The reverse does not hold, but a response may consist of a set or collection of documents.

Query languages and APIs are also connected to other methods of data structuring: for instance file systems (section 3.3) are implemented with a common API (basically POSIX) and many data structuring languages, especially data binding languages (section 3.5.1) were created to express requests and responses of APIs. The connection between query languages and conceptual models (section 3.8) is less developed, although conceptual modeling for API design had already been identified by P. P. Chen, Thalheim, and Wong (1999) as an issue that needs attention.

The conceptual model of most APIs needs to be revealed by reverse-engineering its request and response formats, which may at least be restricted by data types and schemas (for instance an XML Schema). If queries languages are bound to a database or data structuring languages, such as SQL and SPARQL, the conceptual model is equal or very similar to models of this language, for instance the model of RDF (see page 107). In fact it can depend on the viewpoint whether one speaks about an API or about and identifier system or about a data format because API and format are tightly coupled. This coupling also involves trends such as XML, which was later followed by JSON, and the dominance of SQL against alternative methods of access, such as Language Integrated Query (LINQ) and Tutorial D (see section 3.4.4).

Chapter 4

Findings

In the previous chapter, observations were mainly grouped by aspects of practical similarities. File systems, for instance, may differ in their architecture, but all serve the same purpose, despite technical differences. The same applies to databases, schema languages, diagrams types, and other methods of data structuring. This chapter analyzes and jointly groups all methods into independent strategies. In section 4.1 it is found that general prototype categorization better describes what methods of data structuring actually do with data. Section 4.2 then determines typical topics that can be observed as paradigms consistently among all methods.

The outcome of this chapter consists of two categorizations, one based on prototypes and one based on paradigms. The categorizations further help to detect fundamental problems and issues of data structuring and to get candidates and directions for patterns, which will then be elaborated in the next chapter.

4.1. Categorization of methods

Notoriamente no hay clasificación del universo que no sea arbitraria y conjetural. La razón es muy simple: no sabemos qué cosa es el universo.
— Jorge Luis Borges (1952)

The following categorization of data structuring methods is a result of the collection of methods analyzed in chapter 3. Given these methods one can categorize them by history and origin, by type of application, by complexity, and by many other criteria. This approach, however, can result in rather arbitrary classifications, because a single facet has to be chosen and because most facets are not selective for all instances. Another approach, that better fits to how people cognitively perceive and classify things, is grouping based on prototypes which act as cognitive reference points (Lakoff 1987; Rosch 1983). Following this approach, categories of data structuring methods are not defined by selected features, but data structuring methods are clustered by similarity, until prototypical methods emerge. A *prototype* can act as good example of a certain category, while other instances belonging to this category are less central. For instance in western society, a chair is a central prototype of furniture, although other furniture may share little properties with chairs.

category	main purpose	examples
encodings	express data	Unicode, Base64
storage systems	store data	NTFS, RDBMS
identifier and query languages	refer to data	URI, XPath
structuring and markup languages	structure data	XML, CSV, RDF
schema languages	constrain data	BNF, XSD
conceptual models	describe data	Mind Maps, ERM

Table 4.1.: Prototype categorization of data structuring methods

The final prototype categorization of data structuring methods found in this study is summarized in table 4.1. The categorization is a novel result, because comparative studies of data structuring methods, as broad as given in this thesis, have not been conducted yet. The prototypes have partly been anticipated in the division of chapter 3:

- encodings: section 3.1

- storage systems: section 3.3 and 3.4

- identifier and query languages: section 3.2 and 3.10

- structuring and markup languages: section 3.5 and 3.6

- schema languages: section 3.7

- conceptual models: section 3.8 and 3.9

To further validate this result, the prototype categorization was analyzed to find a supporting facet that best divides categories by one aspect of data structuring. As the research question asks for general methods that span a wide range of digital technologies, the supporting facet should be independent from particular use cases and applications. It was found that the *main purpose* of a method can be used as dividing facet. This purpose describes what a method mainly does with data. For instance the main purpose of storage systems like databases and file systems is storage. The data structuring method's main purpose can act as guideline to find the nearest prototype from table 4.1. Still this dividing facet should not be confused with a strict classifier as known from more formal approaches of categorization. Instances from each category can also serve multiple purposes, just like one can use a chair to stand on it when changing a light bulb.

4.2. Paradigms in data structuring

The contemporary meaning of *paradigm* was introduced by Kuhn (1962) in the history of science. He explained fundamental changes in science, like the Copernican

Revolution and Einstein's theories of relativity as shifts in scientific paradigm. A paradigm is "what members of a scientific community, and they alone, share" (Kuhn 1974), especially their basic theories, assumptions, and research methods. The term is now also used in a broader sense for "a philosophical or theoretical framework of any kind" (Meriam-Webster 2011). Paradigms are relevant to analysis of data structuring methods, because they deeply shape the way people talk and think about data. Paradigms in data structuring, however, differ from scientific paradigms, because data structuring and description is more art and engineering practice than science (Simsion 2007). One can identify some paradigm shifts in the history of data structuring (P. P. Chen 1976; Codd 1970; Gamma et al. 1994, to give some examples), but these shifts are less complete and disruptive for data applications as a whole. The reason is that there is less ambition to create one single method to structure and describe all data. Instead it is usual to have many specialized technologies for different use cases, each based on some paradigm and shared by its own community. So the following paradigms do not deal with concrete and influential trends like the relational database model or the Resource Description Framework. They rather describe general kinds of viewing at and dealing with data and with digital documents. These orthogonal perceptions of data come with their own basic and often hidden assumptions. More subliminal than concrete technologies, paradigms in data structuring influence which patterns are used as constituent primitives and which are ignored. Five groups of paradigms are exposed below, each with strengths, weaknesses and related data patterns at the end of each section.

- Documents and objects (section 4.2.1) realize digital documents as given or as created artifacts.

- Standards and rules (section 4.2.2) specify the consistent creation and consumption of data. They show which parts of a document are possible and relevant and how to make use of data.

- Collections, types and sameness (section 4.2.3) group parts of digital documents based on their identities.

- Entities and connections (section 4.2.4) seem to be basic building blocks of all, but they are two sides of the same coin.

- Levels of abstraction (section 4.2.5) separate and combine descriptions of the same document with different granularity.

4.2.1. Documents and objects

The primary question when encountering a piece of data is "what is this digital piece and how can it be described?". Documents and objects are two rivaling approaches to describe digital artifacts, answering the question from two points of view (I). Both views will be illustrated with examples (II) before uniting them as two sides of the coin of data as sign (III).

I. Two points of view

The document view primarily tries to describe the artifact in more or less detail. For instance a document can be described by its format, size, and divisions. One can model the document, for instance as ordered hierarchy, and express it, for instance in a markup language such as TEI. Even alternative descriptions are possible, for instance concurrent hierarchies (Pondorf and Witt 2010; A. Renear, Mylonas, and D. Durand 1996), as long as all descriptions are discoveries of the same concrete document. The object point of view, in contrast, is less interested in the specific details of form: it rather tries to create a broad picture of the document content. An example of the object view is a description of data as set of connected entities and properties. The document approach is mainly found in library information science where cataloging is applied to document artifacts that (are assumed to) already exist. The second approach is mainly found in computer science and in software engineering where digital artifacts are created to solve tasks of computation. Both views, however, always exist together. Neither documents nor objects are better descriptions per se, but both are valid, and both can be found on a large scale and on a small scale. The important question to reveal this paradigm is not whether data is better described as documents or as objects, but where a line between the two is drawn in a particular (application of) data technology.

II. Examples

A visible instance of this separation is the distinction between data values and data objects, for instance in databases and in modeling languages. Example 29 shows a simple ORM data model and a corresponding SQL schema with years, events, places, and names. Years and names are defined as values types in the model, so they are given directly in concrete model instances. Places and events, in contrast, are abstract entity types which are objects without explicit form. In the SQL schema values are expressed by fields with data types, and objects are expressed by tables. Still, objects cannot exist alone, but they need data fields that act as object place-holders, such as the Id fields in example 29. The difficult task is to find out which parts of data are plain documents, and which parts are arbitrary object identifiers.

The line between documents and objects is often less clear than the distinction between value types or field values, and entity types or object identifier in example 29. As described in section 3.2.4, identifiers can also hold information about the objects they refer to — in this case data objects are values. In the same way, most document values can be interpreted as descriptive identifiers for some objects: for instance the YearAD field in example 29 may not only hold a year number but refer to another table that describes Years objects. Both variants can better be shown in RDF which has a clear separation between resources as objects on the one side and literals on the

```
┌ ─ ─ ┐        ╔═══╗        ╭───────╮        ╔═══╗        ┌ ─ ─ ─ ┐
│Year ├────────╢   ╟────────┤ Event ├────────╢   ╟────────┤ Name  │
└ ─ ─ ┘        ╚═══╝        ╰───────╯        ╚═══╝        └ ─ ─ ─ ┘
```

```
CREATE TABLE Event (
   Id       int   PRIMARY KEY IDENTITY,
   YearAD   int   NOT NULL,
   PlaceId  int,
   FOREIGN KEY (PlaceId) REFERENCES Place(Id)
);
CREATE TABLE Place (
   Id       int   PRIMARY KEY IDENTITY,
   Name     char  UNIQUE NOT NULL
);
```

Example 29: Documents as values and objects as entities/tables in ORM and SQL

other.[1] In RDF years are normally be expressed as literals with datatype $xs:integer$ or $xs:gYear$. But in some data sets years are objects, identified by URI references, such as `<http://dbpedia.org/resource/2010>` for the year 2010. The choice is rather arbitrary from a conceptual perspective, but RDF technologies provide no mechanism to switch between document form and object form. A possible mapping in extended RDF would be the Turtle statement

```
"2010"^^xs:gYear owl:sameAs <http://dbpedia.org/resource/2010> .
```

but no common RDF software can make sense of this.[2]

Switching between data as document and data as object is also possible for non-descriptive identifiers. As shown in example 10, an ISBN can be expressed in several variants (ISBN-10, ISBN-13, with/without hyphen or space, etc.). While a general ISBN is an identifier that refers to an abstract publication object, each variant is a distinct document. Another example are number encodings (section 3.1.2) which treat numbers as abstract objects while they are used as concrete values in other context. Number encodings are just one instance of datatypes (section 2.2.2), which are used to tag data pieces as values. One can also find document values combined with the entities and relationships paradigm where objects are seen as as primary objects and values are attached to objects as secondary 'properties' or 'attributes' (paradigm 4.2.4). As discussed in paradigm 4.2.5, levels of abstraction can act as borders between the two forms of a piece of data.

---

[1] A parallel document/object dichotomy in RDF exists with the separation between information resources and non-information resources (Ayers and Völkel 2008).

[2] In an April Fool's joke Vrandečić et al. (2010) provided a similar mapping between numbers as values and numbers as resources. There is some awareness of the dichotomy between documents and objects, but crossing the line in practice seems to be no serious option.

III. Data as sign

Actually both approaches are two sides of a coin: the document may *contain* an object and the object may *be expressed in* a document. In the document view the content of a digital document is taken literally and in the object view it is taken figuratively. A semiotic view helps to better understand the nature of this dichotomy: given a piece of data as sign, the document view corresponds to its nature as signifier and the object view corresponds to its nature as signified. The connection between document and object is an arbitrary result of social convention, so there is not only one digital object in a digital document.

The social grounding of data as signs becomes visible if one looks at the primary purpose of the documents and objects paradigm: both approaches provide analysis models of digital artifacts. In software engineering there are two notions of analysis models, which are often confused in practice (Génova, Valiente, and Nubiola 2005): one models an existing system as selection of the 'real world' (descriptive analysis model) and the other specifies a software system (prescriptive synthesis model). Analysis is done by reverse engineering, it is an act of discovering structures. In simple cases you just 'look at' given data to find out how 'it is' structured. The object approach, on the other hand, tries to create a clever structure that the digital artifact can be be put inside. Again there are simple cases in which there seems to be only one obvious schema. Nevertheless analysis (document to object, signifier to signified) and synthesis (object to document, signified to signifier) is based on experience, intuition, and ad-hoc decisions as usual to the application of signs.

Strength: documents and objects are useful methods to describe a digital artifacts as a whole, either analyzed as concrete, given value, or synthesized as abstract, created reference.

Weakness: it is often not clear whether a particular piece of data is actually used as value or as object. Once the distinction is fixed in a data description language, it is mentally difficult to switch the point of view.

Patterns: The patterns most likely found together with this paradigm include the *label* pattern and the *atomicity* pattern.

4.2.2. Standards and rules

All methods of data structuring can somehow be defined by standards and rules. The term *standard* is used for both, established uniform practices (descriptive standards) and intended practices (prescriptive standards) — both roles may coincide. The main idea of the standards and rules paradigm is that in data there must be some 'right way to do it' and that this way can be described (specification) or enforced (conformance). After an analysis of general properties and data standard types (I), the aspects of specification (II) and conformance (III) will be explained below to highlight strength and weaknesses of the standards and rules paradigm.

I. Properties and types of data standards

General standards help to establish and agree on uniform practices. In society, standards can be norms, laws, and social conventions. A standard specific to digital objects describes an agreed, repeatable way of both, the creation of data and the consumption of data. For instance the Unicode standard (section 3.1.1) defines how to encode written characters as data and how to read them from Unicode data strings. By this a standard is not only a simple sign, but it also affects how other signs are communicated. This semiotic aspect of standards is mostly hidden, although the naming of some data standards refers to an act of communication (*Request for Comments* (RFC), W3C *Recommendations* etc.). A twofold classification of general norms in information systems by Stamper et al. (2000) helps to better understand the semiotic roles of data standards: first, one can distinguish technical (processable automatically), formal (written down to be performed by people), and informal norms. Data standards are always formal with a large technical part, but they cannot be interpreted without informal norms.[3] Second, one can distinguish norms by the kind of task they relate to: substantive norms directly guide to some physical action, communication norms relate to the use of signs, and control norms refer to evaluation of conformity to other norms. Eventually all norms are substantive with layers of communication and control norms above. For instance the specification of a schema language includes norms how to communicate schemas which on their part control other documents (example 30). So in the end all standards refer to some action that can be influenced by human beings — even purely descriptive standards imply the idea of preserving something for later application. Physical laws, for instance, cannot be standardized, but one can only standardize how they are expressed and communicated. These communication standards can be quite arbitrary: we could use the metric system, US customary units, or the Potrzebie System of Weights and Measures as jokingly proposed by Knuth (1957). Finally — a blind spot especially to data standards — questions of standards are inherently questions of power and politics because "standards projects are performed by people, and are not immune from the effect of human relationships" (Meek 1995, p. 254).

II. Specification of data standards

The specification of a data standard describes a particular method of data creation and consumption. The specification must be non-ambiguous, clearly understandable, and it should cover a range of data instances instead of a single document. Different attempts to achieve these goals result in standards that are more or less formal, give more or less degrees of freedom, and provide more or less language-independence.

The most precise method of data specification is to use a formal language or mathematical notation. A formal language, however, does not define the meaning

---

[3] Stamper et al. (2000, p. 20) write that "informal norms are fundamental, because formal norms can only operate by virtue of the informal norms needed to interpret them, while technical norms can play no role in an organization unless embedded within a system of formal norms."

A schema language (e.g. XSD, section 3.7.2) is specified by a standard with:

- rules how to express schemas in the schema language (e.g. the syntax of XSD): communication norms and formal norms;

- rules how to specify other document formats via schemas (e.g. the meaning of XSD elements): control norms and technical norms;

- indications how to make use of schemas in practice (e.g. how to apply and combine XSD schemas): informal norms, that may be substantive, communication or control.

Example 30: Specification of a schema language as standard

of its symbols but only how to combine them to valid words (see section 2.2.1). At the other end of the spectrum of specifications there are general business rules. A business rule is "a statement that defines or constrains some aspect of the business [...] to assert business structure, or to control or influence the behavior of the business" (Business Rules Group 2011). Like other standards, business rules should provide "an enforcement regime what the consequences would be if the rule were broken" (see conformance below), but rules can also exist as less formal agreements. Examples of business rules in bibliographic data are cataloging rules and application profiles.

Most specifications make use of both, formal language and natural language. Without some kind of formalization, natural language is fuzzy, and without further explanation formal languages and notations are precise but meaningless. One strategy to bridge the gap between both is making parts of natural language more precise — again by standardization. Examples include verbalization of ORM and the definition of specific words for mandatory and deontic requirements in RFC 2119 (Bradner 1997) summarized in example 31. Such formalizations create a layering of standards where substantive standards are affected by communication and control standards, which at the top are affected by informal standards.

Independent from the problem how to express rules, a standard should neither be too strict nor too lax for its use case. Examples of common artifacts when data standards collide with real life applications include ad-hoc NULL values, such as "n/a" or "–", in response to mandatory constraints and ad-hoc subfield separators, such as "," or "/", in response to non-repeatable fields. The balance between strict and lax rules in a standard is influenced by many factors. For instance the choice between prescriptive and descriptive rules can result in more or less degrees of freedom in markup types (section 3.6.1). As shown in figure 4.1 only part of the intended meaning of a digital document is explicitly encoded — other parts depend on context. In addition, the document consists of redundant parts. Standards should clearly show which degrees of freedom contribute to the communication of meaning and which parts are irrelevant or predictable. A common example of irrelevant parts

- MUST (or REQUIRED or SHALL) means that the definition is an absolute requirement.

- MUST NOT (or SHALL NOT) means that the definition is an absolute prohibition.

- SHOULD (or RECOMMENDED) means that the full implications of not following
  the definition must be understood and carefully weighted because it is strongly
  recommended.

- SHOULD NOT (or NOT RECOMMENDED) means that the full implications of
  implementing a defined item must be understood and carefully weighted because
  it is strongly discouraged.

- MAY (or OPTIONAL) means that a feature is truly optional. Systems that do not
  implement it MUST be prepared to interoperate with systems that implement the
  feature and vice versa.

Example 31: Summary of precise words defined in RFC 2119

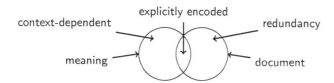

Figure 4.1.: Redundancy and relevance in digital documents[4]

in digital documents is additional whitespace. Examples of predictable parts of
non-choosable elements such as end-tags in XML (for instance in <a>...</a> the
second a>). Standards try to avoid irrelevant and redundant parts, but sometimes
they cannot be removed (for instance unordered collections can only be expressed in
sequences), and sometimes they are wanted to improve readability. In addition to
accepted redundancy many minor violations of a standards occur. These violations
are often tolerated because of the *robustness principle*, also known as Postel's law. In
words of Tim Berners-Lee (1998b) the law says "be liberal in what you require but
conservative in what you do". When consuming data, an implementation should
tolerate some violations of the standard, but when creating data, it should strictly
adhere to the specification. This principle is useful in practice, but it also encourages
laxness in data creation. A clean mapping between specification and implementation
is further complicated because techniques like SQL, XML, or RDF are rarely used
purely. Instead, they bring a whole framework of standards and tools in different
versions and dialects.

---

[4] The diagram is based on a similar illustration used by Pourabdollah (2009, p. 215) to show problems
in expressing data structures (one-to-many relationships in zz-structures in his example).

Across all technologies one finds a request to create generalized, abstract, or *language-independent* specifications which can be applied to different usage scenarios. Concrete approaches include mathematical notation (section 2.1), abstract data types (section 2.2.2), data binding languages (section 3.5.1), generalized markup languages (section 3.6), and modeling languages (section 3.8). In one of the rare works on general language-independence in data, Meek (1995) lists some lessons learned from language independent standardization, some of which apply to standardization in general and some of which to language-independence in particular.[5] Despite the usefulness of language-independent standards, these standards tend to get ignored. For instance ISO 11404 (2007) is referenced by XML Schema datatypes (section IV), but non-XML languages prefer to refer to the latter instead of ISO 11404. Furthermore each language-independent standard, while abstracting from other languages, defines its own language, adding just another layer of abstraction.

III. Conformance of data standards

Given a standard with its specification still there is no guarantee that data will be structured the way it was intended. Standards in practice are interpreted, ignored, and misused in many ways. Unlike propositions, standards can not be true or false, but only valid or invalid, compared to some practice. The relation between practice, actually given as digital documents for the domain of this thesis, and standards is mostly expressed the other way round: we say that some data *conforms* to a standard if the standard contains a valid data description.[6] The importance to "get the conformity rules right" is stressed as critical to every standard by Meek (1995). In particular all requirements must be testable, and implementation-dependent features or extensions should be avoided. Conformance tests (or *validation* tests) which must exactly match the specifications, are found in three forms:

- A *validator* checks whether a particular documents conforms to a selected standard. Validators test the creation of data but they can also be used as membership function to fully define a standard in terms of set theory. In contrast to general implementations, a validator must be strict even on minor errors. For instance a web browser will accept broken HTML code, but a validator such as the W3C Markup Validation service[7] will show all detectable violations of the HTML standard. Most data is created neither with specifications nor with exact validators but with implementations. These implementations may actually

---

[5] The general rules are "don't be too ambitious", "don't let perfection be the enemy of the 'good enough'", "define your target audience", "take related standards into account" and "get conformity rules right". The specific rules are "make yourself language-independent, and recruit others like you", "identify what kind of feature or facility you are trying to define", "get the level of abstraction right" (see section 2.2.2 and 4.2.5), "avoid any representational aspects or assumptions", "promote your standard continually", "decide early on what to do about bindings", and again "get conformity rules right".

[6] One must also take care not to confuse statements of conformance and statements of usefulness: practice and standards can be valid but lunatic, when compared to some goal with common sense.

[7] Available at http://validator.w3.org/.

define a de-facto standard as they unintentionally act as validators. General validators are not specific to a single standard but to a set of languages where the particular language is chosen by a schema (section 3.7). For instance an XML validator checks whether a given XML document matches a given XML schema.

- A *test suite* is a collections of automatic tests to show that a given implementation covers all aspects of a standard. For instance the Web Standard Project's Acid Tests[8] provide complex web pages that make use of many features of HTML, CSS, and related standards. To pass the test, a browser must precisely render the page as required. Tests suits can only test the consumption of data, and for complex languages they only cover the most important aspects. Parts of a test suite can also be used as examples or prototypes of a specification.

- By *verification* the conformance of an implementation with a standard is broken. In its strict sense the prove is exact only with respect to a mathematical model. This process is very laborious and mainly limited to hardware design and critical applications. In a broader sense verification can be done by simply showing that each detail is correct. This strict process is also error-prone. For instance the conformance of a conceptual model to an universe of discourse can only be validated by human beings.

When someone refers to a standard or some rule in data description, one must carefully look at the type (technical, formal, informal and substantive, communication, control), its specification, and how conformance is actually checked. The pure existence of a standard and the simple act of referring to it does not ensure its perfect application. Sometimes one does not even require full conformance: a lot of data in practice only pretends to conform to some standard, for instance HTML, XML, or MARC. On a closer look the data only happens to be parseable in usual application, which do not require full conformance. For instance people can still make use of a document that is 'almost' XML but not well-formed, as specified in the XML specification. Machines and pedants would insist to reject this digital documents while other consumers prefer to fix things after having a closer look at the actual data instances.

Strength: Standards and rules specify the consistent creation and consumption of data. They show which parts of a document are possible and relevant, and how to make use of data.

Weakness: The specific type of a standard and its specification are not as clear as they seem. Standards can only be as exact as their conformance can be tested.

Patterns: The patterns most likely found together with this paradigm include the *schema* pattern and the *derivation* pattern.

---

[8] Available at http://www.acidtests.org/.

4.2.3. Collections, types, and sameness

I love mankind... it's people I can't stand!!
— Linus (in a comic strip by Charles M. Schulz)

Collections, types, and sameness share a principle of grouping, which can be detected in all methods of data structuring. This section will first give examples from chapter 3 and then analyze each of the three paradigm expressions, and how they all depend on questions of identity.

I. Examples

Character encodings classify characters by properties like letter case, character type, and writing system. Different kinds of equivalence and normalization are used to find out when two character sequences are same (section 3.1.1). Identifier systems (section 3.2.3) group objects by giving them same identifiers or by partitioning them in namespaces. File systems (section 3.3) were specifically developed to organize collections of data. Above single files, collections are found in directories, file types or other properties of files. The same applies to databases which are collections of records (section 3.4). Records may further be divided into record types and record fields can be typed, to only hold specific groups of values. Data structuring languages (section 3.5) are essentially build of basic data types and collection types such as records, lists, and tables. Usually these data types are disjoint. Types can also be non-exclusive, for instance RDF's rdf:type property. Schema languages (section 3.7) and type systems of programming languages can be used to define new types by refining existing ones. Schema rules and constraints can also allow to check whether an object belongs to a specific type. The support of specific collection types in conceptual modeling languages is rather poor (T. Halpin and Morgan 2008, ch. 10.4) but they define collections just by appointing them. For instance one can define an entity type 'publication' and virtually create a collection of things that are publications. This way, however, it is also possible to create virtual collections like 'Veeblefetzer' and 'Potrzebie' without indication which things actually belong to these collections.

II. Three appearances of grouping

The grouping paradigm of this section can be detected in three appearances. *Collections* are the most visible appearance of grouping. Independent from the internal structure of a collection (ordered sequence, unordered set, structured graph...) there is the idea of a set of things grouped together. To define this set, one can either list its members one by one, or one can provide a membership function and a universal set to choose from, as described in section 2.1.2. Unfortunately this implies all problems of set theory such as the identification of 'same' elements and non-paradoxical universal sets. As each set defines a property, each collection can also be seen as type and vice versa.

The concept of *types* involves several aspects. Types can:

- combine things that 'belong together' (for instance namespaces)

- classify things according to 'what they are' (for instance types in RDF)

- express 'how things are' by characteristic rules and constraints (for instance derived data types)

- divide things that 'are distinct' (for instance entity types)

These aspects of types can be used independently or combined. Systems of types are studied in library and information science with theory and practice of classification. It is known that classification is no neutral act, but artificial and inherently discriminating because of hidden social assumptions (Bowker and Star 1999). Moreover, classifications must regularly be revised to fit applications. Types neither need to be disjoint and hierarchical but they can be based on multiple facets (faceted classification). Objects of same type do not necessarily share properties and membership of particular objects can be more central than other objects of same type (Lakoff 1987). The connection between types and properties exists in both directions: an object's type may define its properties, and the type of an object may be inferred from how the object is used. In programming the latter is known as *type inference*, if performed at compile-time, or *duck typing*, if performed at run-time.[9]

The concept of *sameness* is related to collections and types in view of the fact that all same objects belong to one type or collection, and every collection or type defines a criterion of sameness. In general one can distinguish identity and equivalence as two kinds of sameness where only the second is directly related to collections and types. For instance all members of the collection of cars of the same type are equivalent, but they are not identical. More precise, the cars of same type are equivalent only by some specific criteria — which is the type. Digital objects can be equivalent by different criteria in the same way, but they can also be identical. Apart from physical storage and technical access, which is irrelevant for this thesis, it makes no sense to distinguish two copies of the same document. Digital data processing relies on the principle that copies of data are indistinguishable. The same document can be stored as file, as record in a database or wrapped in another file format. Different serializations of the same data object are another example. For this reason, the recursive zip file mentioned on page 77 (Cox 2010) contains itself, but *within another system*. The embedding system, however, must be ignored to compare digital documents — otherwise equal documents would not be possible at all. We conclude that equivalence in data results in identity if compared within some system. Identity and equivalence can be aligned by normalization to canonical

---

[9] The term duck typing refers to the phrase "when I see a bird that walks like a duck and swims like a duck and quacks like a duck, I call it a duck", attributed to James Whitcomb Riley. Duck typing in programming does not necessarily include inference of a predefined type like 'duck', but it only ensures the availability of a given set of characteristics.

paradigm	membership function	relationship
collection	part-of	meronomy
type	is-a, instance-of, kind-of	hyponomy
sameness	is, stands-for	identity, metonomy, synecdoche

Table 4.2.: Collections, types, and sameness

representations, which eventually creates a bijection between layers of abstraction. For more complex documents, however, normalization is questioned (A. H. Renear and Dubin 2003) without a clear definition of sameness, and normalization can be hard to compute (for instance see the graph isomorphism problem at page 106).

III. Groupings and identity

In summary, the three paradigm expressions collections, types, and sameness provide different views to the problem of grouping and identity. Table 4.2 lists the expressions, each with its grouping membership function and its underlying relationship. The distinction between meronomy (collection) and hyponomy (type) depends on how one defines groups and members. For instance one can say that an author *is a* creator of a work; but one could also say that an author is *part of* the process of creation of a work, or *member of* the group of all creators. To give another example, documents can be *part of* a library which then *is a* collection of these documents, while each document *is a* collected document only by being part of the library. Identity and synecdoche[10] refer to collections and types in a more subtle way: for instance a library as collection of documents exactly *is* or it *stands-for* its members. Another example is the identity of a single document, based on its parts, as analyzed by A. H. Renear and Dubin (2003). If identity is "that property of an object which distinguishes it from all other objects" (Khoshafian and Copeland 1986), one can construct a membership function based on this property. In programming and databases there are three ways to represent identity (ibid):

- *identity by system* refers to ignorable embedding. For instance files in file system may internally be identified by an inode number.

- *identity by name* is assigned to data, for instance a file name. This kind of identity is best visible in ad-hoc collections of objects.

- *identity by value* is defined by the internal structure of data, for instance the content of a file. It depends on the level of description (see paradigm 4.2.5) what 'content' refers to.

---

[10] *Synecdoche*, or more general *metonomy*, is a figure of speech in which a term is used for instance for a larger whole (pars pro toto), or for the general type it refers to. For instance a 'title' can refer to a document, a work, or its physical copy, although it is a labeling property.

Eventually the identity problem is unsolvable because of theoretical and practical limitations (W. Kent 2003). This also applies to collections and types (W. Kent 1978, ch. 6.3.1).[11] Nevertheless we can deal with domain-specific, partial solutions. We even have to, as soon as there are multiple objects. Still one should carefully look out for the specific limitations and dependencies of existing ideas of collections, types, and sameness, guided by the pattern implied by this paradigm.

Strength: collections, types, and sameness are inevitable to reduce the number of objects by grouping and to allow identification of objects across systems.

Weakness: connections between the paradigms are overlooked. All grouping depends on a domain specific definition of identity.

Patterns: The patterns most likely found together with this paradigm include the *container*, *normalization*, and *identifier*.

4.2.4. Entities and connections

The paradigm of entities and connections is so deeply rooted in most data structuring methods that we hardly question its basic assumptions. Both entities and connections exist in many forms and names — the former for instance as 'objects', 'records', 'files', 'items', or 'resources', and the latter as 'links', 'relationships', 'associations', 'pointers' etc. The idea of structuring and describing data by entities and connections is best visible in conceptual modeling and conceptual diagrams where entities are depicted by circles or rectangles and connections are depicted by lines between them (section 3.8 and 3.9). Some data structuring languages support links based on identifiers that refer to entities (URIs in RDF triples, symbolic links in file systems, foreign keys in databases etc.).[12] More implicit forms of links are attributes, properties, fields, or facets, which do not exist alone but only connected to some object (database record, XML element etc.) that they belong to. Finally, there are hierarchical connections, for instance in XML and file systems, and there are collections and types, which connect a container entity with its member entities. The connections may be more dominant or more hidden, but they always share a common idea of being attached to primary entities.

I. Thinking in graphs

The mathematical model of entities and connections is the graph, so this paradigm assumes that everything could be described in terms of graph theory. This is true in theory, as well as all data could be transmitted by pigeons (Waitzman 1990), and it seems to be true also in practice, where graphs seem to be the natural or the only way

---

[11] For instance the concept of a given type like "employee" does not determine one simple set: There are people who have been employees, or are eligible to become, or have applied to be, or have pretended to be, or have refused to be, and so on, together with various combinations of these sets.

[12] This also includes 'broken links' where no entity can be found for an identifier.

for data description. Once committed to this paradigm, you see graphs everywhere. This fallacy is more obvious if focused on specialized forms of graphs: for instance one tends to see trees everywhere, given tools and technologies such as hierarchical databases, file systems, and XML or given object oriented tools with inheritance, directed acyclic graph seem to fit very well. Even if one broadens its view to general hypergraphs with connections that can span more than two entities, there is the dichotomy between nodes/entities and edges/connections as two types of objects.[13] The dichotomy is not wrong per se, but it comes with two major problems: the choice which piece of data to express as entity and which as connection is rather arbitrary and it is difficult and ambiguous to map between entities and connections if needed.

II. Two problems illustrated

To illustrate the first problem, let us assume you want to store data about people and the year they were born. Example 32 gives several encoding forms in JSON (the principle could also be shown with other data structuring languages). In JSON connections are present as key-value pairs of objects. In the first form (line 1), there is a direct connection of birth between name and year entities. The second form (line 2) moves the birth connection into an entity, and connects this entity to the person. As shown in line 3 and 4 one can follow this procedure further and uses entities for the connection between birth and year and for the connection between year and year value. The choice between entity and connection here depends on which granularity you prefer. Line 5 shows a yet another encoding that groups name and birth in a common entity so there is no explicit connection between the two.

```
1  { "Hannah" : 1906, ... }
2  { "Hannah" : { "birth" : 1906 }, ... }
3  { "Hannah" : { "birth" : { "year" : 1906 } }, ... }
4  { "Hannah" : { "birth" : { "year" : { "AD" : 1906 } } } }
5  [ { "name" : "Hannah", "birth": 1906 }, ... ]
```

Example 32: Rather arbitrary choices between entity and connection

In practice a fixed partition between entities and connections is chosen to avoid confusion. Mapping between both forms is possible in practice, but poorly supported in methods of data structuring. Some technologies, such as reification in RDF and objectification in ORM allow combination and transformation, but these mechanisms are rarely used because of their technical and semantical complexity. For this reason it is difficult to view some matter of affairs as connection, once it has been chosen to be represented by an entity – and vice versa. The semantic difficulties to map between entities and connections are exemplified in example 33. The original model

---

[13] Hypergraphs are mostly represented by bipartite graphs and generalized hypergraphs have not been used for data structuring apart from works by Goertzel (2006).

(figure a) consists of two entity types, Person and Document, that are connected by the binary *n:m* relationship author of. The implicit uniqueness constraint that spans all relationships (every fact can only be given once) is drawn explicitly. For simplicity, some documents may exist without author and some people may exist without having authored a document. The relationship can be objectified as entity Authorship. Can you relate this new entity to Person and Document to fully replace the original author of relationship? First, an Authorship can only exist together with at least one Person and at least one Document, so each connection has a mandatory role constraint (figure b to e).The uniqueness constraint, however, can be transformed in several ways. The most obvious solution is to create two 1:*n* relationships, so both a person and a document can have multiple authorships. Each authorship belongs to exactly one person and one document (figure b). This still allows multiple authorships with the same person and the same document. An external uniqueness constraint can solve the error (figure c) but it is often forgotten in practice. Another solution is to use one 1:1 relationship between Authorship and Document and one *n·m* relationship between Authorship and Person, so each document has at most one authorship, but authorship can consist of a group of people. (figure d). Similarly one could interpret authorship as a 'lifework' of a person, so every Person has at most one Authorship that consists of a set of Document instances (figure e). There are even more possibilities if one makes Authorship an independent entity: one could move both mandatory role constraints to the connection between Authorship and Document to say that every document must be authored, but its authorship may have no person. The example shows that a simple relationship can be transformed to an entity, but multiple models and interpretations exist. The same problem arises on the logical and physical level of data description as shown by W. Kent (1988), who also summarized the motivation for this paradigm as following:

> [It is] difficult to partition a subject like 'information' into neat categories like 'categories', 'entities', and 'relationships'. Nevertheless, in both cases, it's much harder to deal with the subject if we don't attempt some such partitioning.   — W. Kent (1978, p. 15)

Strength: separation of independent, primary elements and dependent, secondary elements.

Weakness: there is no final separation between entities and connections, as both can be transformed into the other.

Patterns: The pattern most likely found together with this paradigm include the *dependence* pattern and the *graph* pattern.

4.2.5. Levels of abstraction

All problems in computer science can be solved by another level of indirection
...except for the problem of too many layers of indirection.
   — David Wheeler

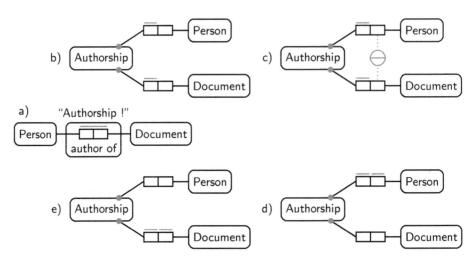

Example 33: Four possible transformations of a binary *n:m* connection

Levels or layers of abstraction are ubiquitous in computer systems. At least since Wheeler invented the subroutine, it is common practice to encapsulate functionality and use it by referencing on a higher level of description (Spinellis 2007). This principle is also omnipresent in stable documents as *data abstraction*. A simple example are character encodings: As shown in section 3.1 a single character can be references by many different sequences of bits or by other symbols. On a closer look (example 34), there can be up to six levels from a sequence of bits to a final Unicode character.

composed character	Å		
decomposed characters	A	°	
codepoints (hexadecimal)	41	30A	
UTF-8 (binary)	_1000001	___01100	__001010
bytes (binary)	01000001	11001100	10001010
bytes (hexadecimal)	41	CC	8A

Example 34: The letter Å with its encoding levels in Unicode

To give another example, one could create a general 'tree-store' that abstracts and integrates the hierarchical content of XML files and the hierarchical directory structures of file systems, as proposed by Wilde (2006) and Holupirek, Grün, and Scholl (2007). On a higher level one could then point to a data element by XPath like expressions without having to deal with details of neither file systems nor XML. The multitude and ubiquity of layers in data formats is often invisible by purpose: full awareness of each level at the same time would mostly result in confusion. In

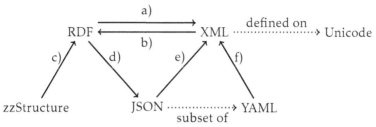

a) RDF/XML (Dave Beckett 2004)
b) RDF Schema for XML Infoset (Tobin 2001)
c) zzStructure in RDF (Gutteridge 2010)
d) RDF/JSON (K. Alexander 2008)
    JSON-LD (Sporny, Kellogg, and Lanthaler 2012)
e) JSONx (Muschett, Salz, and Schenker 2011)
f) YAML in XML (Ben-Kiki, Evans, and Ingerson 2006)

Figure 4.2.: Existing encoding mappings between several data structuring languages

fact, the main purpose of abstraction layers is to hide complexity and irrelevant details. Such abstractions not only hide technical aspects of structuring, but they also subsume concepts of description: a 'data element' in the tree-store example can be a file or an XML element on a lower level, but these concepts are irrelevant one a higher level. Another purpose of abstraction is the translation between different data languages. Depending on the application, abstraction as paradigm also occurs as encoding, wrapping (see section 3.3.3), granularity (C. M. Keet 2008b, 2011), or mapping.

Given a set of precise mapping rules, any formal language can be encoded in, or mapped to any other languages. To give some examples, figure 4.2 shows existing encodings between JSON, RDF, XML, and other data structuring languages. As the mapping graph in figure 4.2 contains circles, one could endlessly encode data in layers (RDF in RDF/XML in JSONx in XML Infoset in RDF ...) without essentially adding value — the existence of layers alone does not guarantee that each layer actually hides complexity and details. In fact, existing data can be compared with stratigraphic deposits in archaeology or geology (see section 6.2.1 for and extension of this comparison). An example is MARCXML, an encoding of MARC in XML keeps irrelevant punctuation and other artifacts from ISBD in MARC. In addition to full encodings that map every relevant aspect of one language in another, there are abstractions which only cover a subset of the original language. By this, a mapping can also be used as specification (see section 4.2.2).

Although each level of abstraction should fully hide the details of implementation on levels below, one sometimes need to take into account several levels, lacking a clean separation between each of them. An example is given by Thomale (2010) for MARC. The general reason why abstraction cannot fully hide levels is the dependency

179

level	domain
1) abstract	conceptual value space
2) computational	representable values and processes
a) linguistic/syntax	how values are expressed
b) operational/semantic	processes which values express
3) representational	value representation

Table 4.3.: Levels of abstraction in language-independent standardization

on context. As "abstraction is deciding which aspects of a problem to consider and which ones to ignore" (Koenig 1998) a specific abstraction only gives you one specific view to a problem. Different views may be required for different applications. An example of different views is given with the paradigms of documents and objects in section 4.2.1. A full separation of levels is also arguable from a semiotic point of view: when one piece of data in language A as sign refers to another piece of data in language B as object, the mode of reference is not necessarily arbitrary: as showed by Peirce, the sign can also resemble the object (iconic sign), or the sign can directly be connected to the object (indexical sign). Examples of iconic signs in data include grouping brackets and descriptive identifiers. Examples of indexical signs include pointers such as positions and hash codes (section 3.2.6). The iconic or indexical connection can also span multiple levels of abstractions.

Although the paradigm of abstraction is omnipresent, applications and encoding levels are often not known explicitly but concealed in the current use of standards. For instance the division of markup in procedural markup, that describes what to do with a given data object, and semantic markup, that describes what a given data object is (section 3.6.1) depends on the level of description one chooses. As Meek (1995) puts it in a nutshell "one language's syntax can be another's semantics"[14] and "most people will shift or mix levels without really noticing that they are there at all". This aspect of abstraction in levels has been identified by Eco (1979) as an unlimited semiosis. Meek, in particular, stresses the importance of clearly distinguishing three levels in language-independent modeling, which are listed in table 4.3. In addition to the levels of data types (section 2.2.2) the levels of data modeling (section 2.2.3) are most vital to this thesis.

A formal theory of abstraction within one method of description is provided by C. M. Keet (2007, 2008b, 2011) as 'granularity'. In Keets model of granularity, different abstraction hierarchies can exist as parallel trees ("perspectives") that each partition a specific subject domain (a point of view) according to specific properties. A simple example is the division of documents in smaller parts or the partition of result sets by faceted browsing. This theory or granularity has been applied to

---

[14] To be honest, this interpretation of Meek may be against his intention as he only tries to avoid the words 'syntax' and 'semantic'. The statement, however, gets an additional meaning if one considers the stacking of multiple languages in layers of abstraction. The term 'language' in Meek's paper mainly refers to programming languages but his results can also be applied to descriptive data languages.

conceptual data models (C. M. Keet 2007) and it can help to map multiple models that partly overlap on different levels of description.

Independent of the kind of abstraction, each abstraction helps to focus on particular properties, but it has a price: as expressed by Yang (2009) "every abstraction layer does not only adds a little over head to the CPU, but also to the poor human who has to read that code." Integration and readability can be improved by redundancy and by precise standards (see section 4.2.2). As standards can be fuzzy, violated, and misinterpreted, there can be confusion about which which level of description is actually used. For instance an RDF document can use predicates from the OWL ontology, but this does not guarantee that the full enforcement of owl-entailment with all of its aspects was actually intended. No abstraction can fully remove the burden of actually reading and interpreting digital documents.

Strength: levels help to separate relevant and irrelevant parts.

Weakness: levels often cannot clearly be separated and too many levels may more confuse then they simplify.

Patterns: The pattern most likely found together with this paradigm include the *encoding* pattern and the *embedding* pattern.

Chapter 5

Patterns in data structuring

> For they say the real is differentiated only by 'rhythm' and 'inter-contact' and 'turning';
> and of this rhythm is shape, inter-contact is order, and turning is position; for A differs
> from N in shape, AN from NA in order, M from W in position.
> — Aristotle· *Metaphysics*, Book I, part 4 (around 350 B.C.)

This chapter contains a language of fundamental patterns in data structuring (for pattern languages in general see section 2.6). Twenty fundamental patterns were identified based on analysis from chapter 3 and findings from chapter 4. The pattern language is introduced with its organization in section 5.1 before the actual patterns are listed in four groups section 5.2 to 5.5. Finally the language is evaluated by comparison with related collections in section 5.6.

5.1. Organization

In short, a pattern is a named description of "a problem which occurs over and over again in our environment" (C. Alexander, Ishikawa, and Silverstein 1977). The pattern guides to ways of solving the problem, independent from particular solutions. Each pattern from this pattern language of data structuring highlights a specific problem that occurs when data is actually organized. As mentioned before, problems of data structuring should not be confused with particular data structures as technical solutions. A pattern refers to particular methods of data structuring (see chapter 3), but it does not adhere to concrete implementations. Instead, each pattern shows general strategies of solutions with its benefits, consequences, and pitfalls.

Each of the patterns is structured similarly to the design patterns presented by Gamma et al. (1994), Cunningham (1995), and other pattern languages.[1] Each pattern consists of four essential elements that imply a set of uniform sections:

- The *name* is a short label for referencing and describing the pattern. A good name should be easy to recognize and communicate the pattern. Additional

---

[1] An informal collection of pattern templates can be found in WikiWikiWeb at `http://c2.com/cgi/wiki?PatternForms`. See also Meszaros and Doble (1997) for patterns in pattern languages.

well-known or helpful names of the pattern may be listed as **alias**. Note that a pattern name may have different meanings and connotations in other context, so it should be taken as technical term with its pattern language as controlled vocabulary.

- The *problem* describes when to apply the pattern. This description consists of the core **idea** with the pattern's rationale and intent, the **context** in which the pattern can be applied and which imposes constraints on solutions, and a **motivation** to illustrate the problem.

- The *solution* lists possible **implementations** as strategies to solve the problem. The solution can be illustrated by **examples** and **counter examples**. Note that there is rarely a single or best solution but each implementation has its strengths and weaknesses.

- The *consequences* are the results and trade-offs of applying the pattern. This includes possible **difficulties** and forces that must be taken into account when choosing a solution. Additional cross-references to **related patterns** include other patterns that describe similar problems or patterns that may coexist unnoticed. Among related patterns there can be **implied patterns** that appear together with a pattern, and **specialized patterns** that solve a more specific problem.

The pattern language is structured in four groups of patterns:

Basic patterns include the most fundamental strategies of describing and structuring data elements (section 5.2). These patterns are named *label*, *atomicity*, *size*, *optionality*, and *prohibition*.

Combining patterns connect multiple data elements to larger structures (section 5.3). These patterns are named *sequence*, *graph*, *container*, *dependence*, and *embedding*.

Relationing patterns relate data elements to each other to solve typical types of problems (section 5.4). These patterns are named *flag*, *derivation*, *encoding*, *identifier*, *normalization*, and *schema*.

Continuing patterns indicate that more data exists (section 5.5). These patterns are named *separator*, *etcetera*, *garbage*, and *void*.

A classification of all patterns is summarized in the last chapter in table 6.1 and appendix C includes a graph to depict connections between patterns.

5.2. Basic patterns

Basic patterns highlight the the most fundamental strategies of describing and structuring data elements. The patterns can be found anywhere at single data elements. The patterns *label* and *atomicity* take an element as such without further inspection. The patterns *size, optionality*, and *prohibition* also include the idea of content which a data element is build of and which can be shaped in a specific way for each of the patterns.

5.2.1. Label pattern

Alias

Name, type, nomenclature.

Idea

Give data elements a name.

Context

Any distinguishable data element.

Motivation

Distinguish the nature of data elements and tell them apart by proper names.

Implementations

A sequence of characters (string) that should have a well-known meaning for human readers. Any documentation (definitions, translations, examples etc.) helps to clarify the interpretation of a label.

Examples

- Domain names in DNS.
- File names in file systems.
- Field names in records and database schemas.
- Object keys in JSON and other data structuring languages.
- Tag names in XML and related markup languages.
- Names of classes and properties in RDF ontologies (`rdfs:label`).
- Names of entity types and relationship types in conceptual models.
- Class names in object orientated modeling.
- URI references within the RDF model do not carry any semantics but they usually include labels for human readers.

Counter examples

Labels have no internal structure. For instance the character sequence "Dublin, Ohio", which refers to a city in the US, is not a pure label but it consists of two labels ("Dublin" and "Ohio"), one acting as qualifier for the other (*flag* pattern). Another counter example is a list of field names such as "address1, address2...", that together refer lists of repeatable objects. Each of these field names is not a label but it consists of a label ("address") and a *sequence* indicator. To test whether a data element is a label, think about whether replacing all of its occurrences with the same random value would make a difference.

Difficulties
Labels are textual signs primarily interpreted by human readers. The label refers to something outside of the domain of data so one cannot find out its referent by looking at the data only but one must analyze its usage in practice. Labels may be both synonymous (multiple labels with same referent) and homonymous (one label used with different referents in different contexts). Labels are often created ad-hoc just because an identifier is needed. A well-considered choice of a label can improve readability of data a lot.

Related patterns
- A label is similar to an *identifier* and often both coincide. An identifier, however, always refers to a specific data element while the referent of a label can be more fuzzy.
- Data elements in an *encoding* also refer to something but their mapping could be changed without making any difference.
- If labels are mutually exclusive, they can also act as *flag*.
- The actual value of a label is irrelevant to most data processing activities (one could replace all of its occurrences with a hash value), so a label may also be *garbage*.

5.2.2. Atomicity pattern

Alias
Black box, brick, encapsulation.

Idea
Take some data as one element without having to deal with its internal structure.

Context
Any data element.

Motivation
Reduce complexity to the smallest unit possible.

Implementations
- If the *size* of a data element is known, one can skip over its content.
- Define an *encoding* to abstract from the actual content of a data element.
- Indicate borders of the element with an *embedding*.

Examples

- In file systems the file is atomic: it's content is one arbitrary piece of data.
- In conceptual modeling the entity is atomic.
- Most data description languages have the notion of "basic" data types.
- An API encapsulates internals of a data element.
- First normal form (1NF) in relational databases.
- The only totally atomic data element is the bit.

Counter examples

A character string delimited by double quotes is not fully atomic. The string must either disallow quotes as content or allow escape sequences (*prohibition*) that force interpretation of the string's internal structure.

Difficulties

- Internals of data elements are rarely hidden in total. As soon as details of an element such as its member elements (see *container*) can be inspected, the element is not fully atomic anymore.
- One cannot refer to parts of an atomic element.
- Although a non-descriptive *identifier* should be atomic, it is common practice to inspect its structure. For instance the actual character string of an URI Reference has no meaning in the RDF model, but it is common to group and interpret these strings for instances based on namespaces.
- Atomicity is broken if levels of abstraction are not fully separated.
- One should be able to replace the content of an atomic element with random data, for instance "XXXXX". In practice the content is often limited by *prohibition*, so the element is not fully atomic.

Related patterns

- A *container* is an alternative strategy to wrap data. Its internal structure is typically visible.
- To achieve atomicity, and as alternative to atomicity, *encoding* can be used.
- If the hidden content of an atomic element does not matter anyway, the element can also be *garbage*.
- Atomic elements may still have properties which can be connected to the atomic elements via *dependence*.

Implied patterns

It must be known where an atomic data element starts and where it ends without having to look into its content, so atomic data elements have a known *size*.

5.2.3. Size pattern

Alias

Number, length, count.

Idea

Quantity before quality.

Context

A data element with some length or another numeric property.

Motivation

Data elements with known size can be arranged and compared independent from their actual content. Size is relevant also because processing and storing data is always limited by size.

Implementations

- Use a special element as end-marker such as the null byte for null-terminated strings (*prohibition*).
- Explicitly encode size value and content in an *embedding*.
- Use fixed size elements only.

Examples

- The size of a byte is 8 bit.
- All finite data types have limited size.
- Numeric data types represent a size.
- UTF-8 is a variable width encoding that expresses the number of bytes of a character with the number of 1 bits in the first byte.
- The possible number of occurrences of a data element can be expressed in *schema* languages, for instance with `:n-m` (BNF), `minOccurs/maxOccurrs` (XSD), and `maxCardinality/minCardinality` (OWL).

Difficulties

- The prohibited end-marker may be allowed to be escaped. For instance the ending double quote in a string may be encoded as `\"`. Such *encoding* requires to parse the full content, contradicting the motivation of the size pattern.
- The conceptual difference between number (multiple elements) and size (one element) is not clear in all data.
- Counting requires to detect boundaries between elements (see *sequence* and *separator* patterns).

Related patterns

- Sizes can be constrained by a *schema*.
- The number of elements in a *container* is a size.
- The size pattern includes the idea of (natural) numbers. Ordinal numbers in contrast are covered by the *sequence* pattern.

Specialized patterns
Knowing the exact size of an element allows to skip its internal structure (*atomicity*).

5.2.4. Optionality pattern

Alias
Possibility, required, mandatory.

Idea
An element may be present but it can also be absent.

Context
A data element as part of a *schema* or *embedding*.

Motivation
Express constraints and possibilities and allow for flexibility.

Implementations
Either optional or mandatory elements must be marked by a special *flag*.

Examples

- Optional parts in regular expressions are indicated by a question mark or with an asterisk.
- Mandatory roles in ORM are marked by a dot.
- Requirement keywords defined in RFC 2119 (MUST, MUST NOT, SHOULD, SHOULD NOT, MAY).
- Elements in regular grammars are mandatory by default. In other systems, such as RDF Schemas, elements are optional by default.
- The end-tag matching to a start-tag in XML is mandatory. The same applies to closing brackets in JSON and other nested structures.
- With a fixed *size* a specific number of elements is mandatory.
- Annotations and qualifiers as optional additional elements (*flag*).

Counter examples

- Default values, for instance default XML namespaces, make optional elements impossible because a default value cannot be omitted.

Difficulties

- Optionality adds deontic logic to the realm of data, with all of its difficulties: constraints on mandatory or optional data elements are not true or false but they can only be fulfilled or violated. Formalization of deontic rules may also lead to unexpected logic results.

- Different levels of obligation may exist: in practice some elements are more optional or more mandatory than others.

- Optional elements can be made mandatory and mandatory elements can be made optional by introducing special *garbage* elements, such as /, n/a, -, 0 etc. Such null values are also created ad-hoc to trick mandatory constraints. For instance 12345 in a number field may indicate that the actual number was not available.

- In a *schema* it is common to either explicitly mark only mandatory only optional, assuming the other case as default. One needs to know which is the default in which context.

Related patterns

- If optional parts are irrelevant, they can also be *garbage*.

- An absent element can still be data as *void* element.

- Instead of or in addition to being mandatory, elements can also be derivable from other elements (*derivation*).

- *prohibition* can be used in a *schema* to express that specific elements must not be present.

Implied patterns

Every optionality is either part of a *schema* or it constitutes a virtual schema consisting of this single optionality.

5.2.5. Prohibition pattern

Alias

Forbidden element, exception.

Idea

Exclude specific elements.

Context

A data element with *embedding* in another element.

Motivation

Define what is *not* allowed instead of listing all possibilities.

Implementations
- Explicitly list all disallowed elements (creating a *container*).
- Refer to a *schema* that tells which elements to avoid.
- Use an *encoding* that does not include prohibited elements.

Examples
- File systems disallow specific characters in file names, such as quotes, brackets, dot, colon, bar, asterisk, and question mark.
- A null-terminated character string must not contain null-bytes.
- Unicode and languages build on top, such as XML and RDF, disallow specific character code points.
- A *separator* element cannot occur as normal content.
- With Closed World Assumption everything is disallowed unless defined as allowed. With Open World Assumption one needs to explicitly state disallowed elements.
- Formal grammars extended by difference operator or negation in boolean grammars allow to express arbitrary forbidden elements in a *schema*.
- In mandatory fields (*optionality*) empty elements are prohibited.
- Specific *graph* types disallow some kinds of vertices, such as loops and circles.

Difficulties
- Prohibitions as "exceptions from a rule" are easy to grasp for human beings but they are more difficult to detect and compute algorithmically. Boolean grammars which support formal expression of exceptions via a negation operator are still more research topic rather than a practical tool for data description.
- Exceptions can have their own exceptions (the world *is* complex).
- Some prohibitions are not stated explicitly but implied by external constraints (*derivation*). For instance numbers in JSON can have arbitrary precision but in practice they are limited to standard floating point and integer representations.

Related patterns
- If the prohibition depends on existence of another element, it is rather an instance of the *flag* pattern.
- *optionality* and mandatory constraints can be used in a *schema* to express whether an element must be present.

Implied patterns
Every prohibition is either part of a *schema* or it constitutes a virtual *schema* consisting of this single prohibition.

5.3. Combining patterns

The primarily purpose of combining patterns is to connect multiple data elements to larger structures. This combination can be done by several methods. Combining patterns include *sequence* and *graph* which structure multiple elements on the same level, and *container*, *dependence*, and *embedding* which include an idea of subsuming elements. As shown in figure 5.1, combining patterns are hierarchically connected to each other by general implications and by the context they occur in (both connections shown by arrows).

The most fundamental and most abstract patterns are *embedding* and *dependence*. More visible data combinations can be found as general collections (*container*), such as sets of files and records, and in form of ordered data (*sequence*) and graph structures (*graph*). Together with these combining patterns one often finds two basic patterns and two continuing patterns, *size* and *atomicity*, which reflect a number of (possibly combined) elements and the indivisible items to be connected, respectively. The continuing patterns *separator* and *etcetera* are needed to indicate borders and connections between elements and to indicate that a combination is incomplete.

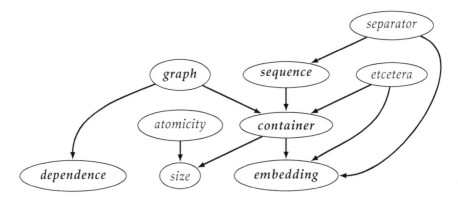

Figure 5.1.: Connections between patterns (combining patterns in bold)

5.3.1. Sequence pattern

Alias
Array, vector, table, list, order.

Idea
Strictly order multiple elements, one after another.

Context
A *container* of multiple elements.

Motivation
Define order and positions among data elements.

Implementations

- If member elements have a known *size*, they can directly be concatenated. If elements further have the same size, their position can directly be used as *identifier*.

- The *separator* pattern can be used to separate each element from its successor element. To distinguish member elements and separators, this implies the *prohibition* pattern. If separators are allowed to occur directly after each other, this can also imply the *void* pattern.

- One can link an element to its successor with an *identifier*. To avoid link structures that result in arbitrary *graph* patterns, additional constraints must be applied.

- Objects can be sorted implicitly by some specific property of each element.

Examples

- A string of ASCII characters.

- A sequence of lines.

- A sequence with separator: 'Kernighan and Ritchie' with separator 'and'.

- A sequence of linked steps: *extract → transform, transform → load*.

- Sequences with multiple dimensions are known as arrays, vectors, tables, and matrices.

Counter examples
Any unordered collection is no sequence. For instance files in a file system and records in a database table have no inherent order.

Difficulties

- Empty sequences (*void* pattern) and sequences of one single element are difficult to spot, like in other *container* patterns.

– Sequences are a natural method to model one-dimensional phenomena, for instance sequences of events in time. As digital storage is structured as sequence of bits, sequences seem to be the natural form of data. Other expressions such as formal diagrams and visual programming languages are often not considered as data also because they are not ordered.

Related patterns

– In the end most data is given as sequence of bits, so many implementations of other patterns use sequences on a lower level.

– The position within a sequence is often used as *identifier*.

– Sequences can be implied by order of some connected property (*derivation*).

– The sequence pattern includes the idea of ordinal numbers. Other kinds of numbers depend on the *size* pattern.

Implied patterns

Without context, sequences are difficult to distinguish from other *container* patterns.

5.3.2. Graph pattern

Idea

Nodes and vertices.

Context

A set of multiple elements and connections between them.

Motivation

Express connected data elements.

Implementations

– *flag* possible nodes (adjacency matrix).

– Store sets of vertices for each node (*container*).

– Trees can be implemented by hierarchic *embedding*.

Examples

– Schemas and conceptual models with entities connected by relations.

– Conceptual diagrams with boxes connected by lines.

– Connected tables in relational databases.

– Directory trees in file systems.

– RDF graphs.

– Specific graph types such as trees.

Difficulties

- For most graphs there is no simple *normalization*. The graph canonization or isomorphism problem is computationally hard because elements in a graph have no natural order. This contrasts with *sequence* as basic method to express data.

- Most practical graphs are more than simple structures build of nodes and vertices. Specialized types and properties of graphs exist, such as directed graphs, multigraphs, hypergraphs, labeled graphs, etc. For instance diagrams likely evolve to generalized hypergraphs with vertices that connect more than two nodes and even other vertices. Additional levels of *encoding* may be necessary to get the common form of a graph with simple nodes and vertices.

Related patterns

Specific graph types such as trees, grids, and lists often indicate alternative patterns such as hierarchies (*embedding*) and order (*sequence*). Bijective and injective graphs may better express *encoding*, *normalization* or *dependence*.

Implied patterns

- Vertices in a graph are secondary elements to nodes (*dependence*).

- The set of all nodes and/or vertices can be used as *container*.

5.3.3. Container pattern

Alias

Collection.

Idea

Combine a number of elements to a larger structure.

Context

A set of multiple data elements.

Motivation

Combine multiple independent elements on the same level to refer to them as a joint group.

Implementations

- Explicitly list all member elements which belong to the container.

- Specify a method to check whether an element belongs to the container.

Examples

- A directory of files in a file system.

- An archive containing a set of files.
- A set of records in a database.
- A repeatable entity or relationship in a schema. In fact the concept of repeatability is an instance of the container pattern.
- An entity type in a schema is the set of all of its instances.

Counter examples
A single record with its properties does not constitute a container because properties depend on the record instead of being independent.

Difficulties
- A container may hold a single member element only, making the collection difficult to distinguish from the element as such.
- A container may be empty, making it difficult to list member elements.

Related patterns
- Explicitly listing member elements requires a *sequence*.
- A membership function is a form of *derivation*.
- Empty containers often involve an implicit element (*void*).
- Collections are used to refer to elements (or to a type of elements) with a human readable *label*.
- Each collection defines the property of "belonging to the collection". An alternative pattern to group by same properties is *normalization*.
- Collections may be abbreviated (*etcetera* pattern).
- Containers are also used to wrap or abstract from sets of data. This goal can better be achieved by *atomicity*.

Implied patterns
- A container is a special kind of *embedding* with member elements embedded into the collection as host element.
- Unless abbreviated, containers have a specific number of member elements which implies the *size* pattern.

Specialized patterns
A *sequence* and a *graph* typically consist of collections of elements.

5.3.4. Dependence pattern

Alias
Secondary element.

Idea
A secondary data element is attached to a primary element.

Context
Two data elements, one more prominent than the other.

Motivation
Structure data by importance and connect elements by affiliation.

Implementations

- The elements are ordered in a *sequence*.
- The primary element acts as *flag* to the secondary element.
- A descriptive *separator* connects the elements.

Examples

- Relations in entity-relationship models are secondary to entities.
- Attributes, properties, and annotations attached to data objects.
- Pointer types are secondary to the elements they point to (unless the pointer is a descriptive *identifier*).
- Directed connections, for instance subclass relationships.
- Attributes of attributes (dependent elements can be stacked).
- Members of a *container*.

Difficulties

- The choice between primary and secondary elements can be rather arbitrary (a connection could also be expressed as entity and some vice versa). For instance members of a *container* are secondary but collections only exist based on their member elements.
- Once fixed, it is difficult to switch primary and secondary.
- The primary element often modifies interpretation of the second (*flag*).
- It is not always clear whether a data element is an integral part of an element or an additional annotation. For instance language tags in RDF look secondary but they are an essential property of literals.

Related patterns

- If multiple secondary elements can exist without a primary element, they are rather structured in a *container*.

- A "connection" between two elements may be a dependence but it could also be a form of *embedding* or *flag*.
- *derivation* looks similar to dependence and both may coincide but neither or both imply the other. Derived elements may also exist independent from the elements that they can be derived from.

Specialized patterns
Sets of dependencies with common elements can form *graph* structures.

5.3.5. Embedding pattern

Alias
Frame.

Idea
Put data elements as part into another element.

Context
At least two data elements, one of them a host or frame, in which the other elements are embedded.

Motivation
Build data hierarchies.

Implementations

- A frame of *separator* elements to put embeddings in between.
- The structure of an embedding can be expressed by a *schema* with placeholders, such as grouped expressions in BNF or non-terminal symbols in other formal grammars.

Examples

- An XML element with embedded child elements.
- The structure "surname, given" with surname and given name embedded into a name element.
- A qualified expression, such as "Marx, Karl, 1818-1883" from the Library of Congress name authority file with qualifier "1818-1883".
- Rules in a formal grammar with non-terminal symbols.
- All kinds of templates and forms that data is put into.
- A namespace with prefix (to specify the context) and embedded local identifier.
- Tree structures and part-whole relationships.

Difficulties

- A clean hierarchy is sign of oversimplification. In practice one has to deal with cross-connections, parallel and overlapping hierarchies (e.g. "({) }").
- Once a template has been filled with values, it becomes invisible. One must know the embedding rules to rediscover embedded elements, otherwise embedding frame and content easily get mixed up.
- Embeddings are part of other embedding, forming a long chain of levels. This chain should contain no circles, but self-referential embeddings may exist both in the conceptual realm and in the data realm (for instance a document that refers to itself or a zip file that contains a copy of itself).

Related patterns

- A hierarchical structure could also be a constrained *graph* instead.
- Hierarchic nesting is also found in *encoding*. While encodings stress the relations between signifier and signified, the purpose of an embedding is more to give context. The relation between encodings and embeddings is similar to the semiotic relation between langue and parole.
- Embedded elements may be mandatory or optional (*optionality*), they may be constrained by *prohibition* and they may be abbreviated (*etcetera*). If an embedding is primarily used to express such constraints, it is likely a *schema*.
- Embedded elements may be secondary to the frame they are embedded in (*dependence*).

Specialized patterns

A *container* embeds multiple member elements.

5.4. Relationing patterns

The following data patterns primarily relate elements to each other. In contrast to combining patterns (section 5.3), which primarily group data to larger structures, the connections established by relationing patterns are more between data elements which serve different purposes. Each pattern solves a general problem in data structuring and description, for instance complexity (solved by *encoding*) and redundancy (solved by *normalization* and *derivation*). Figure 5.2 groups relationing patterns by connections of implication or context in three levels: the most fundamental patterns include *identifier* and *derivation*. Based on these patterns one can find instances of *encoding* and *flag*, among other structures. Finally instances of *normalization* and *schema* are based on patterns of the second level. Figure 5.2 includes more patterns connected to relational patterns by informal implication and context. A full diagram of connections is given in appendix C.

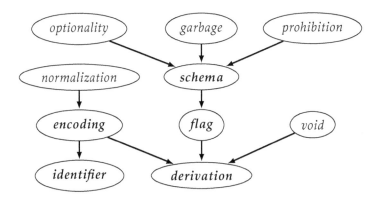

Figure 5.2.: Connections between patterns (relationing patterns in bold)

5.4.1. Flag pattern

Alias
Choice, exclusion.

Idea
The interpretation of a data element is controlled by another element.

Context
At least two data elements, one acting as switch, the other as target.

Motivation
Flags allow to easily add or enrich interpretations and to resolve ambiguity.

Implementations

– One value from a list of possible values (*encoding*).

– A default value (*void*) which can be overridden.

– Markup to turn flags on and off, for instance bold.

– An *identifier* in a key-value record structure.

– An *embedding* that shows which elements are switches and which elements are targets.

Examples

– The bit as basic unit of all digital data is a choice between two possible values. It can be encoded by 0 and 1, by a given value and absence as default.

– Boolean and enumerated data types with type as switch and instance variable as target.

– An exclusive-or constraint in a schema to enforce choice of one possibility.

– A qualified value such as "Dublin, Ohio".

– The statement "license: CC-BY-SA" in contrast to "CC-BY-SA" only.

– Annotations that modify interpretation, such as uncertainty and temporal flags.

– General rules how to read a data element (*schema*).

– A namespace is a flag that gives context to local identifiers.

Difficulties

– Possible values of the switch must be clear. If the first element is ambiguous, interpretation of the target element will also be.

– Default values are not always known or different values are assumed.

– Some flags don't have an independent interpretation, for instance the value "miscellaneous" in a classification.

- In practice flags are created or extended ad-hoc, for instance as additional annotation or as additional switch value to add more interpretations.
- A flag may switch more then one element and an element may be influenced by a combination of flags. It should be made clear, what elements a flag refers to,
- Some flags allow nesting (for instance a qualifier of a qualifier), others do not make a difference when nested (... is simply bold).

Related patterns

- Most flags are based on a *dependence* between switch and target element.
- Instead of exclusion one could also disallow specific combinations of elements *prohibition*.
- A *separator* such as ':' can simultaneously indicate a flag.
- The target data element may not be usable without the flag. In this case, a third element is derived from flag and target (*derivation*).
- If the switch consists of conditions which must be met to make use of the target element, a *schema* is more appropriate.

Implied patterns
A flag is a form of *derivation* as the target's interpretation is implied by the switch.

Specialized patterns
A *schema* defines which choices and exclusions are possible for some data elements. Schemas can further act as flags by telling how to read data.

5.4.2. Derivation pattern

Alias
Implication, functional dependency.

Idea
An element is implied by and derived from other elements.

Context
Two data elements, one of them implied by the other.

Motivation

- Enforce integrity and conformance to some rules.
- Mark redundancy to better find relevant parts in data.
- Provide different views to the same information.

Implementations

- Apply a mathematical model with derivation rules as exact statements.
- Explicitly list derivations, for instance in tables of if-then rules.

Examples

- Given a date of birth and the current date, an age is implied.
- As soon as two elements are related to a third, there is an implicit relation between the two (for instance co-citation for two works that cite a common third).
- RDF-entailment regimes and inference rules add new triples to RDF graphs. These new elements can be expressed or used as implicit, virtual values (*void*).
- The concept of derived types and inheritance is based on derivation: properties of a subclass are derived from another class.
- Hash codes can be calculated from all digital documents.

  An empty string is not given as content but implied by its surroundings.
- The length of a non-empty string can be derived from its content.
- If elements are pairwise comparable, a partial order is implied among them. If the elements are further distinct, a *sequence* is automatically implied.
- A *sequence* implies a position for each element.
- End tags in XML are redundant: <a>...</ can automatically be completed with a>.
- A postal code can be derived from other parts of an address.
- All forms of redundancy originate from possible derivations. If two data elements are redundant then either one of them can be derived from the other or both can be derived from a common third element.

Difficulties

- Data in practice contains errors and inconsistencies. Deriving from these errors can extend negligible anomalies.
- Derivation is not necessarily unique (injective) or revertible (for instance a hash code).
- Chaining inferences can lead to fallacies. For instance each book series could belong to exactly one publisher and each book to exactly one series, so a book implies its series and a series implies a publisher. Both rules do not forbid the inclusion of a book from one publisher as special issue in a series of another, making a chained inference from book to publisher invalid.
- Co-occurrences and correlations look similar to functional dependencies although they generally aren't.
- General implication rules only cover deductive reasoning.

- The existence of an implication does not necessarily tell how data can actually be derived. If derivation rules act like a black box, it is difficult to make use of them.
- There is a continuum between data extraction (infer what can be derived) and data enrichment (extend data with other data) once one realizes that derivation rules have (and/or are expressed in) their own data.

Related patterns

- A derived element may also be dependent to its switch (*dependence*).
- Elements that can be derived do not need to be expressed (*optionality*).

Specialized patterns

- An *encoding* is a special form of derivation that includes a set of implication rules, one for each possible value.
- If an element is not given directly (*void* pattern) it must be implied instead.

5.4.3. Encoding pattern

Alias
Abstraction.

Idea
Data that stands for something else.

Context
Any data element.

Motivation
Hide complexity and irrelevant details.

Implementations
One must define a mapping between each of the elements to be encoded and their particular encoding forms. The definition can make use of a *schema*.

Examples

- Unicode defines which characters exist and how to express them.
- The bit sequence 111000101010000010100001 in bytes encodes the sequence E2 A0 A1 in UTF-8 encodes the Codepoint U+2821 in Unicode 3.0 encodes the character BRAILLE PATTERN DOTS-16 in Swedish Braille encodes the character Á.
- Markup languages encode characteristics of text elements, for instance ..., or **...** for bold.

- MARCXML encodes MARC21 in XML.
- APIs abstract from internal data expressions (for instance SQL) to public, encoded form (for instance in JSON or XML).
- Virtual file systems abstract from different file system access methods.
- Encoding allows mapping between entities and connections and between objects and documents by reification, objectification, and stringification.
- Different serialization forms of RDF define encodings of RDF graphs.
- When a specification of some data format talks about a relation between syntax and semantic, it usually refers to an encoding.

Difficulties

- An encodings is an arbitrary result of social convention: one could modify it (for instance replace angle brackets by square brackets in all specifications and instances of XML) but actual changes are difficult.
- Encodings can also add redundancy.
- The existence and use of an encoding does not ensure that complexity and details are actually hidden.
- Most encoded data elements are encodings by their part, leading to a chain of encodings (unlimited semiosis).
- Encodings are not always one-to-one or reversible at all.
- Encodings only translate from one form of data to another, but the selection of a particular encoding can also be relevant data.
- Any data structuring language can encode any other language by introducing additional rules or constraints, so the particular encoding system may not add any value.

Related patterns

- *atomicity* does also aim at reducing complexity.
- An encoding can also be used as specification (*schema*) and as *normalization*.
- *embedding* is an alternative to encoding if the relation between data elements more depends on its actual context.
- Encoding seems to bridge the semiotic gap between signifier (encoding form) and signified (encoded data element). The common view of encodings as 'semantic', however, hides the fact that encodings must be accompanied by the *label* pattern to make sense.

Implied patterns

- An encoding implies a set of *identifier* but the latter does not include the idea of expressing something at another level.

– Given a full encoding, the referent can automatically be determined (*derivation*).

Specialized patterns
normalization implies encoding.

5.4.4. Identifier pattern

Alias
Pointer.

Idea
An element is used to refer to another.

Context
An element as pointer and another element from a set of possible targets.

Motivation
Identifiers help establishing uniqueness and allow to refer to elements which not are directly available or impractical to express.

Implementations
Identifier systems defines which identifiers exist and what data elements they refer to.

Examples

– Keys or field names in key-value structures or records.

– Queries and requests expressed in data, for instance an XPath expression.

– Data elements originally created for identification, such as URIs and link anchors.

– Parts of an *encoding*, for instance the byte 0x41 that encodes the letter "A" in ASCII.

– Computable hash codes which directly transform the content of an element into an identifier.

– The identity which distinguishes a data element from any other data elements, can only be expressed by an identifier. Every metadata that uniquely refers to this single element is an identifier.

– A geocode, given as WGS 84 coordinate, can identify a place or an address.

Difficulties

– An identifier must only refer to one element. If it refers to multiple elements, it is not clear whether this is an error (for instance collisions of hash codes), or whether all referenced elements are equal, or whether the collection of all referenced elements is actually identified.

- Multiple identifiers may point to the same element, making it difficult to reverse the relation.

- The existence of an identifier does not tell the kind of relation it is used for (e.g. as representation or to indicate a type or membership).

- Identifiers may be meaningless (for instance inode numbers of files or memory addresses), it may be used as *label* or it may be a descriptive identifier with *embedding*.

- The practical requirements of an identifier (unambiguity, uniqueness, persistence, readability, scope, actionability) contradict each other.

Related patterns
An identifier may simultaneously act as *label* or it may have a structure with content that can further be analyzed (*embedding*). If positions are used as identifiers, there must be a *sequence* to refer to.

Specialized patterns
Every *encoding* is based on a set of identifiers.

5.4.5. Normalization pattern

Alias
Canonical form, equivalence, one-to-one.

Idea
Make equal data elements identical by choosing one preferred version, based on relevant distinctions only.

Context
A set of data elements, one of them selected as normalized.

Motivation

- Avoid ambiguity, redundancy and inconsistencies.

- Group multiple data elements with same characteristics.

Implementations

- Avoid *derivation* and *garbage* in the data to be normalized.

- Define normalization rules in a *schema*.

Examples

- Database normalization is recommended to avoid redundancy and inconsistencies.

- Unicode defines several normalization forms (NFD, NFC, NFKD, NFKC).

- XML Schema Datatypes have a canonical lexical representation to establish a one-to-one mapping between value space and literal representations. For instance the boolean value false can be represented as 0 and as `false` but the latter is the canonical, normalized form.
- Approximate data types use a finite (or denumerable infinite) number of distinct values to represent an infinite number of values. The approximation normalizes the infinite set by mapping multiple values to one.
- Whitespace normalization replaces multiple and different whitespace characters by one simple whitespace character.
- An ISBN can have multiple forms (with or without hyphen, or space, as ISBN-10 or ISBN-13 etc.).

Difficulties

- Normalization depends on uniquely identifiable entities but an *identifier* or *label* is often missing.
- Normalization concentrates on the relevant aspects of a data element. It requires to define what variants are considered equivalent and what makes a difference. All these properties, however, may depend on context.
- Normalizing *graph* structures can be very hard both computationally and practically.
- Ordered values (numbers, coordinates...) can be treated as equal if they have a low distance, but they cannot be normalized because distance is not a transitive function.
- Despite its theoretical importance, for instance in database theory, normalization in practice is often applied incompletely or not at all.

Related patterns

- Normalization groups data elements based on sameness of their characteristic properties. More general methods of grouping are examples of the *container* pattern.
- Every normalization defines an *identifier* (the reverse does not apply).
- Normalization may also be virtual, resulting in the *void* pattern. For instance in some file systems file names are case insensitive but case preserving, so the normalized file name is not given directly.

Implied patterns

Every normalization implies a form of *encoding*, as data elements can be encoded by the form they are normalized to. For instance XML documents are encoded by their document model, which gives a normalized form.

5.4.6. Schema pattern

Alias
Specification.

Idea
Specify restrictions and extensions.

Context
One data element (the schema) describes a set of other data elements.

Motivation
Express common structures with requirements and constraints to be applied consistently for creation and consumption of data.

Implementations

- The schema is expressed in a formal schema language.

  The schema is expressed in form of human-readable rules.

- The schema is implicitly given in form of examples.

- A validator or another software is implicitly used as schema by checking whether data elements conform to the specification.

Examples

- Data definition languages and formal schema languages, such as BNF, XSD, RDFS/OWL, parts of SQL etc.

- A class in Object Orientation or the definition of a key-value structure specifies a data element with properties or fields.

- The sequence YYYY-MM-DD to define the structure of a date.

- Upper/lower bounds or other limits on value types.

- Repeatability markers such as * and +.

- A form with fields to fill out.

- An URI template.

- Guides how to construct file system pathes or queries in a query language.

- Any digital document that aims at defining other data.

Difficulties

- Schemas only tell *how* data is structured but not *why*. Some kind of *label* is needed to actually interpret the elements of a schema.

- Many actual definitions in a schema are rather arbitrary. For instance a date could be defined with form YYYY-MM-DD or as DD.MM.YYYY.

- The degree of freedom in a schema can be too lax. For instance the date schema YYYY-MM-DD might not take into account the maximum number of days per month (28-31), leap years, Julian vs. Gregorian dates etc. Another typical example are plain text fields for anything or Unicode fields for strings that must contain letters only.

- The degree of freedom in a schema can be too strict, leading to violations and misuse. For a computer any violations makes the whole data element invalid but in practice errors can be acceptable or recoverable. Common misuse of strict schemas include the ad-hoc introduction of additional rules, such as *garbage* values and *separator* elements.

- Schemas are affected by communication and control standards which eventually are affected by informal standards.

- Applications may select parts of a schema and add rules from multiple schemas. This makes it difficult to find out which schema has actually been used and what exact set of rules is actually meant by a particular schema.

- The trend to express schemas in the same data structuring language that they constrain (for instance schema information tables in SQL, XML schemas in XML, and ontology languages in RDF, etc.) can lead to more complex schemas than necessary.

- Validators hidden in applications are difficult or impossible to analyze.

- Application of schemas on the wrong level of abstraction, for instance conformance to the XML syntax instead of conformance to a specific data format that can be encoded in XML.

Related patterns
Without any human-readable *label* the schema is meaningless. Schema rules mainly refer to questions of *optionality*, *prohibition*, *size*, *garbage*, and shapes of *embedding*. The schema can also specify which elements to use as an *identifier* and what *derivation* is to be expected. Rules can further be given as, or can be transformed into *derivation* statements.

Implied patterns
The same data element is interpreted differently against different schemas. Schemas also contain possible choices and exclusive constraints. For both reasons the *flag* pattern is found in virtually any schema.

Specialized patterns
- *optionality* to express optional and mandatory parts. In fact all schemas include some optionality as degrees of freedom.

- *prohibition* to express constraints.

- *garbage* to express irrelevant and predictable parts.

5.5. Continuing patterns

Continuing patterns are easily overlooked because they don't show explicit encoding. Instead these patterns primarily refer to data that is continued elsewhere, possibly even at another level or another realm of description. The most prominent continuing pattern is the *separator* which indicates a border between data elements. The "punctuation of data" is often visible in form of brackets, delimiters, and whitespace. The *etcetera* pattern is less welcome because it shows that data is rarely complete. Continuation markers such as 'et al.' still have their use because gaps and limits would be hidden without them. In the end all data refers to something in the realm of reality which is never fully encoded in data. The *garbage* pattern can indicate missing data as well but in this case there is nothing more to be encoded. Garbage values such as 'n/a' and 'NULL' make irrelevant or inapplicable values explicit instead of just omitting them. Omission on the other hand is the basic idea of the *void* pattern. If patterns would be given more colloquial nicknames, the continuing patterns could also be named "the glue" (*separator*), "the hint" (*etcetera*), "the ugly" (*garbage*), and "the mystery" (*void*).

5.5.1. Separator pattern

Alias
Delimiter.

Idea
An element indicates the boundary between two other elements.

Context
A *sequence* with at least two elements and a third separator element.

Motivation
Indicate borders and connections between data elements.

Implementations
Select data elements that must not occur in normal content (*prohibition*) or mark an element as (non)separator by a *flag*. A *schema* can tell which separators to use at which places.

Examples

- Whitespace characters separate words.
- Brackets and delimiters, such as {, [, (,),], } and , , |, ;, : etc. are used as separators in JSON, INI, CSV and other data structuring languages. Similar characters are also popular for ad-hoc structuring of values, for instance to create lists and annotations.
- ASCII defines four level separator characters (code 28 to 31).

– Lines in conceptual diagrams are used as borders and connections.

Counter examples
Being a separator is not an inherent property of a data element, so whitespace, brackets and delimiters may also occur as normal content.

Difficulties

– Parts of elements can be misread as separator and vice versa.

– Most elements divided by separators are divided by separators on their parts. Such hierarchic embeddings can be read ambiguously (for instance "({) }").

– It is not obvious whether separators indicate borders and connections between elements on the same level (for instance arrows in a diagram) or whether they also combine elements by subsumption (for instance subfield indicators).

– In sequences it must be clear whether separators occur between, after, or before an element, otherwise one can unintentionally introduce empty elements, for instance by ending a comma-separated list with a comma.

Related patterns

– One can alternatively use data elements of known *size* so no explicit delimiters are needed.

– Separators can simultaneously act as *flag* to indicate the type of a connection.

– If the actual form of a separator does not matter, the separator element is an example of the *garbage* pattern.

Implied patterns
An *embedding* gives context to separating elements and makes clear which data elements are actually separated and connected.

5.5.2. Etcetera pattern

Alias
Ellipsis, partial collection, explicit abbreviating.

Idea
Indicate that a collection of data elements is incomplete.

Context
A *container* or *embedding* of elements.

Motivation
Collections may be too large to be expressed, or parts of a collection may be unimportant or already implied by context. This pattern allows for abbreviating and to show that a collection contains more then explicitly expressed.

Implementations
First, one needs to decide which parts to omit:

- Only express the first or the most important parts.
- Only express mandatory parts and omit the rest (*optionality*).
- Give a random sample of of elements (*garbage*).

Second, the etcetera indicator can be expressed in several ways:

- Use a special element as etcetera indicator. This element must be a *prohibition* to not be confused with normal parts.
- Use obviously wrong elements as placeholders (*garbage*).
- Define a fixed cut, for instance a maximum length.

Examples

- ... or et al. to indicate an abbreviated *sequence*.
- e.g. to indicate that the included elements are examples from a larger set.
- Omission of parts in the middle of an element with [...].
- Library cataloging rules exist to only include three authors in a record, so the list of authors is always abbreviated if there are more then three authors.

Counter examples
Omission of details can also be an example of generalization and abstraction (see *encoding*) instead of abbreviation.

Difficulties

- Type and number of omitted parts and the reason for abbreviating are often unclear.
- An etcetera indicator and normal parts of a collection must not be confused (for instance strings that actually end with ...).
- Indicators could also be used to tell that a collection may be extended or that an element can be repeated (see *container* and *schema* patterns).

Related patterns
With a fixed cut this pattern also uses the *void* pattern instead of an explicit etcetera indicator. The void pattern is also similar because it indicates elements. The etcetera pattern in contrast indicates the existence of more elements.

Implied patterns
The etcetera indicator only makes sense as part of an *embedding* (typically a container or sequence).

5.5.3. Garbage pattern

Alias
Irrelevant, random, null.

Idea
Some data should better be ignored.

Context
Any data element can act as garbage.

Motivation
Garbage elements can act as placeholder for unknown or irrelevant values, as padding to align with specific sizes, or for obfuscation.

Implementations

– Explicitly mark a data element as garbage by some *flag*.

– Use a special data element that acts as *identifier* to garbage, such as the "lorem ipsum" placeholder text.

Examples

– Additional whitespace if it is used only to support readability without adding any informational content.

– Special sample values such as "foo", "bar", "lorem impsum".

– Special values such as /, n/a, -, xxx, 9999 to actually indicate no value.

– NULL values in databases and data structuring languages.

– Position of unordered elements serialized in an sequence.

– Temporary identifiers such as blank node identifiers in RDF.

Counter examples
The empty string and the numerical value zero can be used as garbage elements but they are not more natural as garbage than other values.

Difficulties

– Without additional context it is hard to tell whether data is garbage or whether it only happens to look like irrelevant data.

– Even garbage indicates something: at least the fact that the garbage data element is missing, inapplicable, or should be ignored for some other reason. The specific reason, however, is rarely indicated by garbage elements. Proposals to differentiate kinds of null values contradict the original idea of garbage elements to be ignorable.

– Garbage elements can be introduced against the original purpose of a *schema* to allow *optionality* where no support of optionality was intended. For instance obviously wrong names and email addresses are found if these fields are mandatory.

Related patterns

– While garbage is explicit data that has no content, instances of the *void* pattern have content without explicit data.

– Data that cannot be interpreted as referring to other data may also be a *label* instead of garbage. Eventually all labels are meaningless to a computer.

– Irrelevant data has no internal structure, so *atomicity* is often implied. Atomicity is also an alternative pattern if it turns out that the data is not fully irrelevant.

– Garbage is often used as *separator* which does not need to have a value of its own.

Implied patterns
A *schema* should define the context in which a data element is garbage or not.

5.5.4. Void pattern

Alias
Empty element.

Idea
A data element is given by a gap.

Context
Empty elements may occur everywhere in between other elements.

Motivation
Some elements should not be expressed because they would virtually occur everywhere or because their expression would be confused with other content.

Implementations
An *embedding* or *schema* can indicate the context in which data can be read from gaps. The *separator* pattern is typically applied in form of borders around the gap.

Examples

- An empty string is not given as such but by an empty *embedding* (""). The same applies to other empty instances of *sequence* and *container*.
- Default values are not given explicitly. Even if no default values are defined, one could just omit an element to indicate another value: a missing value is also a value.
- Unit types in data type systems are not visible as data but by referencing them in other structures.
- Assumed rules can lead to implicit *derivation* of data that is not directly expressed (for instance affiliation to superclasses and derived RDF statements).
- Given a comparison rule for equality of elements, one automatically gets an unexpressed normalized form of each element.

Counter examples

A gap can also be a sign of *optionality* where an element does not need to be expressed.

Difficulties

As empty elements may occur virtually everywhere between other elements, it is difficult to spot empty elements and irrelevant empty elements may wrongly be assumed.

Related patterns

- *optionality* is an alternative to the void pattern.
- If elements are cropped to a maximum length or form the original, full form is implicitly given (*etcetera*).
- The *garbage* pattern is kind of the contrary to the void pattern: void is content without form, garbage is form without content.

Implied patterns

A void element is always *derivation* of some other data elements.

5.6. Evaluation

Despite their popularity, there is little research on evaluation of pattern languages and the pattern language paradigm itself (Dearden and Finlay 2006; Petter, Khazanchi, and Murphy 2010). A pattern language is meant to be a tool of communication to describe typical solutions to common problems. Evaluation can therefore concentrate on: first whether and how well the language describes typical solutions to common problems, and second whether and how well the language communicates these problems and solutions. The second question can best be answered with user studies which would go beyond the scope of this thesis. The first question can be answered by direct examination of the patterns and their problems and solutions.

To check whether the pattern language developed in this thesis reflects experience in data description, the pattern language is compared to similar collections and models. If similar approaches have led to similar solutions, this is a strong indicator that the pattern language actually describes common problems and solutions in data structuring and description. Most existing pattern languages such as Gamma et al. (1994) are not comparable because they do not refer to static digital documents but to dynamic behavior of information systems. Literature review led to three models of data that are similar enough to allow for comparison. These models will briefly be compared with the pattern language in the following. Evaluation in greater depth will require more feedback. Evaluation of patterns, as suggested by Petter, Khazanchi, and Murphy (2010), is a conscious continuous improvement activity, which should be applied to the entire life-cycle of a pattern language. The current language should therefore be taken as valid starting point for further improvement.

5.6.1. Honig's analysis model of data structures

Based on a review of 21 programming languages and data base management systems, Honig (1975) in his thesis developed a general analysis model of data structures. The model distilled the major differences out of existing data types as possible axis of variation. Similar to my thesis, Honig's model describes only "the static, unchanging nature of data structures" and it refers to the logical level, independent from particular implementations and naming. In contrast to the broad collection of data structuring methods in chapter 3, elements of the conceptual realm and data structures from other domains, such as markup languages, conceptual modeling languages, and conceptual diagrams are not explicitly included in Honig's model. The final analysis model is a faceted classification with three major classes aggregate, association, and file data structures. Each class has a number of facets, represented as questions in appendix A. Table 5.1 compares Honig's classification with the patterns in data structuring. As the pattern language is no classification, there is no 1-to-1 relationship but a loose mapping between both systems. Their different aims can best be summarized following. While Honig classified data structures to tell out what they actually are, the pattern language of data structuring tells what typical kinds of data structures actually mean.

Both aggregates and files from Honig's model are examples of the *container* pattern as their basic idea is to combine a number of elements to a larger structure. The first facet asks whether an aggregate contains data elements of exactly one kind or type (homogeneous elements). The kind or type can be given by a *flag*, a *schema* or a *label*. The second facet tells whether elements are atomic and indivisible, which is expressed by the *atomicity* pattern. The idea of ordering elements corresponds to the *sequence* pattern (third facet) and constraints on the number of elements are examples of the *size* and the *schema* patterns (fourth pattern). Finally member elements can be identified by different means: if the number or position is used, the *sequence* pattern can be observed and identification by name is an example of the *identifier* pattern. Element identification by pointer is only mentioned briefly by Honig (1975, p. 146) without giving more examples. On a closer look it can be subsumed to identification by name.

The classification of file data types in Honig's model includes three facets, the first of which having a subclass: file selection asks about what method is used to pick one or more entry instances. This facet corresponds to element identification and the *identifier* pattern. If unique entries are specified by file selection, this is eventually based on *normalization*. The second facet (sequential files) corresponds to the *sequence* pattern and the third facet (kinds of entries) best matches to the *flag* pattern.

Associations as third class of data structures basically express instances of the *graph* pattern with some data elements as nodes and connecting data elements as vertices. Cardinalities of connections (first facet) are expressed by a *schema* that puts constraints on a *size*. Kinds of end in an association (second facet) refer to the types of node elements: For instance a kinship association may only exist between people elements. Like the kinds of entries in file data types this question can best be answered with the *flag* pattern but the *derivation* may also be given if one element can have multiple types. Associations with loops allowed correspond to general *graph* structures which may be constrained by a *schema*. Finally complete associations (fourth facet) and exclusive associations (sixth facet) impose mandatory and/or uniqueness constraints on their member elements which maps to the *optionality* and to the *flag* pattern respectively.

5.6.2. Quarks of Object-Orientation

By literature analysis in the field of Object Orientation Armstrong (2006) identified fundamental concepts that define the Object Oriented development approach. She found eight concepts that are mentioned in more then half of the sources, and put them in a simplified Object Orientation taxonomy. The most mentioned concepts are: abstraction, classes, encapsulation, inheritance, objects, message passing, methods, and polymorphism. Table 5.2 shows the structural part of the taxonomy and maps the OO concepts to similar patterns:

Abstraction is used on object orientation to simplify something by concentrating on relevant distinctions only. This methods is found in the *normalization* pattern.

dimension/axis	patterns
aggregates	*container*
homogeneous elements	*flag, schema, label*
basic item elements	*atomicity*
ordered elements	*sequence*
number of elements (fixed, limited, unbounded)	*size, schema*
element identified by number	*sequence*
element identified by name	*identifier*
element identified by pointer	*identifier*
files	*container*
file selection	*identifier*
unique entries	*normalization*
sequential file	*sequence*
kinds of entries	*flag*
associations	*graph*
cardinality (1-1, 1-n, n-m)	*schema, size*
kinds of ends	*flag, derivation*
loops allowed	*graph, schema*
complete associations	*optionality*
exclusive associations	*flag*

Table 5.1.: Comparison of patterns with Honig's model (1975)

A class in object orientation combines a *label* to be referenced and interpreted by humans and a *schema* with possibilities and constraints. Encapsulation hides details of implementation and provides a simplified form of access. This concept maps to both the *atomicity* pattern and the *encoding* pattern. Inheritance connects classes by extension or restriction, which imply an application of the *derivation* pattern. The object concept finally conveys the idea of identifying a single instance, which is expressed by the *identifier* pattern. The OO concepts of message passing, methods, and polymorphism refer to behavior instead of structure so they are left out in the comparison. It should only be noted that data patterns are inherently polymorph: a single patterns rarely describes the nature of one data object but often there are multiple patterns as possible viewpoints to the same artifact.

concept	definition	patterns
Abstraction	Creating classes to simplify aspects of reality using distinctions inherent to the problem.	*normalization*
Class	A description of the organization and actions shared by one or more similar objects.	*label, schema*
Encapsulation	Designing classes and objects to restricts access to the data and behavior by defining a limited set of messages that an object of that class can receive.	*atomicity, encoding*
Inheritance	The data and behavior of one class is included in or used as the basis for another class.	*derivation*
Object	an individual, identifiable item, either real or abstract, which contains data about itself and descriptions of its manipulations of the data.	*identifier*
Message Passing	the process by which an object sends data to another object or asks the other object to invoke a method.	—
Method	A way to access, set, or manipulate an object's information	—
Polymorphism	Different classes may respond to the same message and each implement it appropriately.	—

Table 5.2.: Quarks of Object-Orientation compared to patterns

5.6.3. ISO 11404

ISO 11404 (2007) is one of the rare standards that deal with data types independent from particular (programming) languages. Lessons learned during its specification have been summarized by Meek (1995, 1996). An overview of ISO 11404 is given in section 2.2.2: the standard defines three notions of data types, a set of general datatype properties, a collection of common primitive data types, and some derivation methods to create new types based on existing ones. By this means ISO 11404 defines a set of abstract data type classes of which the actual datatypes used in programming languages are derived. A comparison of these abstract classes and data description patterns is given in table 5.3. The comparison is explained in the following.

First, ISO 11404 distinguishes the fundamental notions value space, value representation, and computational model of a data type. The latter is not relevant to this thesis because it refers to dynamic properties. The relation between value space and value representation is found with the *encoding* pattern as basic semiotic relation between signifier and signified. The equality property is an instance of the *normalization* pattern while order is an applications of the *sequence* pattern. Upper and lower bounds restrict an ordered set with constraints (*schema* pattern). Cardinality in ISO 11404 refers to the property of having either a finite value space, to a denumerable infinite value space ($\aleph_0$) or to an approximate finite or innumerably infinite value space (such as floating point numbers to represent $\mathbb{R}$). Finite and innumerably infinite data types must have some known or derivable *size* while approximate types require a *normalization*. Numeric types combine cardinality with an ordered set, so at least a *sequence* can be found.

Primitive data types from the standard have been summarized in table 2.3. A comparison with data patterns shows that these primitive data types share a set of basic ideas, expressible by a small number of patterns: some basic data types are direct examples of one data patterns, such as Boolean for *flag*, Character for *encoding*, Integer for *size* pattern and Void (also known as unit type) for *void*. Other types share the same fundamental pattern like Enumerated and Ordinal with the *sequence* pattern. The remaining primitive data types combine multiple patterns, the combination established by *embedding* or *encoding*.

Finally, the general derivation methods, identified in ISO 11404 and further described in section 2.2.2 can be mapped to patterns or to combinations of patterns: pointer types are kind of identifiers as secondary elements (*identifier* and *dependence*). Choice types give a direct example of the *flag* pattern. Aggregation types combine multiple elements to one (*container*), possibly with additional structure (*embedding*). Subtypes, like inheritance from the quarks of Object-Orientation, implement a form of *derivation* (properties of a subtype can be derived from properties of supertypes).

221

notions	patterns
value space/representation	*encoding*
properties	**patterns**
equality	*normalization*
order	*sequence*
upper/lower bound	*schema*
cardinality	*size, normalization*
numeric types	*sequence*
primitive data types	**patterns**
Boolean	*flag*
State	*flag, encoding*
Enumerated	*sequence*
Character	*encoding*
Ordinal	*sequence*
Date-and-Time	*sequence, embedding*
Integer	*sequence*
Scaled (fixed point)	*size, embedding*
Real	*size, embedding*
Complex	*size, embedding*
Void	*void*
derivation methods	**patterns**
pointer types	*identifier, dependence*
choice types	*flag*
aggregation types	*container, embedding*
subtypes	*derivation*

Table 5.3.: ISO 11404 concepts and data patterns

Chapter 6

Conclusions

6.1. Summary and results

Many methods, technologies, standards, and languages exist to structure and describe data. The aim of this thesis is to find common features in these methods to determine how data is actually structured and described. The study is motivated by a growing number of purely digital documents and metadata, which both eventually exist as sequence of bits. In contrast to existing approaches, that commit to notions of data as recorded observations and facts, this thesis analyzes data as signs, communicated in form of digital documents. The document approach is rooted in library and information science as documentation science. In this discipline digital documents and metadata are primarily given as stable artifacts instead of processable information like in computer science. The notion of data as documents, as applied in this thesis, excludes statistical methods of data analysis in favour of intellectual data analysis. The study assumes that all data is implicitly and explicitly shaped by a process of data modeling, which is always grounded in the mind of a human being (see figure 6.1 and its unpackaged version in section 2.2.3, figure 2.6). The study also denies a clear distinction between data and metadata because metadata is both a digital document and used to structure and describe digital documents: one's data is the other's metadata and one's metadata is the other's document. Such relations in data, however, are not purely arbitrary but based on conventions that have been analyzed in this thesis.

The plethora of existing ways to structure and describe data was analyzed by a phenomenological research method, which is based on three steps: first, conceptual properties of data structuring and description were collected and experienced critically by phenomenological intuiting. As realized in chapter 2 and chapter 3, data is

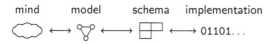

mind   model   schema   implementation

Figure 6.1.: Simplified data modeling process

structured and described in different disciplines (mathematics, computer science, library and information science, philosophy, and semiotics) and by different practices. Examples of these practices include encodings, identifiers, markup, formats, schemas, and models. The most common methods to structure and describe data include data structuring languages (section 3.5) and schema languages (section 3.7). After this empirical part, the methods found were grouped using phenomenological analysis without adhering to known concepts and categories. The result of this second step was presented in chapter 4: the analysis resulted in six prototypes that categorize data methods by their primary purpose (section 4.1). These prototypes can be used to better grasp the actual nature of a method, independent of its originally intended purpose:

1. encodings (most of section 3.1)

2. storage systems (most of sections 3.3 and 3.4)

3. identifier and query languages (most of sections 3.2 and 3.10)

4. structuring and markup languages (most of sections 3.5 and 3.6)

5. schema languages: (most of section 3.7)

6. conceptual models (most of sections 3.8 and 3.9)

The study further revealed five basic paradigms, described in section 4.2, each with its benefits and drawbacks. The paradigms provide general kinds of viewing and dealing with data and they deeply shape the way that people deal with data structuring and description:

1. documents and objects

2. standards and rules

3. collections, types, and sameness

4. entities and connections

5. levels of abstractions

The third step, that is phenomenological describing, resulted in a language of twenty fundamental patterns in data structuring and description (chapter 5). The patterns show problems and solutions which occur over and over again in data, independent from particular technologies. This application of the pattern language approach is novel. Existing design patterns in software engineering refer to dynamic systems instead of static digital documents and the patterns mostly refer to one particular method of data description. The pattern language given in this work consists of twenty patterns, each described with its names, problems, solutions, and consequences. Each pattern shows general strategies in data structuring and description with its benefits, consequences, and pitfalls, and relates this strategy to other patterns. An overview of the pattern language is given below with a classification of the patterns (table 6.1) and with a graph of pattern connections (appendix C). In section 5.6 the pattern language is compared with related works for evaluation.

This thesis collected and analyzed a wide range of traditions (chapter 2), methods (chapter 3), prototypes and paradigms (chapter 4), and patterns (chapter 5) of data structuring and description. The results can help data modelers and programmers to find a trade-off when selecting methods of data structuring and description for their particular application. Patterns can also help to identify solutions that have implicitly been implemented in data. Last but no least the result of this thesis facilitates a better understanding of data. Applications of the results and options for further research will be summarized in the following sections (6.2 and 6.3) before concluding with a final reflection (section 6.4).

1. basic patterns (page 184ff.)
   a) pure data elements
      i. *label*
      ii. *atomicity*
   b) data elements with content
      i. *size*
      ii. *optionality*
      iii. *prohibition*

2. combining patterns (page 192ff.)
   a) combine multiple elements on the same level
      i. *sequence*
      ii. *graph*
   b) combine elements by subsumption
      i. *container*
      ii. *dependence*
      iii. *embedding*

3. relationing patterns (page 200ff.)
   a) primary
      i. *identifier*
      ii. *derivation*
   b) secondary
      i. *encoding*
      ii. *flag*
   c) tertiary
      i. *normalization*
      ii. *schema*

4. continuing patterns (page 211ff.)
   i. *separator*
   ii. *etcetera*
   iii. *garbage*
   iv. *void*

Table 6.1.: Full classification of patterns in data structuring

6.2. Applications

The results of this thesis can be applied virtually everywhere data is intellectually used and created, including the design of automatic methods of data processing. In particular the identified categories, paradigms, and patterns can help to better understand existing data and to improve (the creation of) data models. Ideally, the results will foster a general understanding of methods to describe and structure data, independent from specific technologies and trends, such as programming languages, software architectures, and storage systems. Two specific emerging domains of application will be described below with data archaeology (section 6.2.1) and data literacy (section 6.2.2).

6.2.1. Data archaeology

The domain of *data archaeology* is recovery of digital data in unknown or obsolete formats. This activity is closely related to data recovery, which focuses on recovery of data from damaged media and file systems. Data archaeology includes all methods of interpretation that follow after data recovery. Just like archaeology exposes layers and artifacts by excavation and remote sensing, data archaeology can use many methods to uncover structures in data. The most related existing discipline to data archaeology is digital forensics. Digital forensics has a more specific scope and its application to more complex and heterogeneous methods of data structuring, e.g. databases, is in an early stage of development (Olivier 2009).

The term data archaeology first appeared in 1992 in the Global Oceanographic Data Archaeology and Rescue Project. The goal of this project was to collect, digitize, and consolidate historical data on temperature, chlorophyll, and plankton of the oceans (Data and Exchange 2007). To prevent the need of data archaeology, *digital preservation* or *long-term preservation* has been established as important field in library and information science and archival science. Digital preservation is a set of activities aimed towards ensuring access to digital materials over time (Caplan 2008). This includes creation of descriptive metadata, protection from change, and ensuring that a given digital publication can be read in its original form. Two strategies are followed to manage the variety and change of digital formats: emulation of obsolete software needed to read the data, and conversion of data to newer formats and systems. Both ways are complex and require constant attention. Moreover you can only describe, emulate, and migrate what you currently know — but from a historical view, relevant aspects may emerge only after years and decades.

That said, data archaeology as retrospective analysis of incompletely defined data will gain importance. The paradigms and patterns found in this thesis will help intellectual data analysis, which is needed to underpin and interpret algorithmic data analysis. Algorithmic data analysis with data mining, knowledge discovery, and related applied sciences provides useful tools to discover detailed views on data, but they cannot reveal its meaning as part of social practice. For this reason it is important to locate data archaeology in the (digital) humanities[1] as meaningful data is always a product of human action. It can therefore only be studied involving the cultural context of its creation and usage.

As Steve Hoberman points out in the third edition of W. Kent and Hoberman (2012, p. 63), data archaeology is also an act of reverse-engineering: "Just as an archaeologist must try to find out what this piece of clay that was buried under the sand for thousand of years was used for, so must we try to figure out what these [data] fields were used for when no or little documentation or knowledgeable people resources exist." The data categories, paradigms, and patterns identified in this thesis can help to detect intended shape and purpose of such buried data elements.

6.2.2. Data literacy

The term *data literacy* has gained popularity in recent years to describe the increasing need for reading and writing data, especially among researchers. The focus of data literacy is similar to the needs of "data science" and "data journalism" (Bradshaw and Rohumaa 2011) which mainly include capabilities to aggregate, filter and visualize large sets of data with statistical methods of data analysis. Definitions of data literacy refer to the knowledge "how to obtain and manipulate data" (Schield 2004) and how to "understand, use, and manage science data" (Qin and D'Ignazio 2010).[2] J. Carlson et al. (2011) refer to data literacy as the capability of "understanding what data mean, including how to read graphs and charts appropriately, draw correct conclusions from data, and recognize when data are being used in misleading or inappropriate ways." These definitions and the majority of data literacy literature and curricula focus on numerical data, management of scientific data sets (Haendel, Vasilevsky, and Wirz 2012), common data processing software, file formats, and preservation. Despite the importance of these aspects of data, there is a lack of theory in current data literacy. In particular, current data literacy mostly ignores the semiotic nature of data and the conception of data as communications which are not measured or observed but created (Ballsun-Stanton 2012). Instead the domain is committed to the notions of data as hard numbers or data as observations and emphasises statistical literacy to aggregate and filter large sets of data. This thesis with its focus on data as communications can provide both, a theoretical foundation of data literacy, and guidelines to better appraise practical method of data structuring and description, which are already subject of current data literacy.

---

[1] See Svensson (2010) for a discussion of the scope and definition of digital humanities.

[2] Qin and D'Ignazio (2010) refer to *scientific* or *science* data literacy with the ability of "collecting, processing, managing, evaluating, and using data for scientific inquiry" but they neither provide a separation to general data literacy nor a definition of data.

6.3. Further research

The results of this thesis should not be taken as a final product, but as a starting point. It is natural that in a phenomenological investigation one cannot fully experience a phenomenon in all of its aspects without getting lost in it. The analysis of methods and systems for structuring and describing data (chapter 3) could be extended to additional data structuring languages, more encodings, schema languages etc. Nevertheless it is unlikely that new methods will change the results apart from minor corrections and additions. In particular it may be worth to have a deeper look at the history and practice of forms, as mentioned at page 138, and at patterns in visual notations, such as electrical circuit diagrams (see section 3.9 and Tversky (2011)). Specific technologies not analyzed in more detail in this thesis include zzStructure (Dattolo and Luccio 2009; Gutteridge 2010; McGuffin and schraefel 2004; Nelson 2004; Pourabdollah 2009) and the Data Format Description Language (see page 139). Query languages and APIs (section 3.10) have also received less attention than other methods of data structuring and description.

Especially the pattern language in chapter 5 can be improved continuously by further discussion and evaluation. A promising sample application would be to categorize and analyze the data standards collected by Riley (2010). As noted in section 5.6, evaluation of the pattern language requires user studies with practitioners and experts, which would go beyond the scope of this thesis. A possible methodology for evaluating the pattern language has been proposed by Petter, Khazanchi, and Murphy (2010). To facilitate improvements and applications, the pattern language will be made available under the CC-BY-SA license. Surely understandability and usability can be improved by adding examples and illustrations to better convey the core idea of each pattern.[3]

In addition to the refinement of results of this thesis, the study can be broadened and used as starting point for further research. The following disciplines and activities, among others, might provide additional insights:

- *Information design* and data visualization aim at visual methods to represent and display information and data. Popular examples were given by Tufte (2001) and Bertin (2011).

- Digital forensics already has some history and relevant practice in recovery of structures and descriptions from data.

- Mathematics may guide to applications of non-classical logic to data description.

- In data analysis, linguistic summaries of data can be created based on fuzzy set theory. These summaries provide natural language statements, that capture the main characteristics of data sets (Liétard 2008; Yager and Rubinson 1981).

---

[3] An idea not followed in this thesis was to depict each pattern by an icon for better recognition.

Last but not least, the semiotic background of data could be elaborated in more detail. At best, this thesis provides a 'semiology of data' similar to the semiology of graphics by Bertin (1967, 2011). Expanding the notion of data as sign to data as language, this thesis might also be placed in a new discipline called *data linguistics*. Several linguistic subfields exist, each concerned with particular aspects of human language. For instance anthropological linguistics and sociolinguistics study the relation between language and society, and historical linguistics studies the history and evolution of languages. Although digital documents are used for communication, there is no branch of linguistics dedicated to the study data as language.

6.4. Final reflection

"We do not, it seems, have a very clear and commonly agreed upon set of notions about data" — since George Mealy wrote this in 1967 the world of data processing has changed a lot. Many technologies and models have been proposed and applied, but the basic problem of data modeling remains. As demonstrated by William Kent in his classic "Data and Reality" (1978), the problem is independent from technology and it cannot be solved finally. Given the growing importance of data and digital documents, the lack of current research about foundations of data is surprising. It looks that since the 1980s, when computers became mainstream, the concept of data has been accepted as given. Attention of research is either on efficient implementations with practical value in limited domains, or on sophisticated abstract models, little connected to data practice with its plurality of formats and interpretations. A naive belief in progress is visible in hype cycles around technologies and models such as ERM, Object Orientation, XML and RDF. Despite the usefulness of these methods, they do not reflect a simple progression of improvements. As Ted Nelson (2012) keeps on stressing, "the computer world deals with, imaginary, arbitrary, made-up stuff, that was all made up by somebody". Eventually, all data is created by human beings for human beings. For this reason data is no simple expression of information or even knowledge, but a social artifact, based on convention. This social artifact is called a document. Nelson talks about documents where Tim Berners-Lee and others talk about information.[4] The concept of this document, which is independent from its physical form, can be traced back to founders of library and information science, such as Bush (1945), Otlet (1934), Ostwald (Hapke 1999), Goldberg (Buckland 2006), and Briet (1951). Therefore the phenomenon investigated in this thesis, the way digital data is structured and described, turns out to be inseparable from the nature of digital documents and metadata in general. To understand the latter, it is necessary to understand data, independent from technologies.

To conclude with two of the giants, whose shoulders this thesis is built on, "it's possible to argue that this book hasn't accomplished much" (Gamma et al. 1994,

---

[4] Nelson explicitly coined the term "docuverse". See also Nelson (2010, p. 300) and footnote 2 at page 5 for a comparision. However both, Nelson and Berners-Lee, do not talk about totally different things as one can show with the paradigm of documents and objects (section 4.2.1).

p. 351): this thesis does not present a new and better method to structure and describe data. The contribution, however, is more important than yet another data language. The prototypes, paradigms, and patterns, provide "another look at data" (Mealy 1967) by revealing unspelled assumptions that deeply shape how data is and will be structured and described in practice.

Bibliography

Abiteboul, Serge, Peter Buneman, and Dan Suciu (2000). *Data on the web: from relations to semistructured data and XML*. San Francisco: Morgan Kaufmann.

Alexander, Christopher, Sara Ishikawa, and Murray Silverstein (1977). *A Pattern Language: Towns, Buildings, Construction*. Oxford: Oxford University Press.

Alexander, Keith (2008). "RDF/JSON: A Specification for serialising RDF in JSON". In: *Scripting for the Semantic Web*. CEUR Workshop Proceedings. `http://ceur-ws.org/Vol-368/paper16.pdf`.

Alur, Rajeev and P. Madhusudan (2009). "Adding nesting structure to words". In: *Journal of the ACM* 56.3, 16:1–16:43.

Amazon (2010). *Amazon S3 Developer Guide*. Tech. rep. Amazon. `http://aws.amazon.com/documentation/s3/`.

Ames, Alexander et al. (2005). "Richer File System Metadata Using Links and Attributes". In: *Proceedings of the 13th NASA Goddard Conference on Mass Storage Systems and Technologies (MSST)*. IEEE Computer Society, pp. 49–60.

Andreessen, Marc (1999). *Innovators of the Net: Ramanathan V. Guha and RDF*. (Accessible via Internet Archive). `http://home.netscape.com/columns/techvision/innovators_rg.html`.

Angles, Renzo and Claudio Gutiérrez (Feb. 2008). "Survey of graph database models". In: *ACM Computing Surveys (CSUR)* 40.1, pp. 1–39.

Armstrong, Deborah J. (Feb. 2006). "The Quarks of Object-Oriented Development". In: *Communications of the ACM* 49.2, pp. 123–128.

CODASYL Database Task Group Report (1971). Tech. rep.

Atkinson, M. et al. (Dec. 1989). "The Object-Oriented Database System Manifesto". In: *Proceedings of the First International Conference on Deductive and Object-Oriented Databases*, pp. 40–57.

Austin, John L. (1962). *How to do things with words*. Cambridge: Harvard University Press.

Avram, H.D. (1975). *MARC; its history and implications*. Library of Congress.

Ayers, Danny and Max Völkel (Mar. 2008). *Cool URIs for the Semantic Web*. Interest Group Note 20080331. W3C. `http://www.w3.org/TR/2008/NOTE-cooluris-20080331/`.

Baader, Franz et al. (2010). *The Description Logic Handbook: Theory, Implementation, and Applications*. 2nd. Cambridge: Cambridge University Press.

Bachman, Charles W. (1969). "Data Structure Diagrams". In: *DATA BASE* 1.2, pp. 4–10.

Bachman, Charles W. and Manilal Daya (1977). "The Role Concept in Data Models". In: *Proceedings of the 3rd International Conference on Very Large Date Bases (VLDB)*. IEEE Computer Society, pp. 464–476.

Bagley, Philip Rutherford (1951). "Electronic digital machines for high-speed information searching". M.S. Thesis. MIT. http://hdl.handle.net/1721.1/12185.

– (Nov. 1968). *Extension of programming language concepts*. Tech. rep. 0518086. University City Science Center, p. 222.

Ballsun-Stanton, Brian (2010). "Asking about Data: Experimental Philosophy of Information Technology". In: *5th International Conference on Computer Sciences and Convergence Information Technology*, pp. 119–124.

– (2012). "Asking About Data: Exploring Different Realities of Data via the Social Data Flow Network Methodology". PhD thesis. University of New South Wales.

Balzer, R. M. (1967). "Dataless programming". In: *AFIPS*. ACM, pp. 535–544.

Barker, Richard (1990). *CASE Method Entity Relationship Modeling*. Addison-Wesley.

Barthes, Roland (1967). *Elements of Semiology*. London: Cape.

Beardsmore, Anthony (2007). "Schema description for arbitrary data formats with the Data Format Description Language". In: *IESA*. Ed. by Ricardo Jardim-Gonçalves et al. Springer, pp. 829–840.

Becker, Peter (2007). "Le charme discret du formulaire. De la communication entre administration et citoyen dans l'aprés-guerre". In: *Politiques et usages de la langue en Europe*. Ed. by Michael Werner. Paris: Éditions de la MSH, pp. 217–240.

Beckett, D. (2007). *Turtle - Terse RDF Triple Language*. Tech. rep. http://www.dajobe.org/2004/01/turtle/.

RDF/XML Syntax Specification (Revised) (Feb. 10, 2004). Tech. rep. W3C. http://www.w3.org/TR/2004/REC-rdf-syntax-grammar-20040210/.

Beck, Kent and Ward Cunningham (1987). "Using Pattern Languages for Object Oriented Programs". In: *Conference on Object-Oriented Programming, Systems, Languages, and Applications (OOPSLA)*.

Bell, Alex E (Mar. 2004). "Death by UML Fever". In: *ACM Queue* 2.1, pp. 72–80.

Ben-Kiki, Oren, Clark Evans, and Brian Ingerson (2006). *YAXML, the (draft) XML Binding for YAML*. Tech. rep. http://yaml.org/xml/.

– (Sept. 2009). *YAML Ain't Markup Language (YAML) (tm) Version 1.2*. Tech. rep. YAML.org. http://www.yaml.org/spec/1.2/spec.html.

Extensible Stylesheet Language (XSL) Version 1.1 (2006). Tech. rep. W3C. http://www.w3.org/TR/xsl11/.

Berglund, Anders et al. (Dec. 2010). *XQuery 1.0 and XPath 2.0 Data Model (XDM)*. Tech. rep. http://www.w3.org/TR/2010/REC-xpath-datamodel-20101214/.

Bergman, Michael K. (June 6, 2006). *Sources and Classification of Semantic Heterogeneities*. http://www.mkbergman.com/232/sources-and-classification-of-semantic-heterogeneities/.

Berkeley, Edmund (1949). *Giant Brains, or Machines That Think*. New York: Wiley.

Berners-Lee, T., R. Fielding, and L. Masinter (2005). *Uniform Resource Identifier (URI): Generic Syntax*. Tech. rep.

Berners-Lee, T., J. Hendler, and O. Lassila (May 2001). "The Semantic Web". In: *Scientific American* 284.5.

Berners-Lee, Tim (1989). *Information Management: A Proposal*. Tech. rep. http://www.w3c.org/History/1989/proposal.html.

– (1991). *Document Naming*. http://www.w3.org/DesignIssues/Naming.html.

– (1992). *Basic HTTP as defined in 1992*. http://www.w3.org/Protocols/HTTP/HTTP2.html.

– (June 1994). *Universal Resource Identifiers in WWW*. Tech. rep. 1630.

– (Jan. 1997). *Metadata Architecture*. http://www.w3.org/DesignIssues/Metadata.html.

– (1998a). *Cool URIs don't change*. http://www.w3.org/Provider/Style/URI.html.

– (1998b). *Principles of Design*. http://www.w3.org/DesignIssues/Principles.html.

Berners-Lee, Tim and Dan Connolly (Jan. 14, 2008). *Notation3 (N3): A readable RDF syntax*. Tech. rep. W3C. http://www.w3.org/TeamSubmission/n3/.

Berners-Lee, Tim and Mark Fischetti (1999). *Weaving the web: The original design and ultimate destiny of the world wide web by its inventor*. San Francisco: Harper.

Berners-Lee, Tim, L. Masinter, and M. McCahill (Dec. 1994). *Uniform Resource Locators (URL)*. RFC 1738. IETF.

Bertin, Jacques (1967). *Sémiologie graphique : les diagrammes, les réseaux, les cartes*. Paris: Mouton.

– (2011). *Semiology of Graphics: Diagrams, Networks, Maps*. Redlands: Esri Press.

Biron, Paul V. and Ashok Malhotra (Oct. 28, 2004). *XML Schema Part 2: Datatypes Second Edition*. Tech. rep. http://www.w3.org/TR/2004/REC-xmlschema-2-20041028/.

Bizer, Chris and Richard Cyganiak (July 30, 2007). *The TriG Syntax*. Tech. rep. FU Berlin. http://www.wiwiss.fu-berlin.de/suhl/bizer/TriG/Spec/TriG-20070730/.

Blackman, Kenneth R. (1998). "IMS Celebrates Thirty Years as an IBM Product." In: *IBM Systems Journal* 37.4, pp. 596–603.

Bobrow, Daniel G. et al. (1972). "TENEX, a Paged Time Sharing System for the PDP-10." In: *Communications of the ACM* 15.3, pp. 135–143.

Boole, George (1847). *The mathematical analysis of logic: being an essay towards a calculus of deductive reasoning*. Cambridge: Macmillan, Barclay, & Macmillan.

– (1854). *An Investigation of the Laws of Thought on Which are Founded the Mathematical Theories of Logic and Probabilities*. London: Walton and Maberly.

Borges, Jorge Luis (1952). "El Idioma Analítico de John Wilkins". In: *Otras inquisiciones (1937-1952)*. Buenos Aires: Sur, pp. 139–144.

Cascading Style Sheets Level 2 Revision 1 (CSS 2.1) (Sept. 8, 2009). Tech. rep. W3C. http://www.w3.org/TR/CSS21/.

Bibliography

Bourbaki, Nicolas (1970). *Eléments de mathématique. Théorie des ensembles*. Paris: Hermann.

Bowker, Geoffrey C. and Susan Leigh Star (1999). *Sorting Things Out: Classification and Its Consequences*. The MIT Press.

Boyd, Michael and Peter McBrien (2005). "Comparing and Transforming Between Data Models Via an Intermediate Hypergraph Data Model." In: LNCS 4. Ed. by Stefano Spaccapietra, pp. 69–109.

Boyer, John M. and Glenn Marcy (May 2, 2008). *Canonical XML 1.1*. Tech. rep. http://www.w3.org/TR/2008/REC-xml-c14n11-20080502.

Bradner, Scott (1997). *Key words for use in RFCs to Indicate Requirement Levels*. RFC 2119. IETF.

Bradshaw, Paul and Liisa Rohumaa (2011). *The Online Journalism Handbook: Skills to Survive and Thrive in the Digital Age*. Longman.

Bray, Tim (Feb. 10, 2002). *Extensible Markup Language - SW (XML-SW)*. Tech. rep. http://www.textuality.com/xml/xmlSW.html.

Bray, Tim, Dave Hollander, et al. (Aug. 2009). *Namespaces in XML 1.0*. W3C Recommendation. W3C. http://www.w3.org/TR/2009/REC-xml-names-20091208/.

Bray, Tim, Jean Paoli Paoli, and C.M. Sperberg-McQueen (Feb. 1998). *Extensible Markup Language (XML) 1.0*. Tech. rep. W3C. http://www.w3.org/TR/1998/REC-xml-19980210.

Bray, Tim, Jean Paoli Paoli, C.M. Sperberg-McQueen, et al. (Nov. 2008). *Extensible Markup Language (XML) 1.0*. Tech. rep. W3C. http://www.w3.org/TR/2008/REC-xml-20081126/.

Bray, Tim, Jean Paoli, et al. (Apr. 2004). *Extensible Markup Language (XML) 1.1*. Tech. rep. http://www.w3.org/TR/2004/REC-xml11-20040204/.

Brickley, Dan and Ramanathan V. Guha (Feb. 10, 2004). *RDF Vocabulary Description Language 1.0: RDF Schema*. Tech. rep. http://www.w3.org/TR/2004/REC-rdf-schema-20040210/.

Brier, Søren (2006). "The foundation of LIS in information science and semiotics". In: *Libreas* 2.1. http://www.ib.hu-berlin.de/~libreas/libreas_neu/ausgabe4/001bri.htm.

– (2008). *Cybersemiotics. Why information is not enough!* University of Toronto Press.

Briet, Suzanne (1951). *Qu'est-ce que la documentation?* Paris: Éditions documentaires, industrielles et techniques.

Broder, Andrei Z. (1993). "Some applications of Rabin's fingerprinting method". In: *Sequences II: Methods in Communications, Security, and Computer Science*. Ed. by Renato Capocelli, Alfredo DeSantis, and Ugo Vaccaro. Springer, pp. 143–152.

Brooks, Jr. Frederick P. (Apr. 1987). "No Silver Bullet — Essence and Accidents of Software Engineering". In: *IEEE Computer* 20.4, pp. 10–19.

Buckland, Michael (Sept. 1997). "What is a "document"?" In: *Journal of the American Society of Information Science (JASIST)* 48.9, pp. 804–809.

– (1998a). "Documentation, Information Science, and Library Science in the USA". In: *Historical Studies in Information Science*. Ed. by Trudi Bellardo Hahn and Michael Buckland. Maryland: asis&t, pp. 159–172.

– (1998b). "What is a "digital document"?" In: *Document Numérique* 2.2, pp. 221–230.

– (2006). *Emanuel Goldberg and his knowledge machine: Information, invention, and political forces*. Westport: Libraries Unlimited.

Burke, Sean M. (2003). *RTF Pocket Guide*. O'Reilly.

Burnard, Lou and Syd Bauman, eds. (2007). *Guidelines for Electronic Text Encoding and Interchange (TEI P5)*. The TEI Consortium.

Burstall, Rod M., David B. MacQueen, and Donald Sannella (1980). "HOPE: An Experimental Applicative Language." In: *LISP Conference*, pp. 136–143.

Bush, Vannevar (July 1945). "As We May Think". In: *The Atlantic Monthly* 176.1, pp. 112–122.

Business Rules Group, ed. (2011). *What is a Business Rule?* http://www.businessrulesgroup.org/defnbrg.shtml.

Butler, Judith (1990). *Gender Trouble*. Routledge.

Buzan, Tony and Barry Buzan (1996). *The Mind Map Book: How to Use Radiant Thinking to Maximize Your Brain's Untapped Potential*. Plume.

Campbell, Douglas (2007). "Identifying the identifiers". In: *Proceedings of the DCMI*. Singapore: DMCI, pp. 74–84.

Cao, Lan, Balasubramaniam Ramesh, and Matti Rossi (July 2009). "Are Domain-Specific Models Easier to Maintain Than UML Models?" In: *IEEE Software* 26.4, pp. 19–21.

Caplan, Priscilla (2003). *Metadata fundamentals for all librarians*. American Library Association.

– (Feb. 2008). "What Is Digital Preservation?" In: *Library Technology Reports* 44.2, pp. 7–9.

Capurro, Rafael (Sept. 1, 2008). "On Floridi's metaphysical foundation of information ecology". In: *Ethics and Information Technology* 10.2, pp. 167–173.

Capurro, Rafael and Birger Hjørland (2003). "The concept of information". In: *ARIST* 37.1, pp. 343–411.

Carle, Benjamin and Paliath Narendran (2009). "On Extended Regular Expressions". In: *Proceedings of the 3rd International Conference on Language and Automata Theory and Applications*. Springer, pp. 279–289.

Carlson, Jacob et al. (Apr. 2011). "Determining Data Information Literacy Needs: A Study of Students and Research Faculty". In: *portal: Libraries and the Academy* 11.2, pp. 629–657.

Carroll, Jeremy J. (2003). *Signing RDF Graphs*. Tech. rep. HPL-2003-142. HP Labs. http://www.hpl.hp.com/techreports/2003/HPL-2003-142.html.

Carroll, Jeremy J., Christian Bizer, et al. (2005). "Named Graphs". In: *Journal of Web Semantics* 3.4, pp. 247–267.

Carroll, Jeremy J. and Patrick Stickler (2004). "RDF Triples in XML". In: *Proceedings of the Extreme Markup Languages 2004 Conference.* http://conferences. idealliance.org/extreme/html/2004/Stickler01/EML2004Stickler01.html.

Cayley, Arthur (1857). "On the theory of the analytical forms called trees". In: *Philosophical Magazine* 13, pp. 172–6.

Chamberlin, D. D. and R. F. Boyce (May 1974). "SEQUEL: A Structured English Query Language". In: *ACM SIGMOD*, 249–264.

Chandler, Daniel (2007). *Semiotics: The Basics.* Taylor & Francis.

Chang, Fay et al. (2006). "Bigtable: A distributed storage system for structured data". In: *Proceedings of the 7th USENIX Symposium on Operating Systems Design and Implementation (OSDI'06).* http://research.google.com/archive/bigtable. html.

Chapin, Ned (1968). "A deeper look at data". In: *Proceedings of the 23rd ACM national conference.* New York: ACM, pp. 631–638.

Chen, Chaomei, Il-Yeol Song, and Weizhong Zhu (2007). "Trends in Conceptual Modeling: Citation Analysis of the ER Conference Papers (1975-2005)". In: *Proceedings of the 11th ISSI.* CSIC, pp. 189–200.

Chen, Cindy Xinmin (2001). "Data Models and Query Languages of Spatio-Temporal Information". PhD thesis. Unviersity of California. http://wis.cs.ucla.edu/ wis/theses/thesis_cchen.ps.

Chen, Haitao and Husheng Liao (July 2010). "A survey to conceptual modeling for XML". In: *ICCSIT 2010.* Vol. 8, pp. 473 –477.

Chen, Peter P. (1976). "The Entity-Relationship Model - Toward a Unified View of Data". In: *ACM Transactions on Database Systems* 1.1, pp. 9–36.

Chen, Peter P., Bernhard Thalheim, and LeahY. Wong (1999). "Future Directions of Conceptual Modeling". In: *Conceptual Modeling.* Ed. by G. Goos et al. Vol. 1565. LNCS. Springer, pp. 287–301.

Church, Alonzo (1936). "A Note on the Entscheidungsproblem." In: *Journal of Symbolic Logic* 1.1, pp. 40–41.

XSL Transformations (XSLT) Version 1.0 (Nov. 1999). Tech. rep. http://www.w3.org/ TR/xslt.

Clark, James (2002). *RELAX NG and W3C XML Schema.* http://www.imc.org/ietf- xml-use/mail-archive/msg00217.html.

– (Dec. 13, 2010). *MicroXML.* http://blog.jclark.com/2010/12/microxml.html.

Clark, James and Makoto Murata (Dec. 3, 2001). *RELAX NG DTD Compatibility.* http://relaxng.org/compatibility.html.

Codd, Edgar F. (June 1970). "A Relational Model of Data for Large Shared Data Banks". In: *CACM* 13.6, pp. 377–387.

– (Aug. 1971). *Further Normalization of the Data Base Relational Model.* Tech. rep. RJ909. IBM.

– (Apr. 1974). *Recent Investigations into Relational Data Base Systems.* Tech. rep. RJ1385. IBM.

Compton, Bradley Wendell (2006). "The being of information: a subcategorical development of a continental philosophy of information". In: *Information Research* 12.1. http://InformationR.net/ir/12-1/paper274.html.

Cook, Steve et al. (2007). *Domain Specific Development with Visual Studio DSL Tools*. Addison-Wesley.

Coombs, James H., Allen H. Renear, and Steven J. DeRose (1987). "Markup Systems and the Future of Scholarly Text Processing". In: *Communications of the ACM* 30.11, pp. 933–947.

Cornelius, Ian (2004). "Information and Its Philosophy". In: *Library Trends* 52.3. http://www.ideals.uiuc.edu/bitstream/handle/2142/1679/Cornelius377386.pdf?sequence=2.

Costagliola, G., V. Deufemia, and G. Polese (2004). "A Framework for Modeling and Implementing Visual Notations With Applications to Software Engineering". In: *ACM Transactions on Software Engineering and Methodology* 13, pp. 431–487.

Cowan, John and Richard Tobin (Feb. 2004). *XML Information Set (Second Edition)*. Tech. rep. http://www.w3.org/TR/2004/REC-xml-infoset-20040204.

Cox, Russ (Jan. 2007). *Regular Expression Matching Can Be Simple And Fast*. http://swtch.com/~rsc/regexp/regexp1.html.

– (Mar. 2010). *Zip Files All The Way Down*. http://research.swtch.com/2010/03/zip-files-all-way-down.html.

Coyle, Karen (Jan. 2005). "Catalogs, Card—and Other Anachronisms". In: *The Journal of Academic Librarianship* 31.1, pp. 60–62.

– (2006). "Identifiers: Unique, Persistent, Global". In: *Journal of Academic Librarianship* 32.4, pp. 428–431.

– (2010). "Understanding the Semantic Web: Bibliographic Data and Metadata". In: *Library Technology Reports* 46.1.

– (2011). "MARC21 as Data: A Start". In: *Code4Lib journal* 14. http://journal.code4lib.org/articles/5468.

Crocker, David H. and Paul Overell (Jan. 2008). *Augmented BNF for Syntax Specifications: ABNF*. RFC 5234. IETF.

Crockford, Douglas (2002). *Introducing JSON*. http://www.json.org.

– (July 2006). *The application/json Media Type for JavaScript Object Notation (JSON)*. RFC 4627. IETF.

Definition of the CIDOC Conceptual Reference Model Version 5.0.4 (Nov. 2011). Tech. rep. ICOM/CIDOC CRM Special Interest Group.

Cunningham, Ward (1995). *Portland Pattern Repository*. http://c2.com/ppr/.

Dahl, Ole-Johan and Kristen Nygaard (Sept. 1966). "Simula: An Algol-based Simulation Language". In: *Communications of ACM* 9.9, pp. 671–678.

Daley, R. C. and P. G. Neumann (1965). "A General-Purpose File System For Secondary Storage". In: *Proceedings of the Fall Joint Computer Conference*, pp. 213–230.

Darwen, Hugh and C. J. Date (1995). "The Third Manifesto". In: *SIGMOD Record* 24.1, pp. 39–49.

Data Description Language Committee (1978). "CODASYL: Reports of the Data Description Language Committee". In: *Information Systems* 3.4, pp. 247–320.

Data, International Oceanographic and Information Exchange, eds. (2007). *Global Oceanographic Data Archaeology and Rescue (GODAR)*. http://www.iode.org/index.php?Itemid=57&id=18&option=com_content&task=view.

Date, C. J. and Hugh Darwen (1997). *A Guide to SQL Standard*. 4th edition. Addison-Wesley.

– (2006). *Databases, Types, and The Relational Model: The Third Manifesto*. 3rd. Addison-Wesley.

Dattolo, Antonina, Angelo Di Iorio, et al. (2007). "Structural Patterns for Descriptive Documents". In: *ICWE*. Ed. by Luciano Baresi, Piero Fraternali, and Geert-Jan Houben. Vol. 4607. LNCS. Springer, pp. 421–426.

Dattolo, Antonina and Flaminia L. Luccio (2009). "A State of Art Survey on zz-structures". In: *Proceedings of the 1st Workshop on New Forms of Xanalogical Storage and Function*. CEUR 508, pp. 1–6.

Dau, Frithjof (2009a). "Formal, Diagrammatic Logic with Conceptual Graphs". In: *Conceptual Structures in Practice*. Ed. by Pascal Hitzler and Henrik Scharfe. Chapman and Hall/CRC, pp. 17–44.

– (2009b). "The Advent of Formal Diagrammatic Reasoning Systems". In: *ICFCA*. Ed. by Sébastien Ferré and Sebastian Rudolph. Vol. 5548. LNCS. Springer, pp. 38–56.

Davis, Mark (Oct. 8, 2010). *Unicode Text Segmentation*. Tech. rep. 29.

Davis, Mark, Ken Whistler, and Martin Dürst (2009). *Unicode Normalization Forms*. Tech. rep. Unicode Standard Annex 15. Unicode Consortium. http://unicode.org/reports/tr15/.

Dean, Mike et al. (July 29, 2002). *OWL Web Ontology Language 1.0 Reference*. Tech. rep. W3C Working Draft. http://www.w3.org/TR/2002/WD-owl-ref-20020729/.

Dearden, Andy and Janet Finlay (2006). "Pattern Languages in HCI: A Critical Review". In: *Human-Computer Interaction* 21, pp. 49–102.

Denning, Peter J. (June 2007). "Computing is a natural science". In: *Communications of the ACM* 50.7, pp. 13–18.

DeRose, Steven J., David G. Durand, et al. (1997). "What is text, really?" In: *Asterisk Journal of Computer Documentation* 21.3, pp. 1–24.

DeRose, Steven J., Eve Maler, et al. (Mar. 6, 2010). *XML Linking Language (XLink) Version 1.1*. Tech. rep. http://www.w3.org/TR/2010/REC-xlink11-20100506/.

Dewey, Melvil (1876). *A Classification and subject index for cataloguing and arranging the books and pamphlets of a library*. Massachusetts: Amherst.

Dodds, Leigh (Mar. 13, 2002). *Processing Model Considered Essential*. http://www.xml.com/pub/a/2002/03/13/processing-model.html.

Dougherty, Dale and Tim O'Reilly (1987). *Unix Text Processing*. Hayden Books.

Duerst, M. and M. Suignard (Jan. 2005). *Internationalized Resource Identifiers (IRIs)*. RFC 3987.

Eastlake, D. and P. Jones (Sept. 2001). *US Secure Hash Algorithm 1 (SHA1)*. RFC 3174.

Eastlake, Donald E. (Apr. 1972). *ITS Status Report*. Tech. rep. AIM-238. MIT Artificial Intelligence Laboratory. `ftp://publications.ai.mit.edu/ai-publications/pdf/AIM-238.pdf`.

Eco, Umberto (1976). *A theory of semiotics*. Advances in semiotics. Indiana University Press.

– (1977). *Zeichen: Einführung in einen Begriff und seine Geschichte*. Suhrkamp.

– (1979). *The role of the reader: explorations in the semiotics of texts*. Bloomington: Indiana University Press.

– (1984). *Semiotics and the philosophy of language*. McMillian.

– (1995). *The Search For The Perfect Language*. Blackwell.

Elmasri, Ramez and Shamkant Navathe (2010). *Fundamentals of Database Systems*. 6th ed. Prentice Hall International.

Emtage, Alan (Nov. 1992). *Minutes of the Uniform Resource Identifiers Working Group (URI)*. `ftp://ftp.ripe.net/ietf/uri/uri-minutes-92nov.txt`.

Engelbart, Douglas C. (1963). "A conceptual framework for the augmentation of man's intellect". In: *Vistas in Information Handling*. Ed. by P. Howerton. Vol. 1. Washington: Spartan Books, pp. 1–29.

Eppler, Martin J (2006). "A comparison between concept maps, mind maps, conceptual diagrams, and visual metaphors as complementary tools for knowledge construction and sharing". In: *Information Visualization* 5, 202–210.

Eriksson, Owen and Pär J. Ågerfalk (2010). "Rethinking the meaning of identifiers in information infrastructures". In: *Journal of the Association for Information Systems* 11.8.

Euler, Leonhard (1768). "Lettres à une Princesse d'Allemagne". In:

Fagin, Ronald (Sept. 1977). "Multivalued Dependencies and a New Normal Form for Relational Databases." In: *ACM Transactions on Database Systems* 2.3, pp. 262–278.

Falkenberg, Eckhard D. (1976). "Concepts for Modelling Information". In: *Modelling in Database Management Systems*. Ed. by Gerardus M. Nijssen. North-Holland Publishing, pp. 95–109.

Content Standard for Digital Spatial Metadata. Version 1 (1994). Tech. rep. Federal Geographic Data Committee.

Fielding, Roy Thomas (2000). "Architectural Styles and the Design of Network-based Software Architectures". PhD thesis. University of California. `http://www.ics.uci.edu/~fielding/pubs/dissertation/top.htm`.

Finkelstein, Clive (1989). *An Introduction to Information Engineering: From Strategic Planning to Information Systems*. Addison-Wesley.

Floridi, Luciano (2002a). "On defining library and information science as applied philosophy of information". In: *Social Epistemology* 16.1, pp. 37–49.

Floridi, Luciano (2002b). "What is the Philosophy of Information?" In: *Metaphilosophy* 33.1/2, pp. 117–138.

– (2005). "Is Information Meaningful Data?" In: *Philosophy and Phenomenological Research* 70.2, pp. 351–370.

– (2009). "Trends in the Philosophy of Information". In: *Handbook of Philosophy of Information*. Ed. by Pieter Adriaans and Johan van Benthem. Elsevier, pp. 113–132.

– (2010). *Information – a very short introduction*. Oxford University Press.

Floyd, Christiane (1996). "Choices about choices". In: *Systems Research* 13.3, pp. 261–270.

Fotache, Marin (2006). *Why Normalization Failed to Become the Ultimate Guide for Database Designers?* Tech. rep. 9.

Foucault, Michel (1969). *L'archéologie du savoir*. Paris: Gallimard.

Franssen, Maarten, Gert-Jan Lokhorst, and Ibo van de Poel (2009). "Philosophy of Technology". In: *Stanford Encyclopedia of Philosophy*. Ed. by Edward N. Zalta. Stanford University. http://plato.stanford.edu/entries/technology/.

Frederiks, Paul J. M., Arthur H. M. ter Hofstede, and E. Lippe (1997). "A unifying framework for conceptual data modelling concepts." In: *Information and Software Technology* 39.1, pp. 15–25.

Free Software Foundation (Mar. 2009). *GNU tar: an archiver tool*. Tech. rep. version 1.23. Free Software Foundation. http://www.gnu.org/software/tar/manual/.

Friedl, Jeffrey E. F. (2006). *Mastering Regular Expressions*. 3. O'Reilly.

Friendly, Michael (2009). *Milestones in the history of thematic cartography, statistical graphics, and data visualization*. http://datavis.ca/milestones/.

Fuchs, Norbert E., Uta Schwertel, and Sunna Torge (1999). "Controlled Natural Language Can Replace First-Order Logic." In: *ASE*, pp. 295–298.

Furnas, George W. and Jeff Zacks (1994). "Multitrees: Enriching and Reusing Hierarchical Structure". In: *Proceedings of the CHI*. New York: ACM, pp. 330–336.

Gamma, Erich et al. (1994). *Design Patterns: Elements of Reusable Object-Oriented Software*. 1st ed. Addison-Wesley.

Übersicht der PICA3-Kategorien (Aug. 26, 2010). Tech. rep. VZG. http://www.gbv.de/bibliotheken/verbundbibliotheken/02Verbund/01Erschliessung/02Richtlinien/01KatRicht/pica3.pdf.

Génova, G., M.C. Valiente, and J. Nubiola (2005). "A Semiotic Approach to UML Models". In: *Proceedings of the Workshop on Philosophical Foundations of Information Systems Engineering*. Vol. 13, pp. 547–557.

Giampaolo, Dominic (1999). *Practical File System Design with the Be File System*. Morgan Kaufmann Publishers.

Gil, Joseph, John Howse, and Stuart Kent (1999a). "Constraint Diagrams: A Step Beyond UML". In: *Proceedings of TOOLS 1999*. Ed. by Donald Firesmith et al. IEEE Computer Society, pp. 453–463.

– (1999b). "Formalising Spider Diagrams". In: *Proceedings of IEEE Symposium on Visual Languages*. IEEE, pp. 209–212.

– (2001). "Towards a Formalization of Constraint Diagrams." In: *HCC*. IEEE Computer Society, pp. 72–79.

Glasersfeld, Ernst von (1990). "An exposition of constructivism: Why some like it radical". In: *Journal for Research in Mathematics Education* 4, pp. 19–29.

Gödel, Kurt (1931). "Über formal unentscheidbare Sätze der Principia Mathematica und verwandter Systeme". In: *Monatshefte für Mathematik und Physik* 38.1, pp. 173–198.

Goertzel, Ben (2006). "Patterns, Hypergraphs and Embodied General Intelligence". In: *IJCNN*, pp. 451–458.

Goldfarb, Charles (1996). *The Roots of SGML, A Personal Recollection.* `http://www.sgmlsource.com/history/roots.htm`.

Goldfarb, Charles F. and Yuri Rubinsky (1990). *The SGML Handbook.* Oxford: Clarendon Press.

Gonzalez-Perez, Cesar (2012). "A conceptual modelling language for the humanities and social sciences." In: *RCIS*. Ed. by Colette Rolland, Jaelson Castro, and Oscar Pastor. IEEE, pp. 1–6.

Gonzalez-Perez, Cesar et al. (2012). "Extending an Abstract Reference Model for Transdisciplinary Work in Cultural Heritage". In: *Metadata and Semantics Research*. Springer, pp. 190–201.

Goyvaerts, Jan (2011). *Regular-Expressions.info*. Tech. rep. `http://www.regular-expressions.info/`.

Gradmann, Stefan (1998). "Cataloging vs. Metadata, Old Wine in New Bottles?" In: *Proceedings of the 64th IFLA Conference*. IFLA. Amsterdam. `http://archive.ifla.org/IV/ifla64/007-126e.htm`.

Gradmann, Stefan and Jan Christoph Meister (2008). "Digital document and interpretation: re-thinking "text" and scholarship in electronic settings". In: *Poiesis Praxis* 5.2, pp. 139–153.

Grant, Jan and Dave Beckett, eds. (Feb. 10, 2004). *RDF Test Cases.* `http://www.w3.org/TR/2004/REC-rdf-testcases-20040210/`.

Gray, Robert L. (2003). "Brief Historical Review of the Development of the Distinction Between Data and Information". In: *9th Americas Conference on Information Systems*. Ed. by J. Ross and D. Galletta. Tampa: Association for Information Systems, pp. 2843–2849.

Greibach, Sheila A. (1981). "Formal Languages: Origins and Directions". In: *IEEE Annals of the History of Computing* 3.1, pp. 14–41.

Greimas, Algirdas Julien (1966). *Sémantique structurale: recherche de méthode.* Paris: Larousse.

Grosse, Siegfried and Wolfgang Mentrup, eds. (1980). *Bürger - Formulare - Behörde. Wissenschaftliche Arbeitstagung zum Kommunikationsmittel 'Formular'.* Tübingen: Gunter Narr Verlag.

Grosso, Paul et al. (Mar. 25, 2003). *XPointer Framework.* Tech. rep.

Groth, Paul, Andrew Gibson, and Jan Velterop (2010). "The anatomy of a nanopublication". In: *Information Services and Use* 30.1, pp. 51–56.

Guha, Ramanathan V. (1996). *Towards a Theory of Meta Content*. Apple Technical Report 169. `http://downlode.org/Etext/MCF/towards_a_theory_of_metacontent.html`.

Guha, R.V. and Tim Bray (June 1997). *Meta Content Framework Using XML*. W3C Submission. `http://www.w3.org/TR/NOTE-MCF-XML-970624/`.

Gutteridge, Christopher (2010). *zzStructure Ontology*. Tech. rep. Temple ov thee Lemur. `http://data.totl.net/zz/`.

Haendel, Melissa A., Nicole A. Vasilevsky, and Jacqueline A. Wirz (2012). "Dealing with Data: A Case Study on Information and Data Management Literacy". In: *PLoS Biology* 10.5. `http://www.plosbiology.org/article/info:doi/10.1371/journal.pbio.1001339`.

Halm, Johan van (2005). "Questions and issues about the conversion to 13-digit ISBN and ISSN revision in library systems." In: *Information Services & Use* 25.2, pp. 115–118.

Halpin, Terry (2004). "Business Rule Verbalization". In: *ISTA*. Ed. by Anatoly E. Doroshenko et al. Vol. 48. LNI. Gesellschaft für Informatik, pp. 39–52.

Halpin, Terry and Tony Morgan (2008). *Information Modeling and Relational Databases: From Conceptual Analysis to Logical Design*. 2nd. Morgan Kaufmann.

Hammer, Eric (1994). "Reasoning with Sentences and Diagrams". In: *Notre Dame Journal of Formal Logic* 35.1, pp. 73–87.

Hapke, Thomas (1999). "Wilhelm Ostwald, the "Brücke" (Bridge), and connections to other bibliographic activities at the beginning of the twentieth century". In: *Proceedings of the 1998 Conference on the History and Heritage of Science Information Systems*. Ed. by Mary Ellen Bowden, Trudi Bellardo Hahn, and Robert V. Williams. Information today, pp. 139–147.

Harnad, Stevan (2007). "The Symbol Grounding Problem". In: *Scholarpedia* 2.7, p. 2373.

Hay, David C. (1995). *Data Model Patterns: Conventions of Thought*. Dorset House Publishing.

– (2006). *Data model patterns: a metadata map*. Amsterdam; Boston: Morgan Kaufmann.

Hayes, Patrick J. and Harry Halpin (2008). "In Defense of Ambiguity". In: *Int. Journal on Semantic Web and Information Systems* 4.2, pp. 1–18.

Hayes, Patrick and Brian McBride, eds. (Feb. 10, 2004). *RDF Semantics*. `http://www.w3.org/TR/rdf-mt/`.

Henning, Michi (June 2006). "The Rise and Fall of CORBA". In: *ACM Queue* 4.5, pp. 28–34.

HTML 5: A Vocabulary and Associated APIs for HTML and XHTML (Aug. 25, 2009). Tech. rep. W3C. `http://www.w3.org/TR/2009/WD-html5-20090825/`.

Hirschheim, Rudy, Heinz K. Klein, and Kalle Lyytinen (Oct. 1995). *Information Systems Development and Data Modeling. Conceptual and Philosophical Foundations*. Tracts in Theoretical Computer Science. Cambridge: Cambridge University Press.

Hitchman, S. (1995). "Practitioner perceptions on the use of some semantic concepts in the entity–relationship model". In: *European Journal of Information Systems* 4, pp. 31–40.

Hjelmslev, Louis (1953). *Prolegomena to a Theory of Language*. Baltimore: Wawerly Press.

Hjørland, Birger (Oct. 2007). "Arguments for 'the bibliographical paradigm'. Some thoughts inspired by the new English edition of the UDC". In: *information research* 12.4. http://informationr.net/ir/12-4/colis/colis06.html.

Holmevik, Jan Rune (Dec. 1994). "Compiling Simula: A historical study of technological genesis". In: *IEEE Annals in the History of Computing* 16.4, 25–37.

Holupirek, Alexander, Christian Grün, and Marc H. Scholl (2007). "Melting Pot XML: Bringing File Systems and Databases One Step Closer". In: *Datenbanksysteme in Business, Technologie und Web (BTW 2007), 12. Fachtagung des GI-Fachbereichs "Datenbanken und Informationssysteme" (DBIS)*. Ed. by Alfons Kemper et al. Vol. 103. LNI. GI, pp. 309–323.

Honig, William Leonard (1975). "A model of data structures commonly used in programming languages and data base management systems". PhD thesis. Northwestern University Evanston, p. 423.

Honig, William Leonard and C. Robert Carlson (1978). "Toward an Understanding of (Actual) Data Structures." In: *The Computer Journal* 21.2, pp. 98–104.

Hopcroft, John E. and Jeff D. Ullman (1979). *Introduction to Automata Theory, Languages, and Computation*. 1st. Addison-Wesley.

Horridge, Matthew and Peter F. Patel-Schneider (2009). *OWL 2 Web Ontology Language: Manchester Syntax*. Tech. rep. W3C. http://www.w3.org/TR/owl2-manchester-syntax/.

Horrocks, Ian, Oliver Kutz, and Ulrike Sattler (2006). "The Even More Irresistible SROIQ". In: *Proc. of the 10th Int. Conf. on Principles of Knowledge Representation and Reasoning*. Ed. by Patrick Doherty, John Mylopoulos, and Christopher A. Welty. AAAI Press, pp. 57–67.

Howse, John (2008). "Diagrammatic Reasoning Systems". In: *Proceedings of ICCS 2008*. Ed. by Peter W. Eklund and Ollivier Haemmerlé. Vol. 5113. LNCS. Springer, pp. 1–20.

Huang, Sheng-Cheng (2006). "A Semiotic View of Information: Semiotics as a Foundation of LIS Research in Information Behavior". In: *Proceedings of the 69th Annual Meeting of ASIST*. Ed. by Richard B. Hill. http://hdl.handle.net/10760/8796.

Hull, R. and R. King (Sept. 1987). "Semantic Database Modeling: Survey, Applications, and Research issues". In: *ACM Computing Surveys* 19.3, pp. 201–260.

Husserl, Edmund (1931). *Ideas: General Introduction to Pure Phenomenology*. Allen & Unwin.

Bibliography

Husserl, Edmund (1986). *Die phänomenologische Methode: Ausgewählte Texte I*. Ed. by Klaus Held. Reclam.

IFLA Study Group on the Functional Requirements for Bibliographic Records, ed. (1998). *Funktional Requierements For Bibliographic Records*. K.G. Saur.

Institute of Electrical Electronics Engineers (1988). *Portable Operating System Interface for Computer Environments*. Tech. rep. 1003.1-1988. New York.

– (2008). *IEEE Standard for Binary Floating-Point Arithmetic*. Tech. rep. 754-2008. IEEE.

International Organization for Standardization, ed. (1987). *ISO/TR 9007:1987 Information processing systems – Concepts and terminology for the conceptual schema and the information base*.

– ed. (1996). *ISO/IEC 14977:1996 Information Technology - Syntactic Metalanguage - Extended BNF*.

– ed. (2000). *ISO/IEC 13250:2000 Topic Maps: Information Technology – Document Description and Markup Language*.

– ed. (2005). *ISO/IEC 24824-1 Generic Applications of ASN.1: Fast Infoset*.

– ed. (2006). *ISO/IEC 19757-3:2007 Document Schema Definition Languages (DSDL) – Part 3: Rule-based validation – Schematron*.

– ed. (2007a). *ISO/IEC 11404:2007 Information technology – General-Purpose Datatypes*.

– ed. (2007b). *ISO/IEC 24707:2007 Information technology – Common Logic (CL)*.

– ed. (2008a). *ISO/IEC 19757:2008 Document Schema Definition Languages (DSDL)*.

– ed. (2008b). *ISO/IEC 19757-9:2008 Document Schema Definition Languages (DSDL) – Part 3: Regular-grammar-based validation – RELAX NG*.

– ed. (2008c). *ISO/IEC 19757-9:2008 Namespace and datatype declaration in Document Type Definitions (DTDs)*.

Jakobson, Roman (1963). *Essais de linguistique générale*. Paris: Minuit.

Jarrar, Mustafa, Maria Keet, and Paolo Dongilli (Feb. 2006). *Multilingual verbalization of ORM conceptual models and axiomatized ontologies*. Tech. rep. STARLab Technical Report. Vrije Universiteit Brussel. http://www.meteck.org/files/ORMmultiverb_JKD.pdf.

Jay, Barry (1995). "A Semantics for Shape". In: *Science of Computer Programming* 25.2-3, pp. 251–283.

– (2009). *Pattern Calculus: Computing with Functions and Structures*. Springer.

Jech, Thomas (2003). *Set Theory: The Third Millennium Edition*. Springer.

Jorgensen, Jorgen (1937). "Imperatives and Logic". In: *Erkenntnis* 7, pp. 288–296.

Jr., Thomas B. Steel (1975). "Data Base Standardization - A Status Report". In: *IBM Symposium: Data Base Systems*. Ed. by Helmut F. Hasselmeier and Wilhelm G. Spruth. Vol. 39. LNCS. Springer, pp. 362–386.

Keet, C. Maria (2007). "Enhancing Comprehension of Ontologies and Conceptual Models Through Abstractions." In: *AI*IA*. Ed. by Roberto Basili and Maria Teresa Pazienza. Vol. 4733. LNCS. Springer, pp. 813–821.

– (2008a). "A formal comparison of conceptual data modeling languages". In: *CEUR-WS*, pp. 25–37.

– (2008b). "A formal theory of granularity". PhD thesis. KRDB Research Centre, Faculty of Computer Science, Free University of Bozen-Bolzano.

– (2008c). "Unifying industry-grade class-based conceptual data modeling languages with CMcom". In: *21st International Workshop on Description Logics*. Vol. 353. CEUR-WS.

– (2011). "The granular perspective as semantically enriched granulation hierarchy". In: *IJGCRSIS* 2.1, pp. 51–70.

Kelly, Steven and Juha-Pekka Tolvanen (2008). *Domain-Specific Modeling: Enabling Full Code Generation*. Wiley.

Kent, William (1978). *Data and Reality. Basic assumptions in data processing reconsidered*. North-Holland.

– (1979). "Limitations of Record-Based Information Models". In: *Transactions on Database Systems (TODS)* 4.1, pp. 107–131.

– (1983a). *A Taxonomy for Entity-Relationship Models*. http://www.bkent.net/Doc/ertax.htm.

– (Feb. 1983b). "A Simple Guide to Five Normal Forms in Relational Database Theory". In: *Communications of the ACM 26* 26.2, pp. 120–125.

– (1984). "Fact-based data analysis and design". In: *Journal of Systems and Software* 4.2-3, pp. 99–121.

– (1988). "The Many Forms of a Single Fact". In: *Proceeedings of the IEEE COMPCON*. http://www.bkent.net/Doc/manyform.htm.

– (June 1991). "A Rigorous Model of Object Reference, Identity, and Existence". In: *Journal of Object-Oriented Programming* 4.3, pp. 28–36.

– (2003). "The unsolvable identity problem". In: *Extreme Markup Languages*. http://www.mulberrytech.com/Extreme/Proceedings/html/2003/Kent01/EML2003Kent01.html.

Kent, William and Steve Hoberman (2012). *Data and Reality. A timeless perspective on perceiving and managing in our imprecise world*. 3rd. Westfield: Technics Publications.

Kern, Heiko, Axel Hummel, and Stefan Kühne (2011). "Towards a Comparative Analysis of Meta-Metamodels". In: *11th Workshop in Domain-Specific Modeling*.

Kerschberg, Larry, Anthony C. Klug, and Dennis Tsichritzis (1976). "A Taxonomy of Data Models". In: *Proceedings of the 2nd International Conference on Very Large Date Bases (VLDB)*. Ed. by Peter C. Lockemann and Erich J. Neuhold. North Holland, pp. 43–64.

Khandan, M. (2009). "A comparative study on luciano floridi and rafael capurros informatological thoughts". In: *Research on information science and public libraries* 15.1, pp. 149–183.

Khoshafian, Setrag N. and George P. Copeland (Nov. 1986). "Object Identity". In: *ACM SIGPLAN Notices* 21.11, pp. 406–416.

RIF Overview (June 22, 2010). Working Group Note. `http://www.w3.org/TR/2010/NOTE-rif-overview-20100622/`.

Kimball, Ralph (May 1998). "Surrogate keys". In: *DBMS* 11.5. `http://web.archive.org/web/19990219111430/http://www.dbmsmag.com/9805d05.html`.

Resource Description Framework (RDF): Concepts and Abstract Syntax (Feb. 10, 2004). Tech. rep. W3C. `http://www.w3.org/TR/rdf-concepts/`.

Knublauch, Holger, James A. Hendler, and Kingsley Idehen (2011). *SPIN - Overview and Motivation*. Tech. rep. `http://www.w3.org/Submission/2011/SUBM-spin-overview-20110222/`.

Knuth, Donald E. (June 1957). "Potrzebie System of Weights and Measures". In: *MAD magazine* 33, p. 36.

– (1964). "backus normal form vs. Backus Naur form". In: *Communications of the ACM* 7.12, pp. 735–736.

– (1984). *The TeXbook: a complete user's guide to computer typesetting with TEX*. Addison-Wesley.

Köbler, Johannes (2006). "On Graph Isomorphism for Restricted Graph Classes." In: *CiE*. Ed. by Arnold Beckmann et al. Vol. 3988. LNCS. Springer, pp. 241–256.

Koenig, Andrew (1998). *Programming abstractly*. Lecture slides. `http://www.cs.princeton.edu/courses/archive/spr98/cs333/lectures/19/`.

Korzybski, Alfred (1933). "A Non-Aristotelian System and its Necessity for Rigour in Mathematics and Physics". In: *Science and sanity: an introduction to non-Aristotelian systems and general semantics*. Lancaster.

Kronick, David A. (1962). *A History of Scientific and Technical Periodicals: The Origins and Development of the Scientific and Technological Press, 1665-1790*. New York: Scarecrow Press.

Kuhn, Thomas S. (1962). *The Structure of Scientific Revolutions*. Chicago: University of Chicago Press.

– (1974). "Second Thoughts on Paradigms". In: *The Structure of Scientific Theories*. Ed. by Frederick Suppe. University of Illinois Press, 459–82.

Lakoff, George (1987). *Women, Fire, and Dangerous Things: What Categories Reveal About the Mind*. Chicago: University of Chicago Press.

Lamport, Leslie (1994). *LATEX: a document preparation system: user's guide and reference manual*. 2nd. Addison-Wesley.

Lange, Thomas (2006). "Peenemünde: Analyse einer Technologieentwicklung im Dritten Reich". PhD thesis. Hamburg University.

Resource Description Framework (RDF). Model and Syntax Specification (Feb. 22, 1999). Tech. rep. W3C. `http://www.w3.org/TR/1999/REC-rdf-syntax-19990222`.

Leibniz, Gottfried (1703). "Explication de l'arithmétique binaire". In: *Memoires de l'Académie Royale des Sciences* 3, pp. 85–93.

MARC 21 Format for Bibliographic Data (Sept. 2012). Tech. rep. `http://www.loc.gov/marc/bibliographic/`.

Liétard, Ludovic (2008). "A new definition for linguistic summaries of data". In: *Proceedings of Fuzzy Systems*, pp. 506–511.

Liskov, Barbara (Mar. 1987). "Data Abstraction and Hierarchy". In: *ACM SIGPLAN Notices* 23.5, pp. 17–34.

Liskov, Barbara and Stephen Zilles (Apr. 1974). "Programming with Abstract Data Types". In: *ACM SIGPLAN Notices* 9.4, pp. 50–59.

Loukides, Mike (June 2, 2010). "What is data science?" In: *O'Reilly radar*. http://radar.oreilly.com/2010/06/what-is-data-science.html.

Lund, Niels Windfeld (2009). "Document theory". In: *ARIST* 43.1, pp. 1–55.

Lynch, Clifford (Oct. 1997). "Identifiers and Their Role in Networked Information Applications". In: *ARL: A Bimonthly Newsletter of Research Library Issues and Actions* 194. http://www.arl.org/bm~doc/identifier.pdf.

Mai, Jens-Erik (2001). "Semiotics and indexing: An analysis of the subject indexing process". In: *Journal of Documentation* 57.5, pp. 591–622.

Ma, Lai (Apr. 2012). "Meanings of Information: The assumptions and research consequences of three foundational LIS theories". In: *JASIST* 63.4, pp. 716–723.

Manola, Frank and Eric Miller (Feb. 2004). *RDF Primer*. http://www.w3.org/TR/2004/REC-rdf-primer-20040210/.

Marshall, Catherine C. and Frank M. Shipman III (1995). "Spatial Hypertext: Designing for Change". In: *Communications of the ACM* 38.8, pp. 88–97.

Martinez-Gil, Jorge, Enrique Alba, and Jose F. Aldana-Montes (2010). "Statistical Study about Existing OWL Ontologies from a Significant Sample as Previous Step for their Alignment". In: *International Conference on Complex, Intelligent and Software Intensive Systems*. Los Alamitos, CA: IEEE, pp. 980–985.

Martin, James (1990). *Information engineering*. Englewood Cliffs: Prentice Hall.

Martin, James and Carma MacClure (1985). *Diagramming techniques for Analysts and Programmers*. Prentice-Hall.

Masinter, L. (Aug. 1998). *The "data" URL scheme*. RFC 2397.

McCallum, Sally H. (2002). "MARC: Keystone for Library Automation". In: *IEEE Annals of the History of Computing* 24.2, pp. 34–49.

– (2009). "Machine Readable Cataloging (MARC): 1975-2007". In: *Encyclopedia of Library and Information Sciences*. Ed. by Marcia J. Bates and Mary Niles Maack. 3rd. Taylor & Francis, pp. 3530–3539.

McGee, W. C. (Sept. 1981). "Data Base Technology". In: *IBM Journal of Research and Development* 25.5, pp. 505–519.

McGuffin, Michael J. and m. c. schraefel (2004). "A comparison of hyperstructures: zzstructures, mSpaces, and polyarchies". In: *Proceedings of the fifteenth ACM conference on Hypertext and hypermedia*. New York: ACM, pp. 153–162.

McNamara, Paul (Sept. 2010). "Deontic logic". In: *The Stanford Encyclopedia of Philosophy*. Ed. by Edward N. Zalta. Fall 2010. Stanford University. http://plato.stanford.edu/archives/fall2010/entries/logic-deontic/.

McNaughton, Robert (1999). "An Insertion into the Chomsky Hierarchy?" In: *Jewels are Forever, Contributions on Theoretical Computer Science in Honor of Arto Salomaa*, pp. 204–212.

URIs, URLs, and URNs: Clarifications and Recommendations 1.0 (Sept. 2001). Tech. rep. `http://www.w3.org/TR/uri-clarification/`.

Mealy, George H. (1967). "Another look at data". In: *Proceedings of the 1967, fall joint computer conference*. ACM, pp. 525–534.

Meek, Brian L. (Sept. 1994a). "A taxonomy of datatypes". In: *SIGPLAN Notices* 29.9, pp. 159–167.

– (Apr. 1994b). "Programming languages: towards greater commonality". In: *SIGPLAN Notices* 29.4, pp. 49–57.

– (1995). "The seven golden rules for producing language-independent standards". In: *Software Engineering Standards Symposium*, pp. 250–256.

– (June 1996). "Too soon, too late, too narrow, too wide, too shallow, too deep". In: *StandardView* 4.2, pp. 114–118.

Megginson, David (Apr. 2004). *Simple API for XML (SAX 2.0)*. `http://www.saxproject.org/`.

Meier-Oeser, Stephan (June 2011). "Medieval Semiotics". In: *The Stanford Encyclopedia of Philosophy*. Ed. by Edward N. Zalta. Summer 2011. `http://plato.stanford.edu/archives/sum2011/entries/semiotics-medieval`.

"Paradigm" (2011). In: *Merriam-Webster Online Dictionary*. Ed. by Meriam-Webster. accessed 2011-09-20. `http://www.merriam-webster.com/dictionary/paradigm`.

Meszaros, Gerard and Jim Doble (1997). "A Pattern Language for Pattern Writing". In: *Pattern Languages of Program Design* 3, pp. 529–574.

Mohan, Sriram and Arijit Sengupta (2009). "Conceptual Modeling for XML: A Myth or a Reality". In: *Database Technologies: Concepts, Methodologies, Tools, and Applications*. Ed. by John Erickson. IGI Global, pp. 527–549.

Moltmann, Friederike (2007). "Events, tropes, and truthmaking". In: *Philosophical Studies* 134.3, pp. 363–403.

Monniaux, David (2008). "The pitfalls of verifying floating-point computations". In: *ACM Transactions of Programming Language Systems* 30.3, 12:1–12:41.

Mons, Barend and Jan Velterop (2009). "Nano-Publication in the e-science era". In: *International Semantic Web Conference*.

Moody, Daniel Laurence (2009). "The "physics" of notations: towards a scientific basis for constructing visual notations in software engineering". In: *IEEE Transactions on Software Engineering* 35.6, pp. 756–779.

Mooers, Calvin (July 1960). "Mooer's Law: or, why some retrieval systems are used and others are not". In: *American Documentation* 11.3, p. 204.

Murata, Makoto et al. (Nov. 2005). "Taxonomy of XML Schema Languages Using Formal Language Theory". In: *ACM Transactions on Internet Technology* 5.4, pp. 660–704.

Muschett, Brien, Rich Salz, and Michael Schenker (Mar. 2011). *JSONx, an XML Encoding for JSON*. draft. IETF. http://tools.ietf.org/html/draft-rsalz-jsonx-00.

Directory interchange format manual, version 1.0 (1988). Tech. rep. NASA.

"Revised Report on the Algorithmic Language Algol 60" (Jan. 1963). In: *Communications of the ACM* 6.1. Ed. by Peter Naur, pp. 1–23.

Naur, Peter (July 1966). "The science of datalogy". In: *Communications of the ACM* 9.7, p. 485.

– (1968). "'Datalogy', the science of data and data processes, and its place in education." In: *Proceedings of the IFIP Congress 68*. Ed. by A. J. H. Morrell. North-Holland, pp. 1383–1387.

– (1985). "Programming as Theory building". In: *Microprocessing and Microprogramming* 15.5, pp. 253–261.

– (1992). "Programming Languages Are Not Languages – Why 'Programming Language' Is a Misleading Designation". In: *Computing: A Human Activity*. ACM Press, pp. XX–XX.

– (2007). "Computing versus human thinking". In: *Communications of the ACM* 50.1, pp. 85–94.

Navathe, Shamkant B. (1992). "Evolution of Data Modeling for Databases". In: *Communications of the ACM* 35.9, pp. 112–123.

Nečaský, Martin (2006). "Conceptual Modeling for XML: A Survey". In: *DATESO*. Ed. by Václav Snášel, Karel Richta, and Jaroslav Pokorný. Vol. 176. CEUR Workshop Proceedings. CEUR-WS.org. http://www.ceur-ws.org/Vol-176/paper7.pdf.

– (2008). "Conceptual Modeling for XML". PhD thesis.

Nelson, Ted (1965a). "Complex information processing: a file structure for the complex, the changing and the indeterminate". In: *Proceedings of the 20th ACM National Conference*. Cleveland: ACM, pp. 84–100.

– (1965b). "The Hypertext". In: *Proceedings of the International Federation of Documentation (FID) Congress*. 31. abstract, reprinted in Nelsons Possiplex, p. 154. Washington, DC.

– (1981). *Literary Machines*. 3rd. Sausalito, California: Mindful Press.

– (Dec. 1986). "The Tyranny of the File". In: *Datamation* ?15, ?

– (Dec. 1999). "Xanalogical Structure, Needed Now More Than Ever: Parallel Documents, Deep Links to Content, Deep Versioning, and Deep Re-Use". In: *ACM Computing Surveys* 31.4.

– (2004). "A Cosmology for a Different Computer Universe: Data Model, Mechanisms, Virtual Machine and Visualization Infrastructure". In: *Journal of Digital Information* 5.1. http://journals.tdl.org/jodi/article/viewArticle/131.

– (2010). *Possiplex: Movies, Intellect, and Creative Control. My Computer Life and the Fight for Civilization*. 1st. Mindful Press.

– (May 22, 2012). *Computers for Cynics 0 - The Myth of Technology*. http://www.youtube.com/watch?v=KdnGPQaICjk.

Neward, Ted (June 26, 2006). *The Vietnam of Computer Science.* `http://blogs.tedneward.com/2006/06/26/The+Vietnam+Of+Computer+Science.aspx`.

Nijssen, Gerardus M. and Terry Halpin (1989). *Conceptual Schema and Relational Database Design: A Fact Oriented Approach.* Prentice-Hall.

Novak, Joseph D. and Alberto J. Cañas (2006). *The Theory Underlying Concept Maps and How to Construct Them.* Tech. rep. 2006-01. Technical Report IHMC Cmap-Tools. `http://cmap.ihmc.us/Publications/ResearchPapers/TheoryCmaps/TheoryUnderlyingConceptMaps.htm`.

Open Document Format for Office Applications v1.2 (Jan. 2012). Tech. rep.

Object Management Group (May 2009). *Ontology Definition Metamodel (OMG) Version 1.0.* Tech. rep. formal/2009-05-01. Object Management Group. `http://www.omg.org/spec/ODM/1.0`.

OCLC, ed. (2010). *"info" URI Registry.* `http://info-uri.info/`.

Oei, J L Han et al. (1992). *The Meta Model Hierarchy: A Framework for Information Systems Concepts and Techniques.* Tech. rep. 92-17, pp. 151–159.

Ogbuji (Jan. 12, 2002). "XML class warfare". In: *ADT Magazine.* `http://adtmag.com/articles/2002/12/01/xml-class-warfare.aspx`.

Ogden, Charles Kay and I.A. Richards (1923). *The meaning of meaning.* London: Trubner & Co.

Okhotin, Alexander (2010). "Fast parsing for Boolean grammars: a generalization of Valiant's algorithm". In: *International Conference on Developments in Language Theory.* Vol. 6224. LNCS, pp. 340–351.

Oliver, Ian and Vesa Luukala (2006). "On UML's Composite Structure Diagram". In: *Fifth Workshop on System Analysis and Modelling.*

Olivier, Martin S. (2009). "On metadata context in Database Forensics". In: *Digital Investigation* 5.3-4, pp. 115 –123.

Documents Associated With UML Version 2.4.1 (Aug. 2011). Tech. rep. `http://www.omg.org/spec/UML/2.4.1/`.

Ørom, Anders (2007). "The concept of information versus the concept of document". In: *Document (re)turn. Contributions from a research field in transition.* Ed. by Roswitha Skare, Niels Windfeld Lund, and Andreas Vårheim. Frankfurt: Peter Lang, pp. 53–72.

Otlet, Paul (1918). "Transformations operées dans l'appareil bibliographique des science". In: *Revue Scientifique* 58, pp. 236–241.

– (1934). *Traité de documentation. Le livre sur le livre. Théorie et pratique.* IIB Publication 197. Brussels: Editiones Mundaneum.

– (1990). *International organisation and dissemination of knowledge selected essays of Paul Otlet.* Ed. by W. Boyd Rayward. FID publications. Elsevier.

Palmer, Kent (2009). "Emergent design explorations in systems phenomenology in relation to ontology hermeneutics and the metadialectics of design". PhD thesis. University of South Australia.

Patig, Susanne (2006). "Evolution of entity-relationship modelling". In: *Data and Knowledge Engineering* 56.2, pp. 122–138.

Peckham, J. and F. Maryanski (Sept. 1988). "Semantic Data Models". In: *ACM Computing Surveys* 20.3, pp. 153–189.

Pédauque, Roger T. (2003). "Document: Form, Sign and Medium, As Reformulated for Electronic Documents". In: `http://archivesic.ccsd.cnrs.fr/docs/00/06/22/28/HTML/index.html`.

– (2006). *Le document à la lumière du numérique*. Caen: C & F éditions.

– (Jan. 2007). *La redocumentarisation du monde*. Cépaduès.

– (Feb. 2011). *Le web sous tensions*. `https://espacestemps.co-ment.com/text/vsMAqHUTfIi/view/`.

Peirce, Charles Sanders (1931a). *Collected Papers Volume I: Elements of Logic*. Ed. by Charles Hartshorne and Paul Weiss. Cambridge: Harvard University Press.

– (1931b). *Collected Papers Volume I: Principles of Philosophy*. Ed. by Charles Hartshorne and Paul Weiss. Cambridge: Harvard University Press.

– (1933). *Collected Papers Volume IV: The Simplest Mathematics*. Ed. by Charles Hartshorne and Paul Weiss. Cambridge: Harvard University Press.

Pepper, Steve (Feb. 2010). "Topic Maps". In: *Encyclopedia of Library and Information Science*. 3rd ed. Taylor & Francis.

Petter, Stacie, Deepak Khazanchi, and John D. Murphy (2010). "A design science based evaluation framework for patterns". In: *ACM SIGMIS Databas* 41.3, pp. 9–26.

Phillips, Addison and Mark Davis (Sept. 2006). *Tags for Identifying Languages*. RFC 4646.

Pichler, Reinhard et al. (2010). "Redundancy Elimination on RDF Graphs in the Presence of Rules, Constraints, and Queries". In: *4th International Conference on Web Reasoning and Rule Systems*. Ed. by Pascal Hitzler and Thomas Lukasiewicz. Vol. 6333. LNCS. Springer, pp. 133–148.

Pierce, Benjamin (2002). *Types and Programming Languages*. Cambridge: MIT Press.

Piez, Wendell (2001). "Beyond the 'descriptive vs. procedural' distinction". In: *Proceedings of the Extreme Markup Languages Conference*, pp. 141–172.

PKWARE (Sept. 2007). *ZIP File Format Specification*. Tech. rep. version 6.3.2. PKWARE. `http://www.pkware.com/documents/casestudies/APPNOTE.TXT`.

Pluempitiwiriyawej, Charnyote and Joachim Hammer (Sept. 2000). *A Classification Scheme for Semantic and Schematic Heterogeneities in XML Data Sources*. Tech. rep. TR00-004. University of Florida. `http://ufdcimages.uflib.ufl.edu/UF/00/09/54/63/00001/2000396.pdf`.

Pondorf, Denis and Andreas Witt (2010). "Freestyle Markup Language: Specification of an intuitive, powerful, polyhierarchical new extensible markup language". In: *Proceedings of Balisage Markup Conference 2010*. Vol. 5. Balisage Series on Markup Technologies.

Pourabdollah, Amir (2009). "Theory and practice of the ternary relations model of information management". PhD thesis. University of Nottingham. http://etheses.nottingham.ac.uk/708/.

Powell, Alan, Michael Beckerle, and Stephen Hanson (Jan. 2011). *Data Format Description Language (DFDL)*. Tech. rep. Open Grid Forum. http://www.ogf.org/dfdl/.

Prud'hommeaux, Eric and Andy Seaborne (Jan. 15, 2008). *SPARQL Query Language for RDF*. Tech. rep. http://www.w3.org/TR/2008/REC-rdf-sparql-query-20080115/.

Qin, Jian and John D'Ignazio (June 2010). "Lessons learned from a two-year experience in science data literacy education". In:

Quin, Liam (1996). "Suggestive Markup: Explicit Relationships in Descriptive and Prescriptive DTDs". In: *Proceedings of the SGML 96 conference*. Boston. http://www.holoweb.net/~liam/papers/1996-sgml96-SuggestiveMarkup/.

Raber, Douglas and John M. Budd (2003). "Information as sign: semiotics and information science". In: *Journal of Documentation* 59.5, pp. 507–522.

Ranganathan, Shiyali Ramamrita (1931). *The five laws of library science*. Madras: Madras Library Association.

Rayward, W. Boyd (May 1994). "Visions of Xanadu: Paul Otlet (1868-1944) and Hypertext". In: *Journal of the American Society for Information Science* 45.4, pp. 235–250.

– (Apr. 1997). "The Origins of Information Science and the Work of the International Institute of Bibliography/International Federation for Documentation and Information(FID)". In: *Journal of the American Society for Information Science* 48, pp. 289–300.

Reimer, Jeremy (Mar. 16, 2008). "From BFS to ZFS: past, present, and future of file systems". In: *Ars Technica*. http://arstechnica.com/hardware/news/2008/03/past-present-future-file-systems.ars.

Reiner, Ulrike (1988). "Semantik von Anfragesprachen für Dokumenten-, Fakten- und Erklärungssuchsysteme". PhD thesis. TU Berlin.

– (1991). *Anfragesprachen fuer Informationssysteme*. Frankfurt: DGD.

Renear, Allen H. (2000). "The descriptive/procedural distinction is flawed". In: *Markup Languages: Theory and Practise* 4.2, pp. 411–420.

Renear, Allen H. and David Dubin (2003). "Towards identity conditions for digital documents". In: *Proceedings of the International DCMI Metadata Conference and Workshop*. Seattle: DCMI, pp. 181–189.

Renear, Allen H. and Karen M. Wickett (2009). "Documents Cannot Be Edited". In: *Proceedings of Balisage: The Markup Conference 2009*. Vol. 3. Balisage Series on Markup Technologies. Montréal. http://www.balisage.net/Proceedings/vol3/html/Renear01/BalisageVol3-Renear01.html.

Renear, Allen, Elli Mylonas, and David Durand (1996). "Refining our Notion of What Text Really Is: The Problem of Overlapping Hierarchies". In: *Research in*

Humanities Computing. Ed. by Nancy Ide and Susan Hockey. Vol. 4. Clarendon Press, pp. 263–280.

Repici, Dominic John (2010). *The Comma Separated Value (CSV) File Format*. http://www.creativyst.com/Doc/Articles/CSV/CSV01.htm.

Riley, Jenn (2010). *Seeing Standards: A Visualization of the Metadata Universe*. Tech. rep. http://www.dlib.indiana.edu/~jenlrile/metadatamap/.

Ritchie, Dennis M. (1979). "The Evolution of the Unix Time-sharing System". In: *Language Design and Programming Methodology*. Vol. 79. LNCS. Springer, pp. 25–35.

Rivest, R. (Nov. 1997). *S-Expressions*. Tech. rep. Internet Draft. Network Working Group. http://people.csail.mit.edu/rivest/Sexp.txt.

Rodriguez, Marko A. and Peter Neubauer (Aug. 2010). "Constructions from Dots and Lines". In: *Bulletin of the American Society for Information Science and Technology* 36.6, pp. 35–41.

Rojas, Raúl and Ulf Hashagen, eds. (2000). *The First Computers: History and Architectures*. MIT Press.

Rood, Hendrik (Aug. 2000). "What's in a name, what's in a number: some characteristics of identifiers on electronic networks". In: *Telecommunications Policy* 24.6-7, pp. 533–552.

Rosch, Eleanor (1983). "Prototype classification and logical classification: The two systems". In: *New Trends in Conceptual Representation: Challenges to Piaget's Theory?* Ed. by Ellin Kofsky Scholnick. Erlbaum, pp. 73–86.

Saltzer, J.H. (1965). *CTSS Technical Notes*. Tech. rep. MIT-LCS-TR-016. MIT. http://publications.csail.mit.edu/lcs/specpub.php?id=584.

Saussure, Ferdinand D. (1916). *Cours de linguistique générale*. Paris: Bayot.

Schield, Milo (2004). "Information literacy, statistical literacy, and data literacy". In: *IASSIST Quarterly* 28.Summer/Fall, pp. 6–11.

Schneider, Michael (Oct. 27, 2009). *OWL 2 Web Ontology Language: RDF-Based Semantics*. Tech. rep. http://www.w3.org/TR/2009/REC-owl2-rdf-based-semantics-20091027/.

Schrettinger, Martin (1808). *Versuch eines vollständigen Lehrbuches der Bibliothek-Wissenschaft. Band 1*. München.

– (1829). *Versuch eines vollständigen Lehrbuches der Bibliothek-Wissenschaft, 2. Band*. München: Lindenau.

Schuman, Stephen A. and Philippe Jorrand (1967). "Definition Mechanisms in Extensible Programming Languages". In: *Proceedings of AFIPS*. ACM, pp. 9–20.

Searle, John (1969). *Speech Acts*. Cambridge: Cambridge University Press.

Seibel, Peter (2009). *Coders at Work: Reflections on the Craft of Programming*. New York: Apress.

Sengupta, Arijit and Erik Wilde (Feb. 2006). *The Case for Conceptual Modeling for XML*. Tech. rep. TIK Report 244. Zürich, Switzerland: Computer Engineering and Networks Laboratory, ETH Zürich.

Shafranovich, Y. (Oct. 2005). *Common Format and MIME Type for Comma-Separated Values (CSV) Files*. RFC 4180. IETF.

Shannon, Claude (1938). "A Symbolic Analysis of Relay and Switching Circuits". In: *Transactions of the American Institute of Electrical Engineers* 57, pp. 713–723.

Shannon, Claude Elwood (1948). "A mathematical theory of communication". In: *Bell Systems Technical Journal* 27, pp. 379–423, 623–656.

Shelley, E.P. and B.D. Johnson (1995). "Metadata: Concepts and Models". In: *Proceedings of the Third National Conference on the Management of Geoscience Information and Data*. Adelaide, South Australia: Australian Mineral Foundation.

Sheth, Amit, Cartic Ramakrishnan, and Christopher Thomas (2005). "Semantics for the Semantic Web: The Implicit, the Formal and the Powerful". In: *International Journal on Semantic Web & Information Systems* 1.1, pp. 1–18.

Shin, Sun-Joo (1995). *The logical status of diagrams*. Cambridge: Cambridge University Press.

Signes, Ricardo and John Cappiello (2008). *Rx: Simple, Extensible Schemata*. Tech. rep. `http://rx.codesimply.com/`.

Silberschatz, Abraham, Henry F. Korth, and S. Sudarshan (2010). *Database system concepts*. 6th ed. New York: McGraw-Hill.

Silverston, L. (2001). *The Data Model Resource Book - A Library of Universal Data Models for All Enterprises*. Vol. 1. John Wiley & Sons.

Silverston, Len and Paul Agnew (2009). *The Data Model Resource Book, Vol. 3: Universal Patterns for Data Modeling*. Wiley.

Simsion, Graeme (2007). *Data Modeling Theory and Practise*. Technics Publications.

Skare, Roswitha, Andreas Vårheim, and Niels Windfeld Lund (2007). *A Document (Re)turn. Contributions from a Research Field in Transition*. Frankfurt: Peter Lang.

Smith, David Woodruff (June 2009). "Phenomenology". In: *The Stanford Encyclopedia of Philosophy*. Ed. by Edward N. Zalta. Summer 2009. Stanford University. `http://plato.stanford.edu/archives/sum2009/entries/phenomenology/`.

Solla Price, Derek J. de (1963). *Little science, big science*. New York: Columbia University Press.

Solntseff, N and A Yezerski (1974). "A survey of extensible programming languages". In: *Annual Review in Automatic Programming*. Vol. 7. Elsevier, pp. 267–307.

Sompel, H. Van de et al. (Apr. 2006). *The "info" URI Scheme for Information Assets with Identifiers in Public Namespaces*. RFC 4452.

Souza, Clarisse Sieckenius de (2012). "Semiotics". In: *Encyclopedia of Human-Computer Interaction*. Ed. by Mads Soegaard and Rikke Friis Dam. Aarhus: The Interaction-Design.org Foundation. `http://www.interaction-design.org/encyclopedia/semiotics_and_human-computer_interaction.html`.

Sowa, John F. (July 1976). "Conceptual Graphs for a Data Base Interface". In: *IBM Journal of Research and Development* 20.4, pp. 336–357.

– (1992a). "Conceptual graphs summary". In: *Conceptual structures: current research and practice*. Ed. by P. Eklund et al. Ellis Horwood, pp. 3–51.

– (1992b). "Semantic Networks". In: *Encyclopedia of Artificial Intelligence*. Ed. by Stuart C. Shapiro. 2nd ed. Wiley. http://www.jfsowa.com/pubs/semnet.htm.

– (2000). *Knowledge Representation: Logical, Philosophical, and Computational Foundations*. Brooks Cole Publishing.

– (Apr. 10, 2006). *Concept Mapping*. San Francisco. http://www.jfsowa.com/talks/cmapping.pdf.

– (2008). "Conceptual Graphs". In: *Handbook of knowledge representation*. Ed. by F. van Harmelen, V. Lifschitz, and B. Porter. Elsevier, pp. 213–237.

Spiegelberg, Herbert (1982). *The phenomenological movement: a historical introduction*. 3rd. Nijhoff.

Spinellis, Diomidis (2007). "Another level of indirection". In: *Beautiful Code: Leading Programmers Explain How They Think*. Ed. by Andy Oram and Greg Wilson. O'Reilly. Chap. 17, 279–291.

Sporny, Manu, Gregg Kellogg, and Markus Lanthaler (Dec. 8, 2012). *JSON-LD Syntax 1.0*. Tech. rep. http://json-ld.org/spec/latest/json-ld-syntax/.

Stamper, Ronald et al. (2000). "Understanding the roles of signs and norms in organizations - a semiotic approach to information systems design". In: *Behaviour Information Technology* 19.1, pp. 15–27.

"Interim Report: ANSI/X3/SPARC Study Group on Data Base Management Systems 75-02-08" (1975). In: *Bulletin of ACM SIGMOD* 7.2. Ed. by Thomas B. Steel, Jr., pp. 1–140.

Steels, Luc (2007). "The symbol grounding problem is solved, so what's next?" In: *Symbols, embodiment and meaning*. Ed. by M. De Vega, G. Glennberg, and G. Graesser. New Haven: Academic Press, pp. 223–244.

Steimann, Friedrich (2007). "The role data model revisited". In: *Applied Ontology* 2.2, pp. 89–103.

Steinberg, Dave et al. (2009). *EMF: Eclipse Modeling Framework*. 2nd. Boston: Addison-Wesley.

Stiegler, Marc (Feb. 2005). *An Introduction to Petname Systems*. http://www.skyhunter.com/marcs/petnames/IntroPetNames.html.

Stonebraker, Michael, Samuel Madden, et al. (Sept. 2007). "The End of an Architectural Era (It's Time for a Complete Rewrite)". In: *Proceedings of the 33rd International Conference on Very Large Data Bases (VLDB)*. Ed. by Christoph Koch et al. Vienna: ACM Press, pp. 1150–1160.

Stonebraker, Michael, Lawrence A. Rowe, et al. (1990). "Third-Generation Database System Manifesto - The Committee for Advanced DBMS Function." In: *SIGMOD Record* 19.3, pp. 31–44.

Stroustrup, Bjarne (1997). *The C++ programming language*. 3rd. Addison-Wesley.

Stührenberg, Maik and Christian Wurm (2010). "Refining the Taxonomy of XML Schema Languages. A new Approach for Categorizing XML Schema Languages in Terms of Processing Complexity". In: *Proceedings of Balisage Markup Conference 2010*. Vol. 5. Balisage Series on Markup Technologies.

Suppes, Patrick (1962). "Models of Data". In: *Logic, Methodology and Philosophy of Science: Proceedings of the 1960 International Congress*. Ed. by E. Nagel, P. Suppes, and A. Tarski. Stanford: Stanford University Press, pp. 252–261.

Sutton, Valerie (2002). *Lessons In SignWriting*. La Jolla: Center for Sutton Movement Writing.

Sveinsdottir, Edda and Erik Frøkjær (1988). "Datalogy - The Copenhagen Tradition of Computer Science." In: *BIT* 28.3, pp. 450–472.

Svensson, Patrik (2010). "The Landscape of Digital Humanities". In: *Digital Humanities Quarterly* 4.1. http://www.digitalhumanities.org/dhq/vol/4/1/000080/000080.html.

Sylvester, John Joseph (1878). "Chemistry and Algebra". In: *Nature* 17, p. 284.

Taddeo, Mariarosaria and Luciano Floridi (2005). "The Symbol Grounding Problem: a Critical Review of Fifteen Years of Research". In: *Journal of Experimental and Theoretical Artificial Intelligence* 17.4, pp. 419–445.

– (2007). "A Praxical Solution of the Symbol Grounding Problem". In: *Minds and Machines* 17.4, pp. 369–389.

Tanenbaum, Andrew S. (2008). *Modern Operating Systems*. 3rd. Pearson.

Taverniers, Miriam (Sept. 2008). "Hjelmslev's semiotic model of language: An exegesis". In: *Semiotica* 171, 367–394.

Teichroew, Daniel and Ernest A. Hershey (1977). "PSL/PSA: A Computer Aided Technique for Structured Documentation and Analysis of Information Processing Systems." In: *IEEE Transctions on Software Engineering* 3.1, pp. 41–48.

Tennant, Roy (Oct. 15, 2002). "MARC Must Die". In: *Library Journal*. http://www.libraryjournal.com/article/CA250046.html.

– (2004). "Digital Libraries: Metadata's Bitter Harvest". In: *Library Journal* 12. http://www.libraryjournal.com/article/CA434443.html.

The Unicode Consortium (2011). *The Unicode Standard*. Tech. rep. Version 6.0.0. Mountain View, CA: Unicode Consortium. http://www.unicode.org/versions/Unicode6.0.0/.

Thomale, Jason (Sept. 21, 2010). "Interpreting MARC: Where's the Bibliographic Data?" In: *Code4Lib Journal* 11. http://journal.code4lib.org/articles/3832.

Thompson, Henry S. et al., eds. (Oct. 2004). *XML Schema Part 1: Structures Second Edition*. W3C Recommendation. http://www.w3.org/TR/2004/REC-xmlschema-1-20041028.

Tobin, Richard (Apr. 6, 2001). *An RDF Schema for the XML Information Set*. Tech. rep. http://www.w3.org/TR/2001/NOTE-xml-infoset-rdfs-20010406.

Trabant, Jürgen (1996). *Elemente der Semiotik*. Tübingen: UTB.

Truex, Duane and Frantz Rowe (2007). "Issues at the IS Core: How French Scholars Inform the Discourse". In: *ICIS 2007 Proceedings*. 134. http://aisel.aisnet.org/icis2007/134.

Tufte, Edward R. (2001). *The Visual Display of Quantitative Information*. 2. Cheshire, CT: Graphics Press.

Turing, Alan M. (1936). "On Computable Numbers, with an application to the Entscheidungsproblem". In: *Proceedings of the London Mathematical Society*. 2nd ser. 42, pp. 230–265.

Tversky, Barbara (2001). "Spatial Schemas in Depictions". In: *Spatial Schemas and Abstract Thought*. Ed. by Merideth Gattis. MIT Press, pp. 79–111.

– (July 2011). "Visualizing Thought". In: *Topics in Cognitive Science* 3.3, pp. 499–535.

Vaesen, Krist (2008). "A Philosophical Essay on Artifacts and Norms". PhD thesis. Technical University Eindhoven.

Varda, Kenton (June 2008). *Protocol Buffers: Google's Data Interchange Format*. Tech. rep. Google. `http://google-opensource.blogspot.com/2008/07/protocol-buffers-googles-data.html`.

Vassiliadis, Panos and Timos K. Sellis (1999). "A Survey of Logical Models for OLAP Databases." In: *SIGMOD Record* 28.4, pp. 64–69.

Venn, John (1880). "On the diagrammatic and mechanical representation of propositions and reasonings". In: *The London, Edinburgh and Dublin Philosophical Magazine and Journal of Science* 10.58, pp. 1–18.

Vijay-Shanker, K. and David J. Weir (1994). "The Equivalence of Four Extensions of Context-Free Grammars". In: *Mathematical Systems Theory* 27.6, pp. 511–546.

Vitali, Fabio, Angelo Di Iorio, and Daniele Gubellini (Aug. 2005). "Design Patterns for Descriptive Document Substructures". In: *Proceedings of 2005 Extreme Markup Languages Conference*. Montréal, Canada. `http://www.mulberrytech.com/Extreme/Proceedings/html/2005/Vitali01/EML2005Vitali01.html`.

Vitiello, Giuseppe (Jan. 2004). "Identifiers and Identification Systems An Informational Look at Policies and Roles from a Library Perspective". In: *D-Lib Magazine* 10.1. `http://www.dlib.org/dlib/january04/vitiello/01vitiello.html`.

Vlist, Eric van der (Dec. 2003). *RELAX NG - a simpler schema language for XML*. O'Reilly.

– (Mar. 2007). *Schematron*. O'Reilly.

Voß, Jakob, Hotho Andreas, and Jäschke Robert (2009). "Mapping Bibliographic Records with Bibliographic Hash Keys". In: *Information: Droge, Ware oder Commons?* Ed. by Rainer Kuhlen. Proceedings of ISI. Hochschulverband Informationswissenschaft. Verlag Werner Hülsbusch. `http://eprints.rclis.org/15953/`.

Vrandečić, Denny et al. (2010). "Leveraging Non-Lexical Knowledge for the Linked Open Data Web". In: *Review of April Fool's day Transactions*, pp. 18–27.

Waitzman, David (Apr. 1990). *A Standard for the Transmission of IP Datagrams on Avian Carriers*. RFC 2549.

Walsh, Norman (Apr. 2010). *DocBook: The Definitive Guide*. Ed. by Leonard Muellner. O'Reilly.

Wang, Taowei David, Bijang Parsia, and James Hendler (2006). "A Survey of the Web Ontology Landscape". In: *Proc. of the ISWC 2006*. `http://www.mindswap.org/papers/2006/survey.pdf`.

Bibliography

Warner, Julian (1990). "Semiotics, information science, documents and computers". In: *Journal of Documentation* 46.1, pp. 16–32.

Watzlawick, Paul, Janet Helmick-Beavin, and Don D. Jackson (1967). *Pragmatics of Human Communication - a study of interactional patterns, pathologies, and paradoxes*. New York: Norton.

Weizenbaum, Joseph (1976). *Computer Power and Human Reason: From Judgment to Calculation*. New York: W. H. Freeman & Co.

Wells, Herbert G (1938). *World Brain*. 1st. New York: Doubleday, Doran & Co.

Whistler, Ken and Asmus Freytag (2009). *The Unicode Character Property Model*. Tech. rep. Unicode Standard Annex 23. Unicode Consortium. `http://unicode.org/reports/tr23/`.

Whorf, Benjamin L. (1956). *Language, thought and reality: Selected writings of Benjamin Lee Whorf*. Ed. by J. B. Carroll. Cambridge, MA: MIT Press.

Widder, Oliver (Apr. 17, 2010). "Meta". In: *Geek and Poke*. `http://geekandpoke.typepad.com/geekandpoke/2010/04/meta.html`.

Wieringa, Roel and Wiebren de Jonge (1991). *The identification of objects and roles - Object identifiers revisited*. Tech. rep. IR-267. Faculty of Mathematics and Computer Science, Vrije Universiteit.

Wikipedia (2010). *INI file*. `http://en.wikipedia.org/wiki/INI_file`.

Wilcox-O'Hearn, Zooko (2001). *Names: Distributed, Secure, Human-Readable: Choose Two*. `http://zooko.com/distnames.html`.

Wilde, Erik (Aug. 27, 2003). "A Compact Syntax for W3C XML Schema". In: *XML.com*. `http://www.xml.com/pub/a/2003/08/27/xscs.html`.

– (May 2006). "Merging Trees: File System and Content Integration". In: *15th International World Wide Web Conference*. Ed. by Les Carr et al. Edinburgh: ACM Press, 955–956.

Wilde, Erik and Robert J. Glushko (2008). "XML Fever". In: *Communications of the ACM* 51.7, pp. 40–46.

Winn, William (1990). "Encoding and Retrieval of Information in Maps and Diagrams". In: *IEEE Transactions on Professional Communication* 33.3, pp. 103–107.

Wirth, Niklaus (1976). *Algorithms + Data Structures = Programs*. Prentice-Hall.

– (1977). "What can we do about the unnecessary diversity of notation for syntactic definitions?" In: *Communications of the ACM* 20.11, pp. 822–823.

Wirth, Niklaus and C. A. R. Hoare (June 1966). "A Contribution to the Development of ALGOL". In: *Communications of the ACM* 9.6, pp. 413–432.

Wyssusek, Boris (2007). "A philosophical re-appraisal of Peter Naur's notion of "Programming as theory building"". In: *Proceedings of the 15th European Conference on Information Systems (ECIS)*. St. Gallen, 1505–1514.

Yager, Ronald and Teresa C. Rubinson (1981). "Linguistic summaries of data bases". In: *Proceedings of the Decision and Control conference*, pp. 1094–1097.

Yang, Bill (Oct. 2009). "The problem of too many layers of indirection (abstraction)". In: *Bill Yang's Weblog*. http://billgyang.blogspot.de/2009/10/dark-side-of-abstraction.html.

Yeo, Geoffrey (2010). "'Nothing is the same as something else': significant properties and notions of identity and originality". In: *Archival Science* 10.2, pp. 85–116.

Young, John W. and Henry K. Kent (1958). "An abstract formulation of data processing problems". In: *ACM '58: Preprints of papers presented at the 13th national meeting of the Association for Computing Machinery*. ACM, pp. 1–4.

Zelle, Rintze M. (Sept. 3, 2012). *Citation Style Language 1.0.1*. Tech. rep. http://citationstyles.org/downloads/specification-csl101-20120903.html.

Zeumer, Karl, ed. (2001). *Formulae Merowingici et Karolini aevi*. Hannover: Hahn.

All URLs in this thesis have been checked and updated at January 5th with a script documented at http://tex.stackexchange.com/a/89521/1044. The full bibliography is available at http://www.bibsonomy.org/user/voj.

Appendices

A. Honig's analysis model of data structures

In his dissertation Honig (1975) developed an analysis model of data structures based on a review of 21 programming languages and data base management systems. A partial summary of the model is given by Honig and C. R. Carlson (1978). In Honig's analysis model "data structures are divided into three classes (aggregates, associations, and files) and each class is modeled with a set of questions. Each question delinates one significant characteristic of the data structure and can be viewed as one axis of a n-dimensional universe of data structures." This appendix includes a copy of these questions for better comparision, as applied in section 5.6.1.

```
1.  WHAT KIND OF SELETION IS USED?            SELECTION: NONE, SPECIAL KEY,
        WHAT DOES THE USER SPECIFY TO PICK               BASIC ITEM KEY, CURRENTNESS
        ONE OR MORE ENTRY INSTANCES?

    THE FOLLOWING QUESTION IS
        ANSWERED ONLY WHEN "SELETION" IS BASIC ITEM KEY.

*2. IS THE ENTRY UNIQUE?                       UNIQUE: YES, NO
        DOES EACH SELECTION SPECIFY A SINGLE,
        UNIQUE ENTRY INSTANCE (AS OPPOSED TO
        TWO OR MORE)?

3.  IS THE FILE SEQUENTIAL?                     SEQUENTIAL: YES, NO
        IS ANY KIND OF ORDERING WHATSOEVER
        IMPLIED AMONG THE ENTRY INSTANCES?

4.  HOW MANY KINDS OF ENTRIES?                  KINDS OF ENTRIES: 1, 2, ...
        HOW MANY DIFFERENT DATA DEFINITIONS
        MAY ENTRY INSTANCES BE DRAWN FROM?


*  DATA INTEGRITY
```

FIG. 3-42. MODEL FOR FILES.

1. WHAT IS THE <u>CARDINALITY</u> OF THE ASSOCIATION?
   HOW MANY INSTANCES OF A-END DATA DEFINITIONS ARE
   ASSOCIATED WITH HOW MANY INSTANCES OF B-END DATA
   DEFINITIONS IN ONE INSTANCE OF THE ASSOCIATION?

CARDINALITY: 1-1, 1-N, N-M

2. HOW MANY <u>KINDS</u> OF DATA AGGREGATES AND BASIC ITEMS MAY
   OCCUR AT A-<u>END</u> (AT B-END)?
   HOW MANY DATA DEFINITIONS MAY A-END (B-END) INSTANCES BE
   DRAWN FROM?

KINDS OF ENDS: 1, 2, ...
                (1, 2, ...)

3. MAY THE ASSOCIATION FORM A <u>LOOP</u>?
   MAY A-END AND B-END INSTANCES BE FROM THE SAME GROUP
   OF DATA DEFINITIONS?

LOOP: YES, NO

*4. IS THE ASSOCIATION <u>COMPLETE</u> AT A-END (AT B-END)?
   IS EVERY A-END (B-END) INSTANCE PART OF SOME INSTANCE
   OF THE ASSOCIATION (AS OPPOSED TO BEING UNRELATED)?

COMPLETE: YES, NO
          (YES, NO)

WHEN A DATA AGGREGATE OR BASIC ITEM IS AN END OF MORE THAN ONE ASSOCIATION, THE
FOLLOWING QUESTION MAY BE ANSWERED FOR ANY SET OF TWO OR MORE ASSOCIATIONS
CONNECTED TO THE END.

*5. ARE THE ASSOCIATIONS <u>EXCLUSIVE</u> FOR THIS END?
   MUST EACH INSTANCE OF THE END BE PART OF EXACTLY ONE
   ASSOCIATION (AS OPPOSED TO BEING IN 0, 2, OR MORE)?

EXCLUSIVE: YES, NO

* DATA INTEGRITY

—164—

FIG. 3-19. MODEL FOR ASSOCIATIONS.

1. ARE THE ELEMENTS <u>HOMOGENEOUS</u>?
   ARE ALL INSTANCES OF THE ELEMENTS DRAWN
   FROM THE SAME DATA DEFINITION?

HOMOGENEOUS: YES, NO

2. ARE THE ELEMENTS <u>BASIC ITEMS</u>?
   ARE ALL INSTANCES OF THE ELEMENTS ATOMIC
   AND INDIVISIBLE?

BASIC ITEMS: YES, NO

3. ARE THE ELEMENTS <u>ORDERED</u>?
   IS ANY ORDERING AMONG THE ELEMENT INSTANCES
   IMPOSED OR IMPLIED BY THE STRUCTURE?

ORDERED: YES, NO

4. WHAT IS THE <u>NUMBER</u> OF ELEMENTS?
   HOW MANY INSTANCES OF EACH KIND OF ELEMENT ARE
   COMBINED IN ONE INSTANCE OF THE AGGREGATE?

NUMBER: FIXED, LIMITED, UNBOUNDED

* WHEN "HOMOGENEOUS" IS NO, "NUMBER" MAY BE EXTENDED TO SPECIFY A DIFFERENT COUNT FOR EACH
  KIND OF ELEMENT.

5. HOW IS AN ELEMENT <u>IDENTIFIED</u>?
   HOW IS AN INDIVIDUAL ELEMENT INSTANCE NAMED,
   LABELED, OR IDENTIFIED WITHIN AN AGGREGATE
   INSTANCE?

IDENTIFICATION: NUMBER, NAME,
                POINTER, NONE

* DATA INTEGRITY

—131—

FIG. 3-4. MODEL FOR AGGREGATES.

B. Conceptual diagrams as digital documents

The treatment of conceptual diagrams as form of data is not obvious, so it shall be justified in the following. Figure A2 is used by Moody (2009) to illustrate a specialization of the theory of communication by C. E. Shannon (1948) to the domain of visual notations: diagrammatic communication consists of two complementary processes: encoding and decoding. A diagram (signal) is decoded and encoded using a visual notation, which defines a set of conventions that both sender and receiver understand. The diagram can vary by noise, that are minor differences in sizes, colors, positions etc.

Moody defines the medium (channel) as "the physical form in which the diagram is presented (e.g., paper, whiteboard, and computer screen)". To digitize the diagram from physical form to digital data, we must identify and encode its visual symbols and the rules how symbols are combined (see section 3.9.2). The possibility of such encoding can be shown by mapping the diagram to another notation, such used in figure A3.

The readability differs between both diagrams, but they are formally equal, in the same way as text in different typefaces, size, and layout can be equal if encoded in Unicode (see example 7). Although there is no Unicode standard for conceptual diagrams, an encoding is possible given a set of possible visual symbols and combination rules. For this reason conceptual diagrams can be analyzed as data just like text in Unicode or any other writing system.

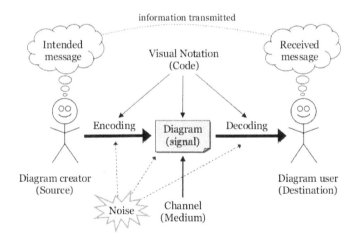

Figure A2.: Theory of Diagrammatic Communication as by Moody (2009)

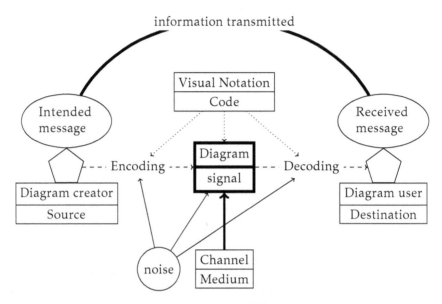

Figure A3.: Figure A2 in different layout

C. A pattern graph

Figure A4 contains a graph that was automatically created from the connections between patterns in chapter 5. Bold arrows indicate connections to implied patterns or to patterns which occur in the context of another pattern: for instance the context of a *separator* pattern is a *sequence* and sequences imply an *embedding*. The relationship, however, is no formal implication in terms of logic. Subsets of this graph are shown in figure 5.1 with focus on combining patterns and figure 5.2 with focus on relational patterns. The full graph in figure A4 further contains dashed arrows that indicate which patterns can be found in implementations of another pattern. One could further draw connections between related patterns, but these links are too dense to make use of it in a static graph with all patterns. A hypertext version will be provided at `http://aboutdata.org` for easier browsing of the pattern language. An alternative overview of the pattern language is given in form of a classification in table 6.1 at page 226.

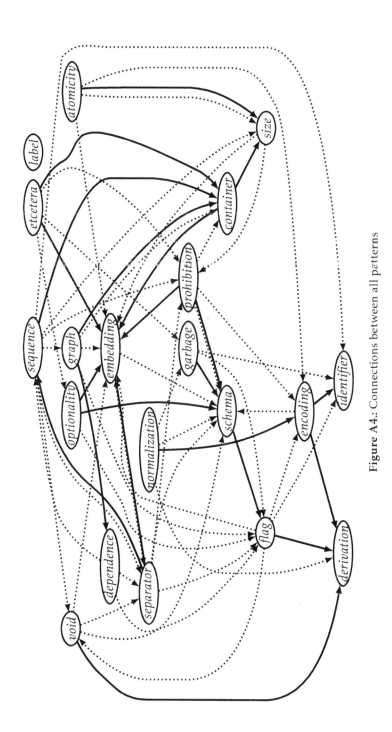

Figure A4.: Connections between all patterns

D. Deconstruction of a MARC record

An application of the results of this thesis shall briefly be illustrated with a fragment of a bibliographic record (figure A5). Similar analyses of MARC have been given by Thomale (2010) and by Coyle (2011). The *Machine-Readable Cataloging* (MARC) standard was developed during the 1960s to support library automation in general and to exchange bibliographic descriptions in particular (Avram 1975; McCallum 2002, 2009). MARC origins in pre-digital data in form of physical catalog cards — the format is also criticized for being suitable only for printing these cards (Coyle 2005; Tennant 2002).[5] Nevertheless MARC is still used widely among library systems today . The brief analysis of the sample record consists of three steps: first, one needs to clarify the main purpose of MARC to find out what a record actually is. This is done by means of the prototype categorization identified in section 4.1. Second, one should ask which basic paradigms have influenced the record (section 4.2). And third, one can identify data patterns in the record (chapter 5).

On a closer look, MARC consists of three methods (Library of Congress 2012): its *record structure* is used as general data structuring and markup language, the *content designation* is based on a rough conceptual model of bibliographic entities (e.g. titles and physical properties), and the actual *content* of data elements is constrained by cataloging rules (ISBD, AACR, RAK, ...). As neither model nor rules are defined in a formal language, and many different MARC variants and interpretations exist, the main use of MARC is limited to a basic record structure (section 3.4.1), similar to methods described in section 3.5 and 3.6.[6] Figure A6 shows a possible model of this structure: parts may be ordered (*sequence* pattern) or indexed (*identifier* pattern).

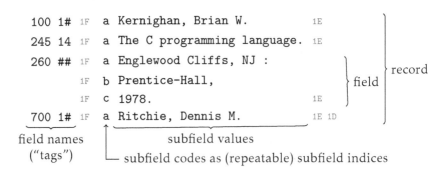

Figure A5.: MARC record and flat file database model with subfields

The governing paradigm of MARC is the paradigm of standards and rules (section 4.2.2), so this paradigm can reveal most defects of the format. It is worth

---

[5] Sure today's formats will be criticized in 40 years for not being suitable then.

[6] Even the basic structure cannot be taken for granted: in 2004 German and Austrian libraries decided to adopt MARC, but they introduced an invalid subfield code (**A**), making some of their records broken MARC. Such violating interpretations also occur at schema and conceptual levels.

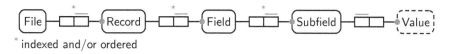

Figure A6.: Flat file record model of MARC

remarking that MARC is neither specified by a formal language nor does it come with a schema language to express subsets and applications of MARC (MARCXML, an encoding of MARC in XML, only defines a schema for the basic record structure but not for particular data elements). Furthermore there is no official validator to check whether records conform to (a specific dialect of) MARC.

The lack of formal specifications and automatic tools for validation increase the importance of intellectual analysis of MARC records. Many actual data patterns do not simply follow the basic record structure of MARC. In particular Thomale (2010) found that "the underlying structure is based on linguistics rather than a format that was designed to be machine-readable", so MARC should better be treated like textual markup. The interpretation of records as markup, which is normally based on element order (*sequence*) contrasts with the requirement select data elements based on the field-subfield-structure (*identifier* pattern). For instance one could combine tag, indicator, and subfield code to a normalized pointer, such as 245 14 a for the title in figure A5. Within MARC fields, Coyle (2011) identified three pattern structures: first, subfields can indepedently and directly describe a resource (so they can be used as part of a pointer). Second, subfields can qualify or modify other subfields (*dependence* pattern or *flag* pattern), and third, multiple subfields can together form a resource description (*sequence, container*, or *embedding* pattern).

An in-depth analysis of MARC in particular is out of the scope of this work, so this appendix ends with some additional pattern instances from the sample record:

- The fields 100 and 700 form a *sequence* of authors.

- Author names are structured by an *embedding* with comma as *separator* (surname, given). Second given names are further abbreviated (*etcetera*).

- Several instances of punctuation are irrelevant (*garbage* pattern).

- NJ in 'Englewood Cliffs, NJ' is an *identifier* that refers to New Jersey.

- Core elements ('Brian', 'Prentice-Hall', ...) are instances of the *label* pattern.

Danksagung

Für die fachliche und praktische Unterstützung bei der Vollendung dieser Arbeit möchte ich mich ausdrücklich bedanken bei Andreas Krausz, Brian Ballsun-Stanton, Ed Summers, Felix Sasaki, Gerald Steilen, Jindřich Mynarz, Kurt Jansson, Peter Becker, Phillip Mayr, Sally Chambers, Silvia Czerwinski, Stefan Gradmann, Sven Porst, Till Kinstler, Thomas Hapke, Ralph Voß, Reiner Diedrichs, Ulrike Reiner, Viola Voß, William Honig sowie den Mitgliedern der Online-Communities Wikipedia und Stack Exchange.